THE YORK CYCLE OF
MYSTERY PLAYS

THE
YORK CYCLE
OF MYSTERY PLAYS

A Complete Version

By the Reverend
J. S. PURVIS, D.D., F.S.A., F.R.Hist.S.

LONDON
S P C K

First published in 1957
First paperback edition 1978
Reprinted 1984
SPCK
Holy Trinity Church, Marylebone Road, London, NW1 4DU

Printed and bound in Great Britain by
William Clowes Limited, Beccles and London

Application for permission to make use of the text of THE YORK CYCLE OF MYSTERY PLAYS in public performances should be addressed to the publishers.

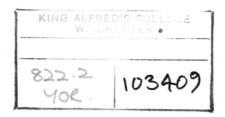
ISBN 0 281 03673 X

CONTENTS

5

CONTENTS

FOREWORD

UNTIL recently, the York Cycle of Mystery Plays was almost unknown except to a comparatively small number of students of Middle English, many of whom showed themselves strangely unresponsive to any kind of merit in the Plays. Some American scholars, certainly, had been more appreciative of their qualities as drama, but in England the almost universal tendency was to dismiss them as crude and immature efforts of the very childhood of literature, possessing little but a certain artless and archaic curiosity, but without much of the force or attraction of primitive art, and on the whole, if not dead, then undoubtedly dull. It was not, in fact, until the Festival of Britain in 1951 that there was any general renaissance of appreciation of the qualities latent in the Cycle. The City of York decided to revive, as part of its share in that Festival, the performance of the Cycle, which had last been presented there in 1572. A version was prepared, by the present writer, which might give a fair idea of the theme of the whole Cycle, while contracting it into a form which might be acted in something under three hours. For a modern and mixed audience it was necessary to translate the original language into its nearest equivalent in modern English, so far as this might be done without sacrificing the form and the verse-systems of the originals, or in any way misrepresenting or over-modernizing them. This version was offered with grave misgivings as to its possible success; the first performance showed how unnecessary those misgivings had been. The performance was hailed by the critics as a quite startling revelation of the power and beauty of the medieval Plays. This was no scientific study by the often patronizing pundits who had regarded the Cycle as a collection of literary fossils, but a plain representation, standing on its own merits as drama. It was not only the critics who were impressed; the effect on the great audiences made up of all sorts of people was truly remarkable in its depth of impact. They saw, not a Passion Play, but something on a plan far more majestic, yet never treated with remote detachment—the whole story of mankind, *sub specie æternitatis*. The actual performance was, indeed, a real revelation, of something fresh, direct, and powerful, and of a greatness hitherto unrecognized. A treasure of English literature had been rediscovered, and the rediscovery was to all who experienced it, in their many various ways and degrees, deeply moving both aesthetically and spiritually.

Far from appearing in general archaic, the Plays sounded often astonishingly modern. The mind or minds which composed the Cycle did so

7

with ideas and for reasons which are no longer ours, but they had handled the common matters of human nature, human experience, and thought which are of timeless appeal. There was a noble simplicity and a direct and powerful handling which belong only to great art, such an art as seems possible only perhaps to ages of faith. Here and there were passages, no doubt, which could not fail to remind that they were medieval and of that kind which Shakespeare parodied in its decrepitude, but these were surprisingly few, and made far less impression on mind or emotions than the many touches of vital dramatic force and lively observation. Above all, there was a sincerity, a natural aptness of expression, a grandeur and unity of theme, a sweeping movement, and a nobility, which are never found together, and seldom even separately, except in great art. The performances of 1951 were indeed a revelation and when the same version of the Cycle was presented again in 1954, the effect produced on the crowded audiences was as deep and marked as before.

Out of this remarkable success came a suggestion that there should be available, not an abbreviated form of the Cycle in modern speech, but the whole Cycle treated in the same way, so that it might be possible to appreciate more fully and in entirety this monument and treasure of early English literature, and to bring this appreciation within the reach of a greater number of readers. That task has now been attempted in the pages of this book.

There is in existence one complete manuscript only of the whole Cycle, that known as the Asburnham Manuscript, now in the British Museum, and edited in 1885 by Miss Lucy Toulmin Smith, with a valuable introduction in which she quoted many important passages from the York Civic records relating to the medieval Cycle and the production of the Plays. This manuscript is emphatically not a "prompt copy", as has been stated sometimes; it is in far too good condition for that. It is a fair copy, made somewhere about the middle of the fifteenth century, or perhaps a little earlier, which is about a century after the first drafting of the Cycle, with some Tudor additions, and gives the version of the Plays which they had acquired after the vicissitudes of about a century of the rough test of performance. That is, there have been additions to the original form of the Cycle, alterations, omissions; some of the additions are quite obviously much later in style than the main part of the work. There are passages which are obviously corrupt, where the original lines have been lost or forgotten. There are places where a page has been torn out, and these tell clearly what happened to the book after it passed into the hands of Archbishop Grindal, who ordered all copies of the Plays to be surrendered to him in order that they might be examined for traces of "superstitious doctrine". There are fairly numerous places with a note "*de novo facto*", and other notes which were no doubt intended for the information and guidance of the Archbishop. But with all these blemishes, the book is undoubtedly a fair copy, from which "prompt" copies were taken as they were needed.

The original manner of production of the Plays is sufficiently well known to need no lengthy discussion here. The Introduction to the Toulmin Smith edition gives copious documentary material on the subject. In brief, the Cycle was produced by the Guilds of York on Corpus Christi Day, the whole production being under the control of the City Corporation. A number of "Stations", varying from nine to twelve or even more, was fixed where the citizens might assemble to see the presentation, and the 48 separate Plays, each on its own "pageant" waggon, were performed in succession at each of the "Stations" throughout the City, all day long. Each Guild, or small group of Guilds, was responsible for its own stage, for the actors in its own Play, the costumes, properties, and all such requirements, while the Corporation exercised a close supervision over the quality of the performances and the financial side of the production. In order to allow time for the whole series of 48 performances, the first presentation took place almost with daylight, at 4.30 in the morning—very fitly, since in the first Play, God is shown creating the light of day. An incidental reference in the Civic records shows that some kind of artificial lighting was needed for the last performance of the last Play—the end of the world.

It may be well to illustrate the nature of the problems involved in the making of a modern version of the medieval text, by taking passages at random from the original, and comparing them with the present "translation". For example, Play 22, lines 25–30 has:

> "For I wotte ilke a dele by-dene,
> Of ye mytyng yat men of mene,
> How he has in grete barett bene
> Sithen he was borne;
> And suffered mekill traye and tene,
> Boye even and morne"

which appears as:

> "For I wot every deal, I ween,
> Of this same minion that men mean,

9

How he has in great trouble been
Since he was born,
And suffered mickle plots and pain
Both even and morn."

Or again, Play 31, at line 278:
"Do karpe on tyte, karle, of thy kynne.
Nay, nedelyngis he neuyns you with none.
Yat shall he bye or or blynne.
A leves lorde! Lattis me alone"

rendered as:

"Come, chat on quick, churl, of thy kin.
Nay, needs must he name to you none.
Yet shall he abide ere he cease.
Ah, stay, lord.—Let me alone."

These are not extreme examples, but may fairly show that to many readers the original form may not be at once intelligible, while the rendering now given may be claimed as close to the text in form and meaning.

The method of translation employed has been that used for the original "Short Version" of 1951. The guiding principles have been to alter nothing that could possibly be retained, either in the words, the arrangement of the words, the verse-forms, or the rhymes and the alliteration, so long as the result might be clear to a modern audience, and the closest faithfulness to the original might be retained. Only words completely archaic or obsolete have been replaced altogether, and even here faithfulness has been carried to the utmost, as where such forms as the following have been retained: "rede" for "advise" or "advice"; "saw" for "saying", "hight", meaning "called"; "promise pight"; "ween" for "think"; "wis"; "learn", in the earlier, and modern dialect, sense of "teach";—archaisms, no doubt, but not too archaic to be intelligible. Occasionally, an unusual word has been retained because it is still used in dialect speech, and understood by many who do not habitually use it. An example of this is "steven", either noun or verb, in the sense of "loud (or clear) sound, or utterance" in either speech or song.

Again, the original authors have two or three words which they introduce frequently because they give easy rhymes at line-ends; a word of this kind regularly found is "seere"; the meaning of this word is "many", or something of that kind—"sorrows sere". In the present version this is represented, not always closely, by "here" where the rhyme is to be preserved, or "sore" in some other cases. A device of a similar kind is the frequent end-use of "bedene" or "by-dene", without any definite meaning. Here sometimes this has been omitted altogether, sometimes replaced by "I ween", or some such token phrase.

In the course of making these versions, it became obvious that the language used in the original has throughout a strong resemblance to that still used in the dialects of North and East Yorkshire, not only in the vocabulary but also in pronunciation. It seemed desirable, therefore, to preserve sufficient indications of this marked general resemblance, and this has been attempted, wherever the result was not likely to be difficulty or confusion for those not acquainted with those Yorkshire dialects.

It should be realized, moreover, that many of the rhymes depend on dialect pronunciation; "among" is to be pronounced "amang", for example. "Know" should be sounded as "knew". This corrects what are apparently defective rhymes. When in Play 4 Adam cries "O Lord, loved be thy name, For now is this a joyful home", there is a true rhyme, as both then and now in dialect speech "home" is sounded "hame". In the passage in Play 25,

> "Yea, Moses' law he knows each deal,
> And all the prophets in a row;
> He tells them so each man may feel
> And that they may entirely know,
> If it were dim.
> What prophets have said in their saw,
> All belongs to him",

"row", "know", and "saw" are true pronunciation rhymes, "raw", and "knaw". "Door" in the dialect is a true rhyme to "poor", which ought not to be thought of as sounding "pore". "As was made there", in Play 38, is a good dialect rhyme with "for ever more (mair)".

Other dialect words which have been retained as still in use in these parts of Yorkshire are: "gainest", "the gainest gate", in Play 10, for "the nearest way"; "take tent", meaning "give attention"; "baaling", in Play 46, to cry like a lamb; "there again", for "against"; Pilate's dismissal of Barabbas, "Let him gang on his gate". A more extreme case but yet defensible on the same grounds is "I'll awand", for "I'll warrant", in Play 9. But those familiar with the still vigorous dialects of North and East Yorkshire will recognize innumerable instances of this character throughout the Plays, even where the pronunciation intended is not indicated so clearly as in Christ's challenge at Hell Mouth, where the original has "Oppen uppe", for "Open up", a phrase still normally used exactly in the same connotation, after six hundred years.

The York Cycle is not only the most complete series of medieval Plays; it is a national monument of medieval thought. Near in date to the *Canterbury Tales*, it is not the work of a courtly poet for a sophisticated audience, but represents the thought of another level of medieval society, the general mass of the people. The theological interest is naturally high—that is to be expected from the circumstances of their composition—but this in itself reveals much relating to normal medieval life, not in England only, for the Plays were written expressly to appeal to the normal range of thought of the normal person in the fourteenth century. Even in this, they open up new and unexpected prospects; for example, the extent to which the Scriptures were familiar to the common man before A.D. 1430, in Latin or in English; the remarkable absence of grossness; the treatment of physical suffering; the reflections of a feudal society. The Cycle therefore is of high significance as an expression of its times, and in that respect perhaps without extravagance may be set alongside the *Canterbury Tales* and *Piers Plowman* for its vivid exposition of the thought and manners of the Middle Ages in England. It approaches life with interests and purposes different from those of Chaucer or Langland, and therefore has a contribution to make without which they are incomplete. On the one hand, it represents the views of the theologian and of the Churchman whose interest is in the education of the laity, an interest not always sufficiently appreciated; on the other, it gives the most complete exposition extant of the religious and secular drama of the day. It is here, perhaps, that the modern reader will find most surprises. As drama, these Plays exhibit many crudities, many faults of inexperience. Yet even here, there is evidence of convention and tradition, as in the introductory speeches in which almost all the main characters explain themselves, or in the end-tags by which the dramatist indicates to the primitive audience that the Play is over, where the Greek drama provides a curious parallel. But along with these crudities of the immature, there are passages of remarkable dramatic power, effective dramatic "situations" carefully prepared, and a sense of characterization and psychology which are part of the "revelation" which the performances of the Plays have brought. These stand by

12

their own right, even with audiences accustomed to all the devices and manners of the modern theatre. There are scenes and speeches of a most deceptive apparent artlessness and simplicity, yet of a quality to test the capacity of even great actors or actresses. That work of such high order could come out of the English Middle Ages is another of the valuable discoveries which this Cycle may reveal to us, and such discoveries throw light all around them. Aspects of medieval life and thought which have been hitherto dimly seen or quite unsuspected begin to claim our notice, and at large may do much to correct our perspective and our sense of proportion, while they reveal a new importance and give us a new pride in our English heritage.

1

THE TANNOURS

Deus pater omnipotens creans et formans celos angelos et archangelos Luciferum et angelos qui cum eo ceciderunt in infernum.[1]

GOD ¶Ego sum alpha et O, Vita, Via,
Veritas, Primus et Novissimus.
I am gracious and great, God without a beginning;
I am maker unmade, and all might is in me.
I am life and way unto weal winning;
l am foremost and first; as I bid shall it be.
My blessing in joy shall be blending,
And falls from harm to be hiding;
My body in bliss aye abiding,
Unending without any ending.
Since I am maker unmade, and most high in might,
And aye shall be endless, and nought is but I,
Unto my dignity dear shall duly be dight
A place full of plenty, at my pleasure to ply.
And therewith as I will I have wrought
Many divers doings amain,
Which my work shall duly contain,
And all shall be made even of nought.
But only the worthy work of my will
In my spirit shall inspire the might of me;
And in the first fitly my thoughts to fulfil,
At hand in my blessing I bid that here be
A bliss all-protecting about me.
In the which bliss I bid that be here
Nine orders of angels full clear,
In love everlasting to lout me.

The Latin descriptions, at the head of each play, give the list of characters from the "Ordo Paginarium ludi Corporis Christi" of A.D. 1415, as recorded in the oldest City Memorandum Book.

15

Then the angels sing: Te Deum Laudamus te
dominum Confitemur.
Here underneath me now an isle do I name,
Which Isle shall be earth now; therefore is all
Earth wholly and Hell, and this high place is
    Heaven.
All that wealth shall wield shall dwell in this hall;
This grant I you, ministers mine,
While steadfast in thought ye remain;
And also all them that are nought
Shall pine in hell-prison in pain.
Of all mights I have made most near after me,
I make thee as master and mirror of my might;
I set thee here by me in bliss for to be,
And name thee now, Lucifer, as bearer of light.
Nought here shall make thee to fear;
In this bliss shall your dwelling remain;
All wealth in your wielding retain,
The while due obedience you bear.
    Then the angels sing: Sanctus, sanctus, sanctus,
    Domine deus Sabaoth.

I ANGEL SERAPHYN   ¶Ah, merciful maker, full mickle is thy might,
That all this world at a word worthily hast
    wrought.
Aye loved be that lovely lord for his light,
That thus us mighty has made, who now were
    right nought.
In bliss for to bide in his blessing,
Everlasting in love let us lout him,
Who sets us thus closely about him,
Of mirth nevermore to have missing.

I ANGEL LUCIFER   ¶All the mirth that is made is marked in me.
The beams of my brilliance are burning so bright,
And so seemly in sight myself I now see.
Like a lord am I lifted to dwell in this light.
More fairer by far I appear;
In me is no point to impair;
I feel me well favoured and fair;
My power is passing my peers.

I ANGEL CHERUBYN   ¶Lord, with a lasting love we love thee alone,
You mightful maker that marked us and made us,

16

And wrought us thus worthily to dwell as thy
    own
Where never feeling of filth may foul us nor
    fade us.
All bliss is here biding about us,
The while we are stable of thought
In the worship of him that us wrought;
Of dread need we never more doubt us.

I ANGEL LUCIFER   ¶Oh what!
I am favoured and fair and figured full fit;
The form of all fairness upon me is fast.
All wealth I am wielding, so wise is my wit;
The beams of my brightness are built with the
    best.
My showing is shimmering and shining,
So bigly to bliss am I brought;
I need to annoy me right nought;
Here shall never pain bring me pining.

ANGEL SERAPHIM   ¶With all the wit that we wield we worship thy
    will,
Thou glorious God that is ground of all grace.
Aye with steadfast sound let us stand still,
Lord, to be fed with the food of thy fair face.
In life that is truly aye-lasting,
Thy dole, Lord, is aye daintily dealing;
And whoso that food may be feeling,
To see thy fair face, is not fasting.

I ANGEL LUCIFER   ¶Oh sure, what!
I am worthily wrought with worship, I wis;
For in a glorious glee my glittering it gleams.
I am so mightily made my mirth may not miss;
Aye shall I bide in this bliss through brightness of
    beams.
I need no annoyance to name;
All wealth at my will am I wielding;
Above all yet shall I dwell in fame,
On height in the highest of heaven.
There shall I set myself, full seemly to sight,
To receive my reverence through right of
    renown.
I shall be like unto him that is highest on height!

Speech hard to fall.
God not judgemental
Lucifer judge on himself
by his actions

Patres them
for the 1st time
= we must always
recognise our
fault etc

Misguided.
Showed only he
guided by God
why be 'mortal'
...indw. God as
...primary.

THE TANNOURS

Oh what! I am perfect and proud. . . .
          Out, deuce! All goes down!
My might and my main are all marring.
Help, fellows! In faith, I am falling.

2 FALLEN ANGEL ¶From heaven are we hurled down on all hand.
To woe are we wending, I warrant.

LUCIFER THE DEVIL ¶Out, out!
Haro, helpless! so hot is it here.
This is a dungeon of dole in which I am dight.
Where are my kin now, so comely and clear?
Now am I loathliest, alas, that ere was so light.
My brightness is blackest of hue now;
My bale is aye beating and burning,
That makes me go griding and grinning.
Out, ay welaway!
I wallow enough in woe now.

2 DEVIL ¶Out, out!
I go mad for woe; my wits are all spent now.
All our food is but filth; we swelter in scorn.
We that were builded in bliss, in bale are we
    burnt now.
Out on thee, Lucifer, lurdan! Our light has thou
    lorn.
Thy deeds to this dole now have drawn us;
To spoil us thou hast been our speeder,
For thou wast our light and our leader,
Who highest in heaven had called us.

LUCIFER ¶Welaway!
Woe is me now; now is it worse than it was.
Uncomfortless carp ye; I said but a thought.

2 DEVIL ¶Yah, lurdan! You lost us.

LUCIFER   Ye lie! Out, alas!
I wist not this woe should be wrought.
Out on ye, lurdans; ye smother me in smoke.

2 DEVIL ¶This woe hast thou wrought us.

LUCIFER   Ye lie, ye lie!

2 DEVIL ¶Thou liest, and that shalt abide by.
Here, lurdans; have at ye. Let's look!

ANGEL CHERUBIM ¶Ah, Lord,
Loved be thy name, that us this light lent,
Since Lucifer our leader is lighted so low,

18

For his disobedience in bale to be burnt,
Thy righteousness in right order to show.
Each work even as it is wrought
Through grace of thy merciful might
The cause I see it in sight,
Wherefore into bale he is brought.

GOD ¶These fools from their fairness in fantasies fell,
And made nought of might that marked them and made
them;
Wherefore as their works were in woe shall they dwell;
For some are fallen into filth that evermore shall fade
them,
And never shall have grace for to shade them.
So passing of power they thought them,
They would not me worship that made them.
Wherefore shall my wrath e'er go with them.
And all that me worship shall dwell here, I wis.
Wherefore in my work go forward I will,
Since their might is marred that meant all amiss,
Even to mine own figure this bliss to fulfil.
Mankind out of mould will I make.
But first before him I create
All things that shall strengthen his state,
To which his own nature shall take.
And in my first making to muster my might,
Since earth is vain void and darkness doth dwell,
I bid by my blessing the angels give light
To the earth, for it faded when fiends fell;
In hell never darkness is missing.
The darkness thus name I for "night",
And "day" do I call this clear light;
My after works soon shall ye know.
And now in my blessing, I part them in two,
The night from the day, so that they meet never,
But each on its course their gates for to go.
Both the night and the day, do duly your devoir
To all I shall work, without ceasing.
This day's work is done every deal,
And all this work likes me right well,
And straightway I give it my blessing.

19

2

THE PLAYSTERERS

Deus Pater in sua substancia creans terram et omnia que in ea sunt per spacium v dierum.

GOD ¶*In altissimis habito.*
In the highest heaven my home have I,
Eterne mentis et ego,
Without end everlastingly.
Since I have wrought this world so wide,
Heaven and air and earth also,
My high godhead I will not hide,
Although some fools fell from me so.
When they assented with sin of pride
Up for to climb my throne unto,
In heaven they might no longer bide,
But swiftly went to dwell in woe;
And since they wrong have wrought
I choose to let them go
To suffer sorrow unsought,
Since they deserved so.
Their miss they never may amend,
Since they assent me to forsake;
For all their force none may defend;
They shall be fiends full foul and black;
And they that will on me depend
And true attention to me take,
Shall dwell in wealth without an end
And always joyful with me wake.
They shall have for their bliss
Solace that never shall slake.
This work methinks full well,
And more now will I make.
Since that this world is ordained even,
Forth will I publish all my power.

THE PLAYSTERERS

Not by my strength but voice's might,
A firmament I bid appear;
Among the waters, lightning light,
Their courses truly for to learn,
And that same shall be naméd heaven,
With planets and with clouds all clear.
The water I will be set,
To flow both far and near,
And then the firmament,
In midst to set them here.
The firmament shall not move away,
But be a mean; thus I decide;
Over all the world to hold and stay,
And you two waters to divide.
Under the heavens and also above
The waters separate shall be seen;
And so I will my power prove
By creatures of all kinds clean.
This work glads me today
Right well without my gain.
Thus ends the second day
Of my doings again.
More subtle works assay I shall
For to be set in service sure.
All ye waters great and small
That under heaven are ordained here,
Go ye together and hold you all,
And be a flood fastened secure,
So that the earth both down and dale
In dryness plainly may appear.
The dryness "land" shall be
Named both far and near;
And then I name the "sea",
Gathering of waters clear.
The earth shall foster and bring forth
Obediently as I shall bid
Herbs and all other thing,
Well for to wax and worthily clad.
Trees too thereon shall spring,
With branches and with boughs abroad;
With flowers fair on height to hang,

And fruit also to fill and feed.
And then I will that they
Of themself have the seed
And matter, that they may
Last long in land at need.
And all these matters are in mind,
For to be made of mickle might,
And to be cast in divers kind,
So for to bear their burgeons bright.
And when their fruit are fully fined
And fairest seeming unto sight,
Then the weather's wet and wind
Away I will it wend full right;
And of this seed full soon
New roots shall rise upright.
The third day thus is done;
These deeds are duly dight.
Now since the earth thus ordained is,
Measured and made by my assent,
All goodly for to grow with grass,
And weeds that soon away be sent,
Forth of my goodness will I pass,
That to my works no harm be meant—
Two lights, one more and one less,
To be fast in the firmament.
The more light to the day
Full soothly shall be sent,
The lesser light alway
To night shall take intent.
These figures fair that forth shall run,
On many sides thus serve they shall.
The more light shall be named the "sun",
Dimness to waste by down and dale.
Herbs and trees that are begun
All shall he govern great and small;
With cold if they be closed or bound,
Through heat of sun shall they be whole.
And as I have honours
To choose of every wealth,
So shall my crèatures
Ever abide in health.

THE PLAYSTERERS

Ye sun and moon in fair manner
Now goodly go in your degree;
As ye have taken your courses clear,
To serve henceforth look ye be free.
For ye shall set the seasons here,
Kindly to know in each country,
Day from day and year from year
By certain signs soothly to see.
The heaven shall be overceiled
With stars to stand plenty.
The fourth day is fulfilled;
This work well liketh me.
Now since these works with joy begin,
So founded forth by frith and fell,
The sea now will I set within
Whales all quick there for to dwell,
And other fish to flit with fin,
Some with scale and some with shell.
Of divers matters great and less
In many manners so I deal;
Some shall be mild in peace,
And some both fierce and fell.
This world thus I increase;
By wit I make all well.
Also up in the air on height
I bid now that there be ordained
For to be fowls full fair and bright,
Duly in their degree contained;
With feathers fair to try their flight
From stead to stead where they will stand,
And also lightly to alight
Whereso they like in every land.
Thus fish and fowls all here,
Kindly I you command
To move in your manner
Both by sea and by sand.
These matters more yet will I mend,
So for to fulfil my forethought;
All divers beasts on land I send,
To breed and be with pain forth brought;
And with the beasts I will to blend

23

Serpents to be seen unsought,
And worms upon their wombs shall wend
To woe in earth and worth to nought.
And so it shall be kenned
How all is made that ought;
Beginning, midst and end
I with my word have wrought.
For as I bid must all things be,
And duly done as I will dress.
Now beasts are set in their degree,
On mould to move, both more and less.
Then, fowls in air and fish in sea,
And beasts of earth of bone and flesh,
I bid ye wax forth fair plenty,
And goodly grow each in your place.
So multiply ye shall
Aye forth in fair process.
My blessing have you all.
The fifth day ended is.

3

THE CARDMAKERS

Deus pater formans Adam de lymo terre, et faciens Evam de costa Ade et inspirans eos spiritu vite.

GOD ¶In heaven and earth the course is seen
Of five days' work even unto the end,
I have completed by courses clean;
Methinks the space of them well spent.
In heaven are angels fair and bright,
Stars and planets their course to go;
The moon serveth unto the night,
The sun to light the day also.
In earth are trees and grass to spring,
Beasts and fowls both great and small,
Fishes in flood, each other thing . . .
Thrive they, and have my blessing all.
And yet can I here no beast see
That accords by kind and skill,
And for my works might worship me.
For perfect work now were it none,
Save that were made to give it care.
For love made I this world alone;
Therefore my love shall there appear.
To keep this world both more and less
A skilful beast then will I make
After my shape and my likeness, /
The which shall worship to me take.
Of the simplest part of earth that's here
I shall make man: My motive still,
For to abate his haughty cheer,
Both his great pride and other ill,
And also to have in his mind
How simple he is at his making,
His feeble state still shall he find

When he shall die, at his ending.
For this reason and cause alone
I shall make man like unto me.
Rise up, thou earth, in blood and bone,
In shape of man, I command thee.
A female shalt thou have for mate,
Whom here I make of thy left side,
That thou alone be not desolate
Without thy faithful friend and bride.
Take ye now here the breath of life,   v
And receive both your souls of me.
This female take thou to thy wife;
Adam, and Eve, your names shall be.

ADAM ¶Ah, Lord, full mickle is thy might,
And that is seen on every side.
For now is here a joyful sight,
To see this world so long and wide.
Many diverse things here now there is,
Of beasts and fowls, both wild and tame,
Yet none is made to thy likeness
But we alone. Ah, loved be thy name.

EVE ¶To such a lord in all degree
Be evermore lasting loving,
That to us such a dignity
Has given before all other thing.
And wondrous things may we see here
In all this world so long and broad,
Where beasts and fowls so many appear.
Blessed be he that has us made.

ADAM ¶Ah, blessed Lord, now at thy will,
Since we are wrought, vouchsafe to tell,
And also say unto us still,
What we shall do, and where to dwell.

GOD ¶For this cause made I you this day—
My name to worship evermore.
Love me therefore, and love me aye;
For my making I ask no more.
Both wise and witty shalt thou be,
As man that I have made of nought.
Lordship in earth then grant I thee,
Each thing to serve thee that is wrought.

In Paradise ye both shall dwell;
Of earthly things get ye no need;
Evil and good both shall ye tell;
I shall learn you your lives to lead.

ADAM   ¶Ah, Lord, since we shall do no thing
But love thee for thy great goodness,
We shall obey to thy bidding
And fulfil it, both more and less.

EVE   ¶His sign since he has on us set
Before all other thing certain,
Him for to love we will not let,
And worship him with might and main.

GOD   ¶At heaven and earth first I began,
And six days wrought ere I would rest.
My work is ended now with man;
All likes me well, but this the best.
My blessing have they ever and aye.
The seventh day shall my resting be;
Thus will I cease, soothly to say,
Of my doing in this degree.
To bliss I shall you bring;
Come forth, you two, with me;
You shall live in liking.
My blessing with you be.

4

THE FULLERS

Deus prohibens Adam et Evam ne comederent de ligno vite.

GOD ¶Adam and Eve, this is the place
That I have granted of my grace
To have your dwelling in.
Herbs, spices, fruit on tree,
Beasts, fowls, all that ye see,
Shall bow to you therein.
It is called Paradise;
Here shall your joys begin.
And if that ye be wise,
From this need ye never part.
All your will here shall you have,
Living for to eat or save
Flesh, fowl or fish,
And for to take at your own wish.
All other creatures at your will,
Your subjects shall they be.
Adam, of more and less
Lordship in earth here grant I thee.
This place that worthy is,
Keep it in honesty;
Look that ye rule it witfully.
All other creatures shall multiply,
Each one in tender hour.
Look then that ye both sow and set
Herbs and trees, and nothing let,
So that ye may endeavour
To sustain beast and man
And fowl of each stature.
Dwell here if that ye can;
This shall be your endeavour.

ADAM ¶O Lord! loved be thy name.

For this is now a joyful home
That thou has brought us to,
Full of solace calm and mirth,
Herbs and trees and fruit on earth,
With spices many a one, too.
Lo, Eve, now are we brought
To rest and comfort too;
We need to take no thought,
But look all well to do.

EVE ¶Loving be aye to such a lord
To us has given so great reward,
To govern both great and small,
And made us after his own mind
(Such pleasure and such play to find)
Amongst the mirths here all.
Here is a joyful sight
Wherein now dwell we shall.
We love thee, most of might,
Great God, on whom we call.

GOD ¶Love then my name with good intent
And hearken to my commandment;
My bidding both obey.
Of all the fruit in Paradise
Take ye thereof in your best wise,
And make you right merry.
But the tree of good and ill—
What time you eat of this,
You speed yourselves to spill,
And be brought out of bliss.
All things be made, man, for thy gain;
All creatures bow to thee amain
That here are made earthly.
In earth I make thee lord of all,
And beasts unto thee shall be thrall;
Thy kind shall multiply.
But this one tree alone,
Adam, thus outtake I.
The fruit of it come near none;
For if ye do, ye die.

ADAM ¶Ah, Lord, that we should do so ill.
Thy blessed bidding we shall fulfil,

Both in thought and in deed.
We come not nigh this tree nor bough,
Nor yet the fruit that on it grow,
Therewith our flesh to feed.

EVE ¶We shall do thy bidding;
We have no other need.
The fruit full still shall hang,
Lord, that thou hast forbid.

GOD ¶Look that ye do as ye have said.
Of all that here is hold you glad,
For here is wealth at will.
This tree that bears the Fruit of Life,
Look neither thou nor Eve thy wife
Lay no hands on it still.
Wherefore do my bidding.
It is known both of good and ill;
This fruit save ye let hang,
You speed yourselves to spill.
Wherefore this tree that I outtake,
Now keep it closely for my sake,
That nothing nigh it near.
All other at your will may be;
I outtake nothing but this tree,
To feed you with in fear.
Here shall you lead your life
With dainties that are dear.
Adam, and Eve thy wife,
My blessing have you here.

5

THE COWPERS

Adam et Eva et arbor inter eos, serpens decipiens eos cum pomis; Deus loquens eis et maledicens serpentem, et angelus cum gladio eiciens eos de paradiso.

SATAN ¶For woe my wit works wildly here,
　　　Which moves me mickle in my mind.
　　　The Godhead that I saw so clear,
　　　And perceived that he would take kind
　　　　　　Of a degree,
　　　　　That he had wrought,
　　　And I denied that angel kind
　　　　　　Should it not be.
　　　For we were fair and bright;
　　　Therefore methought that he,
　　　Take one of us he might . . .
　　　Yet he disdained me.
　　　The kind of man he thought to take,
　　　And thereat had I great envy.
　　　But He has made to him a mate,
　　　And hard to her I will me hie——
　　　　　That ready way——
　　　That purpose how to put it by,
　　　And try to pluck from him that prey.
　　　My travail were well set,
　　　　Might I him so betray,
　　　His liking for to let. . . .
　　　And soon I shall essay.
　　　In a worm's likeness will I wend,
　　　And try to feign a likely lie.
　　　Eve! Eve!
EVE 　　　　　　Who is there?
SATAN 　　　　　　　　　I, a friend.

And for thy good is the coming
    I hither sought.
Of all the fruit that ye see hang
In Paradise, why eat ye not?

EVE   ¶We may of them each one
Take all that we good thought,
Save one tree out alone,
Which harms to nigh it ought.

SATAN   ¶And why that tree, that would I wit,
Any more than all other by?

EVE   ¶For our Lord God forbids us it,
The fruit of it, Adam nor I,
    To nigh it near;
And if we did, we both should die,
He said, and cease our solace here.

SATAN   ¶Ah, Eve, to me take tent;
Take heed, and thou shalt hear
What that same matter meant
He moved on that manner.
To eat thereof forbade he you—
I know it well; this was his skill—
Because he would none other knew
Those great virtues that belong to it.
    For wilt thou see?
Who eats the fruit of good and ill
Shall have knowing as well as he.

EVE   ¶Why, what kind of thing art thou,
That tells this tale to me?

SATAN   ¶A worm, that wots well how
That ye may worshipped be.

EVE   ¶What worship should we win thereby?
We have lordship to make mastery
Of all things that in earth are wrought.

SATAN   ¶Woman, away!
To greater state ye may be brought,
If ye will do as I shall say.

EVE   ¶To do we are full loath
Or displease God this way.

SATAN   ¶Nay, sure; no harm for both;
Eat it safely ye may.
For peril, there none in it lies.

But worship and a great winning;
For right as God shall ye be wise,
And peers to him in everything.
Ay, great gods shall ye be,
Of ill and good to have knowing,
For to be all as wise as he.

EVE ¶Is this sooth that thou says?

SATAN ¶Yea; why believe not me?
I would by no kind of ways
Tell ought but truth to thee.

EVE ¶Then will I to thy teaching trust,
And take this fruit unto our food.

SATAN ¶Bite boldly on; be not abashed.
Give Adam some, to amend his mood
And eke his bliss.

EVE ¶Adam, have here of fruit full good.

ADAM ¶Alas, woman! Why took thou this?
Our Lord commanded us both
To tend this tree of his.
Thy work will make him wroth;
Alas, thou hast done amiss.

EVE ¶Nay, Adam, grieve thee nought at it,
And I shall say thee reason why.
A worm has given me to wit
We shall be as gods, thou and I,
        If that we eat
Here of this tree. Adam, thereby
Fail not this worship for to get.
For we shall be as wise
As God that is so great,
And also mickle of price;
Therefore eat of this meat.

ADAM ¶To eat it would I not eschew,
Might I be sure in thy saying.

EVE ¶Bite on boldly, for it is true.
We shall be gods, and know all thing.

ADAM   To win that name
I shall it taste at thy teaching.
Alas! What have I done? For shame!
Ill counsel! Woe worth thee!
Ah, Eve, thou art to blame;

33

To this enticed thou me.
My body does me shame,
For I am naked, as I think.

EVE ¶Alas, Adam, right so am I.

ADAM ¶And for sorrow sore why might we not sink?
For we have grieved God almighty
That made me man;
Broken his bidding bitterly—
Alas, that ever we began!
This work, Eve, hast thou wrought,
And made this bad bargain.

EVE ¶Nay, Adam; blame me not.

ADAM ¶Away, love Eve; who then?

EVE ¶The worm to blame were worthy more;
With tales untrue he me betrayed.

ADAM ¶Alas, that I list to thy lore,
Or trusted trifles that you said;
So may I bid.
For I may ban that bitter trade
And dreary deed that then I did.
Our shape for dole me grieves.
Wherewith shall they be hid?

EVE ¶Let us take these figleaves,
Since it is thus betide.

ADAM ¶Right as thou says so shall it be,
For we are naked and all bare.
Full wondrous fain would I hide me
From my Lord's sight, if I wist where—
I care not where.

GOD ¶Adam! Adam!

ADAM   Lord!

GOD   Where art thou,
                                   there?

ADAM ¶I hear thee, Lord, and see thee not.

GOD ¶Say, whereto does it belong,
This work? Why hast thou wrought?

ADAM ¶Lord, Eve made me do wrong,
And to this breach has brought.

GOD ¶Say, Eve, why hast thou made thy mate
Eat fruit I bade thee should hang still,
And commanded none of it to take?

34

EVE   ¶A worm, Lord, enticed me thereto.
      So welaway!
      That ever I did deed so ill!

GOD   ¶Ah, wicked worm! Woe worth thee aye!
      For thou on this manner
      Hast made them such affray.
      My malison have thou here,
      With all the might I may.
      And on thy womb then shalt thou glide,
      And be aye full of enmity
      To all mankind on every side,
      And earth it shall thy sustenance be
           To eat and drink.
      Adam and Eve, also ye
      In earth now shall ye sweat and swink
           And travail for your food.

ADAM   ¶Alas, when might we sink,
      We that had all world's good?
      Full grievous may we think.

GOD   ¶Now, Cherubin, mine angel bright,
      To middle earth swift go drive these two.

ANGEL   ¶All ready, Lord, as it is right,
      Since thy will is that it be so
           And thy liking.
      Adam and Eve, set you to go,
      For here may ye make no dwelling.
      Go ye forth fast to fare.
      Of sorrow may ye sing.

ADAM   ¶Alas! For sorrow and care
      Our hands now may we wring.

6

THE ARMOURERS

Adam et Eva, angelus cum vanga et colo assignans eis laborem.

ANGEL ¶All creatures here to me take tent.
From God in heaven now am I sent
Unto these wretches that wrong have bent
Themselves to woe;
The joy of heaven that them was lent
Is lost them fro.
For them is lost both game and glee.
He bade that they should masters be
Over all things except one tree;
So taught he still;
And thereto went both he and she
Against his will.
Against his will thus have they wrought.
To grieve great God gave they right nought
Of any heed or faithful thought;
That well wit ye.
And therefore sorrow is to them sought,
As ye shall see.
Ye fools that faith is fallen fro,
Take tent to me now ere ye go.
From God in heaven am I sent now
Unto you two,
For to warn you what kind of woe
Is wrought for you.

ADAM ¶For us is wrought, so welaway,
Dark dole enduring night and day;
The wealth we thought to have dwelt in aye
Is lost us fro;
For this mischief full well may we
Ever mourning go.

ANGEL ¶Adam, thyself made all this spite;

For to the tree thou went full right,
And boldly on the fruit 'gan bite
My Lord forbid.

ADAM   ¶Alas, my wife I there indict,
For she me led.

ANGEL   ¶Adam, because thou trowed her tale,
He sends his word and says you shall
Fare forth in fear, and for thy fall
Live aye in sorrow,
Abide and be in bitter bale
For many a morrow.

ADAM   ¶Alas, wretches, what have we wrought?
To bounteous bliss we both were brought;
While we were there
We had enough; now we have nought.
Alas, for care!

EVE   ¶Our cares are come both keen and cold,
With fellest fortunes manifold.
Alas, that tyrant to me told,
Throughout his guile,
That we should have all wealth in hold.
Woe worth the while!

ANGEL   ¶That which ye wrought unwittily,
So for to grieve God almighty,
That must ye abide full heavily,
Ere that ye go,
And lead your life, as is worthy,
In want and woe.
Adam, have this; look how ye think;
[*gives him the spade*]
(With sorrow must ye sweat and swink,)
And till withal thy meat and drink
For evermore.

ADAM   ¶Alas, for shame might I not sink;
So shames me sore.

EVA   ¶Sore shames us now sorrow severe;
And felly fare we both from here.
Alas, that ever we nighed it near,
That tree unto.
With dole now must we abide full dear
Ill deeds we do.

37

ANGEL   ¶Eva, since thou beguiledst him so,
Travail hereafter shalt thou know,
Thy bairns to bear with mickle woe;
This I warn thee.
Obedient thou and other mo
To man aye be.

EVA   ¶Alas, for dole what shall I do?
Now must I never have rest or rue.

ADAM   ¶Nay, such a tale is told me too,
Of swinking sore.
Now we are ruined, I and she too.
Shame evermore!
Alas, for shame and sorrow sad.
Mourning makes me amazed and mad;
To think in heart what help I had,
And now have none;
On ground may I go never glad;
My games are gone.
Gone are my games all without glee.
Alas, in bliss could we not be?
For we were put to great plenty
At prime of day.
By time of noon all lost had we.
So welaway.
So welaway! Hard pain I see.
All beasts were to my bidding free,
Fish and fowl fain willingly
To me were found.
Now all things shall against me be
That go on ground.
On ground ungainly may I gang,
To suffer pains and shame so strong;
All is for deed that I did wrong,
Through wicked will.
Alive methinks I live too long.
Alas the while!
Ah Lord, I think what thing is this,
That is ordained me for my miss.
If I work wrong, who guides me in this
By any way?
How best will be, so have I bliss, I will assay.

Alas for bale! What may this be?
In world unwisely wrought have we.
This earth it trembles for this tree,
And thunders so.
All this world now is wroth with me;
This well I know.
Full well I wot my wealth is gone.
Earth elements now every one
For my sin sorrow have put on;
This well I see.
Was never wretch so woebegone
As now are we.

EVA ¶We were full well worthy, I wis,
To have this mischief for our miss;
For brought we were to wondrous bliss
Ever to be.
Now my sad sorrow sure is this—
Myself to see.

ADAM ¶To see it is a sinful sight.
We both that were in bliss so bright,
We must go naked every night
And day also.
Alas! How woman's wit was light.
That well I know.

EVA ¶Since it was so, it frets me sore.
But since that woman witless were,
Man's mastery should have been the more
Against the guilt.

ADAM ¶Nay, at my speech wouldst thou never spare;
That has us spilt.

EVA ¶If I had spoken ought to you,
(In wicked ways to walk for woe,)
You should have taken good tent thereto,
And turned my thought.

ADAM ¶Away, woman! (That was vain to do,)
So name it not.
For at my bidding thou wouldst not be.
And thus my woe blame I to thee.
Through ill counsel outcast are we
In bitter bale.
Now God let ne'er man after me

Trust woman's tale.
For certain I repent full sore
That ever I should learn thy lore;
That counsel has cast me in care
That thou didst lend.

EVA ¶Be still, Adam; name it no more
It may not mend.
For well I wot I have done wrong,
And therefore ever I mourn among.
Alas, the while I live so long;
Dead would I be.

ADAM ¶On ground may I never glad gang,
But without glee.
All without glee since I must go,
And since this sorrow will me slay,
This tree I take to me, that so
For me is sent.
He that us wrought guide us from woe,
Where'er we wend.

7

THE GAUNTERS (GLOVERS)

Sacrificium Cayme et Abell.
Abel et Kaym immolantes victimas.

ANGEL ⁋The Lord of life loyal aye lasting,
Whose might unmeasured is to be seen,
He shaped the sun, both sea and sand,
And wrought this world with word, I ween.
His angel clear as crystal clean
Here unto you thus am I sent
        This tide.
Abel and Cayne, ye both I mean,
To me entirely take intent;
To move my message have I meant,
        If that you bide.
Almighty God of might the most,
When he had wrought this world so wide,
Nothing him thought was wrought in waste,
But in his blessing bound to bide.
Nine Orders for to tell that tide
Of angels bright he bade there be
        For pride.
And soon the tenth part it was tried
And went away as was worthy;
They haled to hell all that meiny,
        Therein to bide.
Then made he man in his likeness,
That place of pride for to restore;
And since he shewed him such kindness,
Somewhat will he require therefor.
The tenth to tithe he asks, no more,
Of all the goods he has you sent,
        For true.
To offer readily prepare,

And to my tale take you intent;
For every man that life has lent
    Shall follow you.

ABEL   ¶Gramercy, God, of thy goodness,
That me on mould has marked thy man.
I worship thee with worthiness,
With all the comfort that I can,
Me to defend from work so wan.
For to fulfil thy commandment,
    The tithe
Of all the good since I began
Thou shalt it have, since thou it sent.
Come, brother Cayme, I would we went
    With heart full blithe.

CAYME ¶What! Whither now, in mere malison?
Trowest thou I think to truss from town?
Go jape thee, ribald; jangle on.
I list not now to bend or groan.

ABEL   ¶Dear brother, let us be ready found
God's bidding blithely to fulfil,
    I tell to thee.

CAYME ¶Yah! Dance in the devil's way; dress thee down!
For I will work even as I will.
What masters thee, in good or ill,
    To meddle with me?

ABEL   ¶To meddle with thee mildly I may;
But, good brother, go we in haste;
Give God our tithe duly this day.
He bids us thus; be nought abased.

CAYME ¶Yah! Devil me thinks, that work were waste—
That he us gave, give him again
    To see.
Now fickle friendship for to taste
Methinks there is in him certain.
If he be most in might and main,
    What need has he?

ABEL   ¶He has no need unto thy good.
But it will please him principal
If thou mildly in main and mood
Grudge not to give tenth part of all
 . . . . . .

42

. . . . . .
It shall be done even as you bid,
And that anon.

[*A large section of the Play, including the actual killing of Abel, has been lost here. The Play resumes with an entirely new character, that of Cain's servant Brewbarret* (=*Strife-brewer*), *and Cain is apparently becoming intoxicated.*]

BREWBARRET ¶Lo, Master Cayme, what shares bring I,
Even of the best for to bear seed,
And to the field I will me hie
To fetch thee more, if thou have need.
CAYME ¶Come up, sir knave! The devil thee speed!
Ye will not come but to be prayed.
BREWBARRET ¶O Master Cayme, I've broken my toe!
CAYME ¶Come up, sir, come; for, by my thirst,
You shall drink ere you go.
ANGEL ¶Thou cursed Cayme, where is Abell?
What hast thou done thy brother dear?
CAYME ¶What asks thou me that tale to tell?
For yet his keeper was I ne'er.
ANGEL ¶God has sent thee his curses down
From heaven to hell, maledictio Dei.
CAYME ¶Take that thyself even on thy crown,
Quia non sum custos fratris mei,
Nor thine.
ANGEL ¶God has sent thee his malison,
And inwardly I give thee mine.
CAYME ¶The same curse light upon thy crown,
And right so might it worth and be.
For he that sent that greeting down . . .
The devil might speed both him and thee.
Foul might thou fall.
Here is a cursed company;
Therefore God's curse light on you all.
. . . . . . [*Three lines lost.*]
ANGEL ¶What has thou done? Behold and hear,
The voice of his blood cries vengeance
From earth to heaven with voice entire
This tide.
That God is grieved with thy grievance,

43

Take heed, for tidings I announce,
    Therefore abide.
You shall be cursed upon the ground.
God has given you his malison.
If thou would till the earth so round,
No fruit to thee shall there be found,
Of wickedness since thou art son.
Thou shalt be wayfaring here and there
    This day.
In bitter bale now art thou bound;
An outcast shalt thou be for care;
No man shall pity thy misfare,
    For this affray.

CAYME ¶Alas, for shame; so may I say.
My sin it passes all mercy.
For ask it thee, Lord, never I may;
To have it I am not worthy.
From thee shall I be hid in high;
Thou castest me, Lord, out of my kith
    In land.
Both here and there outcast am I.
For every man that meets me with,
They will slay me, by fen or frith,
    With dint of hand.

ANGEL ¶Nay, Cayme, not so; have thou no dread.
For he that slays shall punished be
Seven times for doing of that deed.
Therefore a token shalt thou see;
It shall be printed so in thee,
That all men know thee certainly.

CAYME ¶Alas! Then will I further flee
    For shame.
Since I am set from bliss to be,
That curse that now is come on me,
    I give to you the same.

8

THE SHIPWRIGHTES

Deus premuniens Noe facere archam de lignis levigatis.

GOD ¶First when I wrought this world so wide,
Wood and wind and waters wan,
Heaven and hell was not to hide;
With herbs and grass thus I began,
In endless bliss to be and bide.
And to my likeness made I man;
Lord and sire on every side
Of all mid-earth I made him then.
A woman also with him wrought I,
All in law to lead their life.
I bade them wax and multiply,
To fill this world full, without strife.
Since, men have wrought so wofully,
And sin is now running so rife,
That I repent and rue thereby
That ever I made or man or wife.
But since, they make me to repent
My work I wrought so well and true,
And without cease will not assent,
But ever be bound more bale to brew.
So for their sins shall they be shamed
And undone wholly, hide and hue.
Of them shall no more none be named,
But work this work I will all new.
All new I will this world be wrought,
And waste away that wend therein.
A flood above them shall be brought,
To drown the earth and all therein,
But Noe alone; leave shall it nought,
To be all sunken for their sin.
He and his sons—thus is my thought—

And with their wives, away shall win.
Noe, my servant grave and clean,
For thou art stable in stead and stall,
I will thou work with cunning keen
A work to save thyself withal.

NOE ¶O mercy, Lord! What may this mean?

GOD ¶I am thy God of great and small,
Who comes to tell thee of thy pain,
And what wonder shall after fall.

NOE ¶Ah, Lord, I love thee loud and still,
That unto me, wretch unworthy,
Thus with thy word, as is thy will,
Likes to appear so properly.

GOD ¶Noe, as I bid thee, do fulfil.
A ship I will have wrought in high.
Although thou can but little skill,
Take it in hand, for help shall I.

NOE ¶Ah, worthy Lord, would thou take heed!
I am full old and out of heart,
So that I list do no day's deed
Without great mastery on my part.

GOD ¶Begin my work behoves thee need,
If thou wilt pass from pains so smart.
I shall thee succour and thee speed,
And give thee health in head and heart.
I see such ire among mankind
That of their works vengeance I take;
They shall be sunken for their sin.
Therefore a ship I will thou make.
Thou and thy sons shall be therein;
They shall be saved for thy sake.
Therefore go boldly and begin
Thy measures and thy marks to take.

NOE ¶Ah, Lord, thy will shall ever be wrought,
Who counsel gives to every clerk.
But of shipcraft can I right nought;
Of their making have I no mark.

GOD ¶Noe,
I bid thee heartily have no thought;
I shall thee guide in all thy work,
And even till it to end be wrought;

46

Therefore to me take heed and hark.
Take thee high trees and hew them clean,
All by the square and nought a a-sqwyn;
Make of them boards and wands between,
Thus thrivingly and not too thin.
Look that thy seams be subtily sewn
And nailed well that they not part.
Thus I devise each to start;
Therefore do forth, and leave thy din.
Three hundred cubits shall it be long
And fifty broad, all for thy bliss;
The height of thirty cubits strong;
Look truly that thou think on this.
Thus give I goodly ere I gang
Thy measures that thou do not miss.
Look now that thou work nothing wrong
Thus wittily, since I thee wish.

NOE ⁋Ah, blissful Lord, that all may hold,
I thank thee heartily ever and aye.
Five hundred winters I am of old;
Methinks those years as yesterday.
Full weak I was and all unbold;
My weariness is gone away;
To work this work here in this field
All by myself I will assay.
To hew this board will I begin—
But first I will lay on my line.
Now must it be all in like thin,
So that it neither part nor pine.
Thus shall I join it with a gin,
And set it sound with cement fine.
Thus shall I work each whit therein
Through teaching of God, master mine.
More subtily can no man sew;
It shall be clenched in every deal
With nails that are both noble and new;
Thus shall I fix it fast to feel.
With the bows there now work I well;
This work I warrant both good and true
And rightly wrought, the truth to tell.
Full fair it is, who will attend.

47

But fast my force begins to fail.
A hundred winters away do wend
Since first I did this work assail,
And in such travail to be bent
Is hard to him that is thus old.
He that to me this message sent,
He will be my help; thus am I bold.

GOD ¶Noe, this work is near an end,
And wrought right as I warned thee.
But yet in manner you must it mend;
Therefore this lesson learn of me.
For divers beasts in must thou send,
And fowls also in their degree.
That they shall not together blend,
Divers stages therein must be.
And when it is ordained so,
With divers stalls and stages here,
Of every kind shalt thou take two,
Male and female in consort clear.
Thy wife, thy sons, shall with thee go,
And their three wives, all free from fear.
These eight bodies and no mo
Shall thus be saved on this manner.
Therefore to my bidding be fain;
Till all be harboured, haste thee fast.
After the seventh day it shall rain
Till forty days be fully past.
Take with thee gear, such as may gain
To man and beast their lives to last.
I shall thee succour for certain,
Till all thy care away be cast.

NOE ¶Ah lord, that each amiss may mend,
I love thy lore both loud and still;
I thank thee both with heart and hand
That will me help from angers ill.
About this work now must I wend,
With beasts and fowls my ship to fill.
He that to me this skill did send,
He guide me with his worthy will.

48

9

THE FYSSHERS AND MARYNARS

Noe in Archa et uxor eius, tres filii Noe cum uxoribus suis,
cum diversis animalibus.

NOYE ¶Thou Lord that lives everlasting life,
I love thee ever with heart and hand,
That would me rule by reason rife
Six hundred years to live in land.
Three seemly sons, a worthy wife,
I have ever at my sound to stand.
But now my cares are keen as knife,
Because I know thy high command.
There come to each country,
  Yea, cares both keen and cold.
For God has warned me,
This world wasted shall be,
And sure the sooth I see,
As forefathers have told.
My father Lamech who likes to name
Here in this world thus long did dwell,
Seven hundred years, seventy and seven
In such a space his time did tell.
He prayed to God with stable steven,
That he to him a son should send;
And at the last there came from heaven
Such promise that made much amend;
And made him grub and grave,
  And ordained fast before;
For he a son should have,
After which he did crave
And as God did vouchsafe.
  In world then was I born.

When I was born, Noye named he me,
And said these words with mickle glee,
"Lo," he said, "this same is he
That to mankind shall comfort be."
Now, sirs, by this well wit may ye,
My father knew all truth herein;
By certain signs he could well see
That all this world should sink for sin;
How God should vengeance take,
    As now is seen certain,
An end of mankind make
That sin would not forsake,
And how then it should slake,
    And a world wax again.
I would God that it wasted were,
That I should not attend thereo.
    My seemly sons and daughters dear,
Take ye intent unto my skill.

I SON   ¶Father, we are all ready here
Thy bidding straightway to fulfil.

NOYE   ¶Go call your mother, and come near,
And speed us fast that we nought spill.

I SON   ¶Father, we shall not stay
Till your bidding be done.

NOYE   ¶To pine shall full soon pass away
All that live under sun.

I SON   ¶Where are you, mother mine?
Come to my father soon.

WIFE   ¶What sayest thou, soon?

I SON   Mother, certain
My father thinks to flit full far.
He bids you haste with all your main
Unto him, that nothing you mar.

WIFE   ¶Yea, good son! Hie thee fast again
And tell him I will not come near.

I SON   ¶Dame, I would do your bidding fain
But you must wend, ere worse things are.

WIFE   ¶"Must"? That would I wit—
    We wrangle wrong, I ween.

I SON   ¶Mother, I tell you yet,
My father is bound to flit.

WIFE ¶Now, sure, I shall not sit,
      Ere I see what he mean.
1 SON ¶Father, I have done now as you command;
      My mother comes to you this day.
NOYE ¶She is welcome, I well warrant;
      This world shall soon all waste away.
WIFE ¶Where art thou, Noye?
NOYE   Lo, here at hand.
      Come hither fast, dame, I thee pray.
WIFE ¶Trows thou that I will leave dry land,
      And turn up here in such array?
      Nay, Noye, I am not bound
      To trudge now over these fells.
      Come, bairns; go we and truss for town.
NOYE ¶Nay, sure, soothly then must ye drown.
WIFE ¶In faith, thou were as good come down
      And go do somewhat else.
NOYE ¶Dame, forty days are nearhand past
      And gone since it began to rain;
      Alive shall no man longer last
      But we alone; that is full plain.
WIFE ¶Now, Noye, 'faith, thou grows fond too fast.
      I ask no more, nor will remain.
      Thou art nigh mad. I am aghast.
      Farewell! I will go home again.
NOYE ¶O woman, art thou mad?
      Of my works knowest thou nought.
      All that has bone or blood
      Shall be overflowed with the flood.
WIFE ¶In faith, ye were as good
      As let me go my gate.
      Oh! Out! Haro!
NOYE   What now? What cheer?
WIFE ¶I will no nearer for no kin's need.
NOYE ¶Help me, my sons, to hold her here,
      For to her harms she takes no heed.
2 SON ¶Be merry, mother, and mend your cheer.
      This world will all be drowned indeed.
WIFE ¶Alas! That I this lore should hear.
NOYE ¶Thou spoils us all—ill might thou speed!
3 SON ¶Dear mother, wend with us;

There shall nothing you grieve.

WIFE ¶Nay, nay; needs home I must,
For I have tools to truss.

NOYE ¶Woman, why dost thou thus,
To make us more mischief?

WIFE ¶Noye, thou might have let me wit,
Early and late when you went out,
And aye at home you let me sit,
To look not what you were about.

NOYE ¶Dame, hold thou me excused of it;
It was God's will, without a doubt.

WIFE ¶What? Thinkest thou so for to go quit?
Nay, by my troth, thou gettest a clout.

NOYE ¶I pray thee dame, be still;
Thus God would have it wrought.

WIFE ¶Thou shouldest have known my will,
If I would assent to ought,
And, Noye, for that same skill,
Bad bargain shall be bought.
For now I find and feel certain
Where thou hast to the forest sought;
You should have told me for our gain,
When we were to such bargain brought.

NOYE ¶Now, dame, you need not dread it so,
For to account it cost you nought.
A hundred winters, well I know,
Are gone since I this work have wrought.
And when I made ending,
God gave me measure fair
Of every kind of thing;
He bade that I should bring
Of beasts and fowls that sing
Of every kind a pair.

WIFE ¶Now, sure, if we win free from woe
And so be saved as you say here,
My comrades and my cousins also,
I would they went with us in here.

NOYE ¶'Tis danger through the flood to go;
Look! Without doubt that may appear.

WIFE ¶Alas! Life is to me full loath;
I live over long this lore to hear.

1 DAUGHTER	¶Dear mother, mend your mood.
	For we wend with you here.
WIFE	¶My friends from whom I went
	Are overflowed with flood.
2 DAUGHTER	¶Now thank we God all good
	That he his grace would grant.
3 DAUGHTER	¶Mother, of this work would you not ween,
	That all should waste to waters wan?
2 DAUGHTER	¶Father, what may this marvel mean?
	Whereto made God mid-earth and man?
1 DAUGHTER	¶So wondrous sight was never none seen,
	Since first that God this world began.
NOYE	¶Go now, and spar your doors, I say;
	For better counsel can I none.
	This sorrow is sent for sinful way.
	Therefore to God we pray
	From woe that we are in.
3 SON	¶O king of all man's kin
	Out of this woe us win,
	As thou art Lord that may.
1 SON	¶Yea, Lord; as thou lettest us be borne
	In this great bale, send help with speed.
NOYE	¶My sons, see ye, mid-day and morn
	To these cattle take ye good heed.
	Keep them up well with hay and corn;
	And women, take these fowls and feed,
	So that they be not lightly lorn,
	As long as we this life shall lead.
2 SON	¶Father, we are full fain
	Your bidding to fulfil.
3 SON	¶Nine months are past, 'tis plain,
	Since we were put to pain
	He that is most of main
	May mend it when he will.
NOYE	¶O bairns! It waxes clear about!
	That may ye see there where you sit.
1 SON	¶Aye, father dear; look now thereout,
	If that the water wane ought yet.
NOYE	¶That shall I do without a doubt,
	For by the waning may we wit.
	Ah Lord! to thee I loving lout!

The cataracts, I trow, are knit.
Behold, my sons all three,
The clouds are waxen clear.

2 SON ¶Ah, lord of mercy free,
Aye loved might thou be.

NOYE ¶I shall essay to see
How deep it is yet here.
Loved be that Lord that gives all grace,
That kindly does our cares compel.

NOYE ¶I shall cast lead, and look the space,
How deep the water is each deal.
Fifteen cubits of height it has
Over every hill fully to feel.
But be well comforted in this place;
Waning it is, that know I well.
Therefore a fowl of flight
Full soon shall I forth send
To seek, if he have sight,
Some land whereon to light;
Then may we know full right
When our mourning shall mend.
Of all the fowls that men may find,
The raven is strong, and wise is he.
Thou art full crabbed, and all thy kind;
Wend forth thy course, I command thee,
And warily watch, and hither wind,
If thou find either land or tree.
Nine months now here have we been pined,
But when God will, better may it be.

1 DAUGHTER ¶That lord that lends us life
To learn his laws in land,
Who made both man and wife,
Help us to stint our strife.

3 DAUGHTER ¶Our cares are keen as knife;
Now God good tidings send.

1 SON ¶Father, this fowl is forth full long;
Upon some land he lights indeed,
His food on earth to find along;
That makes him failing friend in need.

NOYE ¶Now, son, if he did so forth gang,
Since he for all our weal did wend,

54

Then be he for his works so wrong
Evermore wearied without end.
And surely for to see
When our sorrows shall cease,
Another fowl full free
Our messenger shall be.
Thou dove, I command thee
Our comfort to increase.
A faithful fowl to send art thou
Of all within these waves so wide.
Wend forth, pray, for our profit now,
And surely seek on every side
To see if floods be falling now,
That thou on earth may build and bide.
Bring some token that we may trow
What tidings shall of us betide.

2 DAUGHTER   ¶Good Lord, on us now look,
And cease our sorrows sore,
Since we our sins forsook
And to thy lore us took.

3 DAUGHTER   ¶A twelvemonth but twelve week
Have we been hovering here.

NOYE   ¶Now, bairns, we may be blithe and glad,
And love our Lord of heavens king.
My bird has done as I him bade;
An olive branch I see him bring.
Blest be thou, fowl never afraid,
That in thy force makes no failing.
More joy in heart never I had.
We may be saved, now may we sing.
Come hither, my sons, on high;
Our woe away is spent.
I see here certainly
Armenia's hills near by.

I SON   ¶Loved be that Lord thereby,
That us our lives has lent.

WIFE   ¶I care not now, if we may win
Out of this woe that once we bore.
But Noye, where are now all our kin
And company we knew before?

NOYE   ¶Dame, all are drowned. Let be thy din,

For soon they bought their sins full sore.
Good living let us now begin
So that we grieve our God no more.
He was grieved in degree,
And greatly moved in mind
For sin, as men may see,
Dum dixit penitet me;
Full sore regretted he
That ever he made mankind.
That makes us now to toil and truss.
But, sons, he said, I well know when,
Arcum ponam in nibibus;
He set his bow clearly to ken
As a token betwixt him and us,
For knowledge to all Christian men,
That since this world was finished thus
With water would be ne'er waste again.
Thus has God most of might
Set up his sign full clear,
Up in the air in height;
The rainbow it is right,
As men may see in sight,
In seasons of the year.

2 SON   ¶Sir, now since God our sovereign sire
Has set his sign thus in certain,
Then may we wit this world's empire
Shall evermore last, for that is plain.

NOYE   ¶Nay, son; that shall we not desire,
For if we do we work in vain;
For it shall once be waste with fire,
And never work to world again.

WIFE   ¶Ah, sir, our hearts may fear
These sayings ye say here,
That mischief must be more.

NOYE   ¶Be not afraid therefore;
Ye shall not live so long
By many a hundred year.

I SON   ¶Father, how shall this life be led,
Since none are in the world but we?

NOYE   ¶Sons, with your wives shall ye be stead,
And multiply your seed shall ye;

Your bairns shall then each other wed,
And worship God in good degree.
All beasts and fowls shall forth be bred,
And so a world begin to be.
Now travel shall you taste,
To win you bread and wine,
For all this world is waste.
These beasts must be unbraced.
Then wend we hence in haste
   In God's blessing and mine.

10

THE PARCEMYNERS AND BOKEBYNDERS

Abraham immolans filium suum Isaac super altare, garcio cum bosco et angelus.

ABRAHAM ¶Great God that all this world has wrought,
And wisely wots both good and ill,
I thank him throughly in my thought
For all his love he lends me still,
That thus from bairnhood has me brought,
A hundred winters to fulfil:
Now grant me power so that I might
Ordain my works after thy will.
For in this earthly life
Are none to God more bound
Than am I and my wife
For friendship we have found.
Unto me told God on a tide
Where I was tented under a tree,
He said my seed should multiply
Like to the gravel of the sea,
And as the stars were strewed wide,
So said he that my seed should be;
And bade I should be circumcised
To fulfil the law; thus learned he me.
In world wherein we run
He sends us riches rife;
As far as shines the sun
He is stinter of strife.
Abram first named was I,
And then he set a syllable more,
And my wife called Sarai,
And then was named Sara.

But Sara was uncertain then
That ever our seed should suchwise yield,
Because herself she was barren,
And we were both gone in great eld.
But she wrought as a wise woman,
To have a bairn us for to shield;
Her servant privily she won
Unto my bed, my will to wield.
Soon after then befell,
When God our deed would dight,
She brought forth Esmaell,
A son seemly to sight.
Then after, when we were waxen old,
My wife, she fell in fear for same;
Our God then tidings to us told,
When we were in our house at home;
To have a son should we be bold,
And Isaak should be his name,
And his seed should spring manifold.
If I were blithe, who would me blame?
And since I trusted this tiding
That God told to me then,
The ground and the beginning
Of truth that time began.
Now ought I greatly God to yield,
That so would tell me his intent,
And not gainstanding our great eld
A seemly son to us has sent.
Now is he light himself to wield,
And from me long all lightness went;
Therefore shall he be all my shield.
I love him that this loan has lent;
For he may stint our strife,
And fend us from all ill.
I love him as my life,
With all my heart and will.

ANGEL ¶Abraham! Abraham!
ABRAHAM   Lo, I am here.
ANGEL ¶Now bidding unto thee I bring.
God will assay thy will and cheer,
If thou wilt bow to his bidding.

Isaak, thy son that is so dear,
Whom thou loves over all thing—
To the Land of Vision now repair,
And there of him make offer'ng.
I shall shew thee full soon
The place of sacrifice.
God wills this deed be done,
And therefore thee advise.

ABRAHAM   ¶Lord God, that lends everlasting light,
This is a marvel strange to tell:
To have a son seemly to sight,
Isaak, that I love so well—
He is of age, to reckon right,
Thirty years and more some deal—
And unto death must he be dight.
God tells me so for my sure weal,
And bids me wend thuswise
To the Land of Vision,
There to make sacrifice
Of Isaak that is my son.
And that is hence three days' journey
The gainest gate that I can go.
And sure, I shall not say him nay,
If God command myself to slay.
But to my son I will nought say,
But take him and my servants two,
And with our ass wend forth our way;
As God has said, it shall be so.
Isaak my son, I understand
To wilderness now wend will we,
And there will make our offering,
For so has God commanded me.

ISAAK   ¶Father, I am ever at your will,
As worthy is; I do not feign.
All God's commandments to fulfil
Ought all folks always to be fain.

ABRAHAM   ¶Isaak my son, thou sayest good skill—
But all the truth is not to say—
Go we then, since we must, our way.
I pray God send us back here well.

ISAAK   ¶Children, lead forth our ass,

60

With wood that we shall burn.
Even as God ordained has,
To work will we begin.

1 SERVANT ¶At your bidding we will be bound;
What way in the world ye will is well.

2 SERVANT ¶Why, shall we truss ought forth o' town,
In any unknown land to dwell?

1 SERVANT ¶I hope thou have in this season
From God in heaven some solace sent.

2 SERVANT ¶To fulfil it is good reason,
And kindly keep what he has lent.

1 SERVANT ¶But what they mean certain
Have I no knowledge clear.

2 SERVANT ¶It may not greatly gain
To move of such matter.

ABRAHAM ¶Annoy you not in no degree
So for to deem here of our deed.
As God commanded, so work we;
Unto his tales we must take heed.

1 SERVANT ¶All those that will his servants be,
Full specially he will them speed.

ISAAK ¶Children, with all the might in me
I praise that God of every land,
And worship him certain;
My will is ever thereto.

2 SERVANT ¶God give you might and main
Right here so for to do.

ABRAHAM ¶Son, if our Lord God almighty
Of my self would have his offering,
I would be glad for him to die,
For all our health hangs in his hand.

ISAAK ¶Father, forsooth even so would I,
Liever than long to live in land.

ABRAHAM ¶Ah, son, thou sayest full well thereby;
God give thee grace ready to stand.
Children, bide ye here still;
No further shall ye go.
For yonder I see the hill
That we shall wend unto.

ISAAK ¶Keep well our ass and all our gear,
To time we come again to you.

61

ABRAHAM ¶My son, this wood behoves thee bear,
Till thou come high upon yon hill.

ISAAK ¶Father, that may do no hurt here,
So God's commandment to fulfil;
For from all ills defends he clear,
Whereso we wend to work his will.

ABRAHAM ¶Ah, son, that was well said.
Lay down that wood even here,
Till our altar be prepared;
And, my son, make good cheer.

ISAAK ¶Father, I see here wood and fire,
But whereof shall our offering be?

ABRAHAM ¶Sure, son, good God our sovereign sire
Shall ordain it in good degree.
For soon, if we do his desire,
Full good reward therefor get we.
In heaven, there must we have our hire,
For unto us so promised he.
Therefore, son, let us pray
To God, both thou and I,
That we may make this day
Our offering here duly.
Great God, that all this world has wrought
And goodly governs good and ill,
Now grant me might, that as I ought
Thy commandments I may fulfil.
And if my flesh grudge or grieve ought,
Though sure my soul assenteth still
To burn all that I hither brought,
I shall not spare, . . . whate'er I kill.

ISAAK ¶Lord God of power so free,
To whom all people prays,
Grant both my father and me
To work thy will all ways.
But, father, now would I ask full fain
Whereof our offering is prepared?

ABRAHAM ¶Sure, son, I may no longer feign.
Thyself is bitter offering made.

ISAAK ¶Why, father, . . . will God I be slain?

ABRAHAM ¶Yea, soothly, son; so has he said.

ISAAK ¶Then I shall not grudge thereagain;

To work his will I shall be glad.
Since it is his desire,
I am prepared to be
Broken and burnt in fire;
Therefore mourn not for me.

ABRAHAM ¶Nay, son, this gate must needs be gone.
My Lord God will I not gainsay,
Nor never make mourning nor moan
To make offering of thee this day.

ISAAK ¶Father, since our Lord God All One
Vouchsafed to send when you did pray
A son to you, when you had none,
And now wills that he wend his way,
Be ready me to fell
As offering in this place;
But first I shall you tell
My counsel in this case.
I know myself by course of kind
My flesh for death will be dreading.
I am afraid that you shall find
My power your purpose to withstand.
Therefore 'tis best that ye me bind
In bands full fast, both foot and hand,
Now, whilst I am in might and mind;
So shall you safely make offering.
For, father, when I am bound,
My might may not avail.
Here shall no fault be found,
To make your purpose fail.
For you are old, and weak to wield,
And I am strong, and wild of thought.

ABRAHAM ¶To bind him that should be my shield!
Out on God's will! That would I not.
But lo, here shall no force be felt;
So shall God have what he has sought.
Farewell, my son, I shall thee yield
To him that all this world has wrought.
Now kiss me heartily, 1 pray.
Isaak, I take my leave for aye.
My blessing have thou entirely—
           Thee must I miss.

And I beseech God Almighty
To give thee his.
Thus do we both assent
After thy words so wise.
Lord God, to this take tent;
Receive thy sacrifice.
This is to me a peerless pain,
To see mine own dear child thus bound.
I had far liever I had been slain,
Than see this sight thus of my son.
It is God's will; it shall be mine;
Against his sending shall I ne'er shun.
To God's commandment I incline,
That in me fault shall none be found.
Therefore, my son so dear,
If thou wilt anything say,
Thy death it draweth near.
Farewell, for once and aye.

ISAAK   ¶Now, father dear, I would thee pray,
Hear me three words; grant me my boon.
Since I from this shall pass away,
I see mine hour is come full soon.
In word, in work, or any way
That I have trespassed or ought misdone,
Forgive me, ere I die this day,
For his love that made sun and moon.
Here since we two shall part,
First God I ask mercy,
Then you, with all my heart,
This day ere ever I die.

ABRAHAM   ¶Now, my great God and Adonay,
That all this world has worthily wrought,
Forgive my son, for thy mercy,
In word and work, in deed and thought.
Now, son, as we are told,
Our time may not miscarry.

ISAAK   ¶Now farewell, middle earth.
My flesh grows faint and cold.
Now father, take thy sword;
Methinks full long you tarry.

ABRAHAM   ¶Nay, nay, son; I beseech you yet;

That do I not, for doubt or fear.
Thy words do make my cheeks to wet,
And change, my child, full oft my cheer.
Therefore lie down now, hands and feet.
Now mayest thou wit thine hour is near.

ISAAK   ¶Ah, father dear, life is full sweet.
The dread of death now daunts me here.
But as I am your son,
God's bidding to fulfil,
Now am I laid here bound;
Do with me what you will.
Father, I ask no more respite ;
But hear a word that I advise.
I do beseech you, ere you smite,
Lay down this kerchief on mine eyes.
Then may your offering be perfect,
If you will work as I advise.
And here to God my soul I plight,
My body a burnt sacrifice.
Now, father, be not missing,
But smite fast as ye may.

ABRAHAM   Farewell, in God's dear blessing
And mine, for ever and aye.
That peerless prince I pray
Mine offering here to have it.
My sacrifice this day,
I pray thee, Lord, receive it.

ANGEL   ¶Abraham! Abraham!

ABRAHAM   Lo, here, I wis.

ANGEL   ¶Abraham, abide, and hold thee still.
Slay not thy son; do him no miss.
Take here this sheep; this offering kill;
'Tis sent thee from the King of bliss,
That faithful aye to thee is found.
He bids thee make offering of this,
Here at this time, and save thy son.

ABRAHAM   ¶I love that Lord with heart entire,
That of his love this loan has lent,
To save my son, my darling dear,
And sent this sheep to this intent,
That we shall offer it to thee here.

So shall it be as thou hast meant.
My son, be glad, and make good cheer;
God has to us good comfort sent.
He wills not thou be dead,
But to his laws take keep;
And see, son, in thy stead
God has sent us a sheep.

ISAAK ¶To make our offering at his will
All for our sake he has it sent.
To love that God I hold great skill,
That to his servants thus has meant.
That death I would have suffered still
Full gladly, Lord, to thine intent.

ABRAHAM ¶Ah, son, thy blood would he not spill;
Therefore this sheep thus has he sent.
And soon I am full fain
Of our speed in this place;
But go we home again,
And love God for his grace.

ANGEL ¶Abraham! Abraham!

ABRAHAM   Lo, here indeed.

ANGEL ¶God says thou shalt have mickle meed
For this good will in which you were.
Since thou for him wouldst do this deed,
To slay thy son and not to spare,
He means to multiply thy seed
On every side, as he said ere.
And yet he promises this,
That your same seed shall rise
Through help of him and his
Overhand of all enemies.
Look ye love him; this is his list;
And loyal live after his law;
For in your seed all men be blest
That there be born by night or day.
If ye will in him trow and trust,
He will be with you ever and aye.

ABRAHAM ¶Full well were us, if we but list
How we should work his will alway.

ISAAK ¶Father, that shall we attain
From wiser men than we,

And fulfil it full fain,
In deed after our degree.

ABRAHAM ¶Now, son, since we thus well have sped,
That God has granted me thy life,
It is my will that thou be wed
And take a woman to thy wife.
So shall thy seed spring and be spread
In the laws of God by reason rife.
I know in what place she is stead
That thou shalt wed, and with no strife.
Rebek that damozel;
Her father is now gone;
The daughter of Batuell,
That was my brother's son.

ISAAK ¶Father, as you like my life to spend,
I shall assent unto the same.

ABRAHAM ¶A servant then soon shall I send
Unto that bride, to bring her home.
The gainest gate now will we wend.
My bairns, ye are not to blame,
If ye think long that we remain.
Gather up our gear now, in God's name,
And go we home again,
Even unto Barsabe.
God that is most of main
Guide us and with you be.

·11

THE HOSIERS

Moyses exaltans serpentem in deserto, Pharao Rex, viij
Judei admirantes et expectantes.

KING PHARAO ¶O peace! I bid that no man pass,
But keep the course that I command;
And take good heed to him that has
Your life all wholly in his hand.
King Pharao my father was,
And led the lordship of this land;
I am his heir, as age will ask,
Ever in his stead to stir and stand.
All Egypt is mine own,
To lead after my law;
I will my might be known
And honoured, as they owe.
Therefore as king I command peace
To all the people of this empire,
That no man put him forth in press
But that will do as we desire.
And of your saws I bid you cease
And list to me your sovereign sire,
That may your comfort most increase,
And as I list take life entire.

1 COUNCILLOR ¶My lord, if any were
That would not work your will,
If we wist who they were
Full soon we shall them spill.

KING PHARAO ¶Throughout my kingdom would I ken,
And know them thank that could me tell
If any were so wicked then
That would ought work our force to fell.

2 COUNCILLOR ¶My lord, there are a manner of men
That muster great masteries to tell—

The Jews that dwell here in Jessen
And are named children of Israel.
They multiply so fast
That soothly we suppose
They are like, if they last,
Your lordship for to lose.

KING PHARAO ¶Why, devil! What gauds have they begun?
Are they of might such riot to raise?

1 COUNCILLOR ¶These felon folk, sir, first were found
In King Pharo your father's days
They came of Joseph, Jacob's son
That was a prince worthy to praise;
And since in increase forth they run,
Now are we like to lose our laws.
They shall confound us clean,
Unless they sooner cease.

KING PHARAO ¶What the devil ever may it mean
That they so fast increase?

2 COUNCILLOR ¶How they increase full well we ken,
As our elders before us found.
They were told but sixty and ten,
When they entered into this land.
Since they have sojourned in Jessen
Four hundred year, this we warrant;
Now are they numbered of mighty men
Well more than three hundred thousand
Without or wife or child
And herds that keep their fee.

KING PHARAO ¶So might we be beguiled;
But sure, that shall not be;
For with cunning we shall them quell,
So that they shall no further spread.

1 COUNCILLOR ¶Lord, we have heard our fathers tell
How cunning clerks, that well could read,
Said one should wax with them and dwell,
That should fordo us and our deed.

KING PHARAO ¶Fie on them! To the devil of hell!
Such destiny shall we not dread;
We shall make midwives them to spill,
Whenever Hebrew child is born,
All them that are mankind to kill;

So shall they soon be lorn.
For of the other I have no awe,
Such bondage shall we to them bid,
To dike and delve, to bear and draw,
And do all such unhonest deed;
Thus shall the lads be holden low,
As worthless ever their life to lead.

2 COUNCILLOR ¶Sure, lord, this is a subtle saw;
So shall the folk no further spread.

KING PHARAO ¶Yaa! Help to hold them down,
That we no faintness find.

1 COUNCILLOR ¶Lord, we shall be ready anon
In bondage them to bind.

II

MOSES ¶Great God, that all this ground began
And governest ever in good degree,
That made me Moyses unto man,
And saved me since out of the sea—
King Pharao he commanded then
So that no sons should saved be.
Against his will away I won;
Thus has God shewed his might in me.
Now here I am to keep
Set under Synay side
The Bishop Jethro's sheep;
So best behoved to bide.
Ah mercy, God! Mickle is thy might.
What man may of thy marvels tell?
I see yonder a wondrous sight,
Whereof before no sign was seen:
A bush I see there burning bright,
Yet the leaves last aye in like green.
If it be work of worldly wight
I will go wit, doubt to dispel.

GOD ¶Moses! Come not too near,
But still in that stead dwell,
And take heed to me here;
Attend what I shall tell.
I am thy Lord without mistake,

To length thy life even as I list;
And the same God who sometime spake
Unto thy elders, as they wist.
But Abraham and Ysaac
And Jacob, said I, should be blest
And multiply, and them to make
So that their seed should not be missed.
And now King Pharao
Fells their childer full fast;
If I suffer him so,
Their seed should soon be past.
Go, make the message I intend
To him that them so harmed has.
Go, warn him now with word full kind,
So that he let my people pass,
That they to wilderness may wend
And worship me as whilom was.
And if he longer make them attend
His song full soon shall be "Alas!"

MOSES   ¶Ah Lord, since, with thy leave,
That lineage loves me nought;
Gladly they would me grieve,
If I such bidword brought.
Therefore, Lord, let some other test
That has more force to make them fear

GOD   ¶Moyses, be not abased
My bidding bold to bear
If they with wrong ought would thee wrest,
Out of all harms I shall thee bear.

MOSES   ¶Ah Lord! They will not to me trust,
For all the oaths that I may swear.
To name such note anew
To folk of wicked will,
Without some token true,
They will not heed me still.

GOD   ¶And if they will not understand
Nor take heed how I have thee sent,
Before the king cast down thy wand,
And it shall seem as a serpent.
Then take the tail into thy hand;
Handle it hardy in intent;

In the first state as thou it found,
So shall it turn to my intent.
Hide thy hand in thy breast—
Like serpent it shall be;
Hale it as ye will best;
These signs shall of thee be.
And if he will not suffer then
My people to pass forth in peace,
I shall send vengeance nine or ten,
To serve him sorrow ere I cease.
But the Jews that dwell in Jessen
Shall not be marked with such as these.
As long as they my laws will ken
Their comfort shall I ever increase.

MOSES   ¶Ah Lord! Loved be thy will,
That makes thy folks so free;
Unto them shall I tell
All you tell unto me.
But to the king, Lord, when I come
And he ask me what is thy name,
And I stand still then, deaf and dumb—
How shall I be without a blame?

GOD   ¶I say thus: EGO SUM QUI SUM:
I am he that I am the same.
And if thou might not move as dumb
I shall thee save from sin and shame.

MOSES   ¶I understand this thing
With all the might in me.

GOD   ¶Be bold in my blessing;
Thy shield aye shall I be.

MOSES   ¶Ah, Lord of life, learn me thy lore,
That I thy tales may truly tell.
Unto my friends now will I fare,
The chosen children of Israel,
To tell them comfort in their care
And of their danger that they in dwell.

III

MOSES   ¶God maintain you and me evermore,
And mickle mirth be your having.

1 JEW   ¶Ah, Moyses, master dear,
        Our mirth is all mourning.
        We are hard holden here
        As bondmen by the king.

2 JEW   ¶Ah, Moyses, we may mourn and pine;
        There is no man that mirth us makes.
        And since we come all of a kin
        Give us some comfort in this case.

MOSES   ¶Of mourning may you end herein;
        God will defend you of your foes.
        Out of this woe he will you win,
        To please him in more plainer place.
        I shall speak to the king,
        And seek to make you free.

3 JEW   God send us good tiding,
        And all well with you be.

IV

MOSES   ¶King Pharao, to me take tent.

KING PHARAO   ¶Why now, what tidings can you tell?

MOSES   ¶From God of heaven thus am I sent,
        To fetch his folk of Israel;
        To wilderness he would they went.

KING PHARAO   ¶Yaa! wend thou to the devil of hell!
        I make no force how thou hast meant,
        For in my danger shall they dwell.
        And, false one, for thy sake
        They shall be put to pain.

MOSES   ¶Then will God vengeance take
        On thee and on all thine.

KING PHARAO   ¶Fie on thee! Lad, out of my land!
        Thinks thou with wiles to loose our law?
        Whence is this warlock with his wand
        That would thus win our folk away?

2 COUNCILLOR   ¶It is Moyses, we well warrand;
        Against all Egypt is he aye.
        Your father great fault in him found
        Now will he mar you if he may.

KING PHARAO   ¶Nay, nay; that dance is done;
        That lurdan learned too late.

MOSES ¶God bids thee grant my boon,
And let me go my gate.

KING PHARAO ¶Bids God me? False lurdan, thou lies!
What token told he, took thou tent?

MOSES ¶Yea, sir; he said thou should despise
Both me and all his commandment.
In thy presence cast on this wise
My wand he bade, by his assent;
And that thou shouldst thee well advise
How it should turn to a serpent.
And in his holy name
Here shall I lay it down.
Lo, sir, see here the same.

KING PHARAO ¶Ah dog! The devil thee drown!

MOSES ¶He said that I should take the tail,
So for to prove his power plain;
And soon he said it should not fail
For to turn to a wand again.
Lo, sir, behold! Hop illa hail!

KING PHARAO ¶Now sure this is a subtle swain.
But these boys shall abide in bail;
For all their gauds shall nought them gain,
But worse both morn and noon
Shall they fare for thy sake.

MOSES ¶God send some vengeance soon,
And on thy work take wreak.

1 EGYPTIAN ¶Alas, alas! This land is lorn;
Alive we may no longer stay.

2 EGYPTIAN ¶So great mischief is made this morn;
No medicine now amend us may.

1 COUNCILLOR ¶Sir King, we curse that we were born;
Our bliss is all to sorrow grown.

KING PHARAO ¶Why cry you so, lads? List you scorn?

1 EGYPTIAN ¶Sir King, such care was never known.
Our water that was once ordained
To men and beasts as food,
Throughout all Egypt land
Is turned now to red blood.
Full ugly and full ill it is
That was full fair and fresh before.

KING PHARAO ¶This is great wonder for to wit

74

	Of all the works that ever were.
2 EGYPTIAN	¶Nay, lord, there is another yet
	That suddenly pursues us sore.
	For toads and frogs we may not flit;
	Their venom poisons less and more.
I EGYPTIAN	¶Lord, great lice both morn and noon
	Bite us full bitterly;
	And we trow all is done
	By Moyses our enemy.
2 COUNCILLOR	¶Lord, while we with this people live,
	May never mirth be us among.
KING PHARAO	¶Go, say we shall no longer grieve—
	But they shall never the sooner gang.
2 EGYPTIAN	¶Moyses, my lord has granted leave
	To lead thy folk to liking long,
	So that we mend of our mischief.
MOSES	¶I wit full well these words are wrong;
	That shall full soon be seen.
	My promise I repeat—
	If he of malice mean,
	More marvels must he meet.
I EGYPTIAN	¶Lord, alas, for dole we die;
	We dare not look out at no door.
KING PHARAO	¶What the devil ails you so to cry?
2 EGYPTIAN	¶We fare now worse than ever before;
	Great lops over all this land they fly,
	That with biting make blain and sore.
I EGYPTIAN	¶Lord, our beasts lie dead and dry,
	As well on midden as on moor.
	Both ox and horse and ass
	Fall dead down suddenly.
KING PHARAO	¶Thereof no man harm has
	Half so much as I.
2 COUNCILLOR	¶Yes, lord. Poor men have mickle woe
	To see their cattle be out cast.
	The Jews in Goshen fare not so;
	They have all liking that may last.
KING PHARAO	¶Go, say we give them leave to go
	Till time these perils be o'er past.
	But e'er they flit over far us fro,
	We shall them bind four times as fast.

75

2 EGYPTIAN	¶Moyses, my lord gives leave Thy men for to remove.
MOSES	¶He must have more mischief, Unless his tale be true.
1 EGYPTIAN	¶Woe, Lord! We may not lead this life.
KING PHARAO	¶Why, is there grievance grown again?
2 EGYPTIAN	¶Such powder, lord, upon us drives, That where it beats it makes a blain.
1 EGYPTIAN	¶Like lepers makes it man and wife. Since they are hurt with hail and rain, Our vines in mountains may not thrive, So are they threshed and thunder-slain.
KING PHARAO	¶How do they in Goshen, The Jews? Can ye ought say?
2 EGYPTIAN	¶This care nothing they ken; They feel no such affray.
KING PHARAO	¶No, devil! And sit they so in peace, And we each day in doubt and dread?
1 EGYPTIAN	¶My lord, this care will ever increase, Till Moyses have leave them to lead.
1 COUNCILLOR	¶Lord, were they gone then would it cease, So should we save us and our seed, Else be we lorn: this is no lies.
KING PHARAO	¶Let him go forth? The devil him speed! Though he should rave and curse, His folk not far shall go.
2 COUNCILLOR	¶Then will it soon be worse, It were better that they go.
2 EGYPTIAN	¶Woe, lord! New harm is come to hand.
KING PHARAO	¶No, devil! Will it no better be?
1 EGYPTIAN	¶Wild worms are laid o'er all this land; They leave no fruit nor flower on tree. Against that storm may nothing stand.
2 EGYPTIAN	¶Lord, there is more mischief, thinks me, And three days has it yet endured. Such murk no man might other see.
1 EGYPTIAN	¶My lord, great pestilence Is like full long to last.
KING PHARAO	¶Comes that in our presence? Then is our pride all past.
2 EGYPTIAN	¶My lord, this vengeance lasteth long,

	And must till Moyses have his boon.
I COUNCILLOR	¶Lord, let them wend, else work we wrong;
	It may not help to hover nor have.
KING PHARAO	¶Go, say we grant them leave to go—
	In the devil's way—since it must be done.
	We shall take them—it may fall so—
	And mar them ere tomorn at noon.
I EGYPTIAN	¶Moyses, my lord has said
	You shall have passage plain
	And to pass am I glad.
MOSES	¶My friends, be now full fain,
	For at our will now shall we wend,
	In land of liking for to dwell.
I JEW	¶King Pharao, that felon fiend,
	Will have great care when this is kenned.
	Then will he shape to smite us down,
	And soon his host after us send.
MOSES	¶Be not afeared; God is your friend,
	From all our foes us to defend.
	Therefore come forth with me;
	Have done, and dread you nought.
2 JEW	¶My Lord, loved might thou be
	That thus from bale has brought.
3 JEW	¶Such friendship never before we found.
	But in this doing defaults may fall;
	The Red Sea is right near at hand;
	There must we bide till we be thrall.
MOSES	¶I shall make us way with my wand.
	For God has said, to save us all,
	On either side the sea shall stand,
	Till we be gone, right as a wall.
	Therefore have ye no dread,
	But seek aye God to please.
I JEW	¶That Lord to land us lead.
	Now wend we all at ease.

V

I EGYPTIAN	¶King Pharao, those folk are gone.
KING PHARAO	¶How now? Is there annoyance new?
2 EGYPTIAN	¶The Hebrews are gone every one.

KING PHARAO	¶How sayest thou that?
I EGYPTIAN	These tales are true.
KING PHARAO	¶Quick harness horse, that they be ta'en.
	This riot rapidly shall they rue.
	We shall not cease till they be slain,
	For to the sea we shall pursue.
	So charge our chariots with speed,
	And fearless follow me.
2 EGYPTIAN	¶My lord, we are all blithe indeed
	At your bidding to be.
2 COUNCILLOR	¶Lord, to your bidding are we bound
	Our bodies boldly for to bid.
	We shall not bide, but ding them down,
	And have no fear, till all be dead.
KING PHARAO	¶Heave up your hearts aye to Mahound;
	He will be near us in our need.
	Out, help, haro! Devil! I drown!
I EGYPTIAN	¶Alas, we die, for all our deed.
I JEW	¶Now are we won from woe,
	And saved out of the sea.
	Cantemus domino:
	To God a song sing we.

12

THE SPICERS

Doctor declarens dicta prophetarum de nativitate Christi futura. Maria, Angelus salutans eam, Maria salutans Elizabetham.[1]

DOCTOR ⁋Lord God, great marvel this may mean,
How man was made with nought amiss,
And set where he should ever have been
All without bale, biding in bliss;
And how he lost that comfort clean,
And was put out from Paradise,
And since what sorrows sore were seen,
Seen unto him and to all his,
And how they lay long space
In hell lockèd from light,
Till God granted them grace
Of help as he had hight.
Then is it needful for to name
How prophets could God's counsel tell,
As prophet Amos of the same
Taught while he in this life did dwell,
     Deus pater disposuit salutem fieri in medio terre, etc.
He saith thus: God the Father in heaven
Ordained in earth mankind to mend;
And to grace it with godhead even,
His Son he said that he should send
To take kind of man's kin
In a maiden full mild.
So was many saved of sin,
And the foul fiend beguiled.
And that the fiend should be so fed

---

[1] A marginal note in a sixteenth-century hand says, "Doctor, this matter is newly mayde, wherof we haue no coppy." This may refer to the whole of the Prologue, spoken by a "Doctor".

By grief and to no truth take tent,
God made that maiden to be wed,
Ere He his son unto her sent.
So was the Godhead closed and clad
In weeds of wedding where they went.
And that our bliss should be so bred
Full many matters may be meant.
    Qoniam in semine tuo benedicentur omnes gentes,
    etc. Gen. xxii. 18.
God himself said this thing
To Abraham as he list,
"Of thy seed shall upspring
Wherein folk shall be blest."
To prove these prophets ordained were,
Even as I say to old and young,
He moved our mischiefs for to mar,
For thus he prayed God for this thing:
Orate celi desuper,
Lord, let thou down at thy liking
The dew to fall from heaven so far,
For then from earth shall spread and spring
A seed that shall us save
That now in bliss are bent.
Of clerks whoso will crave,
This may thus wise be meant:
The dew to God the Holy Ghost
May be comparèd in man's mind;
The earth unto the maiden chaste,
Because she comes of earthly kind.
Those wise words were not wrought in waste,
To waft and wend away as wind,
For this same prophet soon in haste
Said furthermore, as folks may find:
    Propter hoc dabit dominus ipse vobis signum, etc.
    Isa. vii.14.
Lo, he says thus: God shall give
Hereof a sign to see,
To all that loyal live,
And this their sign shall be:
    Ecce virgo concipiet et pariet filium, etc. Isa. vii.14.
Lo here, he says a maiden soon

Here on this mould where mankind dwell
Shall clear conceive and bear a son,
And name his name Emmanuell.
His kingdom that ever is begun
Shall never cease, but dure and dwell;
On David's seat shall he sit down,
His dooms to deem and truth to tell.
 Zelus domini faciet hoc, etc. Isa. ix.7.
He says: love of our Lord
All this shall ordain then,
Man's peace and full accord
To make with earthly men.
More of this maiden then moves he;
This prophet says for our succour:
 Egredietur virga de Jesse:
A wand shall breed of Jesse's bower;
And of this same also says he,
Upon that wand shall spring a flower,
Whereon the Holy Ghost shall be,
To govern it with great honour.
That wand means unto us
This maiden even and morn,
And the flower is Jesus,
That of that bliss is born.
The prophet Johell, a gentle Jew,
Sometime has said of the same thing;
He likens Christ even as he knew,
Like to the dew in downcoming:
 Ero quasi ros et virgo Israel germinabit sicut lilium.
 Hos. xiv.6.
The maiden of Israel all new,
He says, shall bear one and forth bring,
As the lily flower full fair of hue.
This meaneth so to old and young
That the high Holy Ghost
Comes our mischief to mend
In Mary maiden chaste,
When God his Son would send.
This lady the lily equalling,
That is because of her clean life—
For in this world was no such thing,

One to be maiden, mother and wife;
Her son in heaven's realm be king,
As oft is read by reason rife;
And her husband both master and meek
In charity, to stint all strife.
This passed all earthly wit,
How God ordained them then;
In her one to be knit
Godhead, maidenhead and man.
But of this work great witness was—
Our forefathers all folk may tell—
When Jacob blessed his son Judas,
Between them was this tale to tell:

> *Non auferetur sceptrum de Juda: Veniat qui
> mittendus est. Gen. xlix.10.*

He says, the sceptre shall not pass
From Juda land of Israel,
Ere he come that God ordained has
To be sent, fiend's force for to quell.

> *Et ipse erit expectacio gencium. Gen. xlix.10.*

Him shall all folk abide,
And stand unto his steven.
These saws were signified
To Christ, God's Son in heaven.
For how he was sent, see we more,
And how God would his place purvey:
He said, "Son, I shall send before
Mine angel to make ready thy way."

> *Ecce mitto angelum meum ante faciem tuam qui
> preparabit viam tuam ante te. Mark i.2.*

Of John Baptist he did mean there,
For in earth he was ordained aye,
To warn the folk that whilom were
Of Christ's coming, who thus did say,

> *Ego quidem baptizo in aqua vos autem baptiza-
> bimini spiritu sancto. For Matth. iii.11.*

"After me shall come now
A man of might the most,
And he shall baptize you
In the high Holy Ghost."
Thus of Christ's coming may we see

How St. Luke speaks in his Gospel:
"From God in heaven is sent," says he,
An angel is named Gabriel,
To Nazareth in Galilee,
Where then a maiden mild did dwell,
That with Joseph should wedded be;
Her name Mary: thus did he tell.
God's grace was then arrayed
To man in this manner;
And how the angel said,
Take heed, all that are here.

Then the angel sings.

GABRIEL ¶Hail, Mary, full of grace and bliss;
Our Lord God is with thee,
And has chosen thee for his;
Of all women blest might thou be.

MARY ¶What manner of hailing is this
That privily comes to me?
For in my heart a thought it is,
The tokening that I here see.

GABRIEL ¶Now dread thou nought, thou mild Mary,
For nothing that may thee befall,
For thou hast found all sovereignly
Of God a grace over others all.
In chastity of thy body
Conceive and bear a child thou shall.
This bidding bring I thee thereby . . .
His name Jesu shalt thou call.
Mickle of might then shall he be,
He shall be God and called God's Son,
And David's seat, his father free,
Shall God give him to sit upon.
As king for ever reign shall he,
In Jacob's house aye for to dwell;
Of his kingdom and dignity
Shall no man earthly know nor tell.

MARY ¶O thou God's angel meek and mild,
How should it be, I do thee pray,
That I should so conceive a child
Of any man by night or day?
I know no man that has defiled

83

My maidenhood, the sooth to say;
Without a will of workings wild
In chastity have I been aye.

GABRIEL ¶The Holy Ghost in thee shall light,
High virtue shall he to thee hold;
The holy birth of thee so bright,
The Son of God shall he be called.
Lo, Elizabeth thy cousin might
No child conceive, for she is old—
This is the sixth month now full right
With her that barren has been told.

MARY ¶Thou angel, blessed messenger,
Of God's will do I hold me glad.
I love my Lord with heart full dear,
For grace that he has on me laid.
God's handmaiden, lo, I am here,
To do his will all ready arrayed.
Be done to me in all manner
Through thy word even as thou hast said.

GABRIEL ¶Now God that all our hope is in,
Through the might of the Holy Ghost,
Save thee, good dame, from stain of sin,
And guide thee from all workings waste.

II

The house of Zacharias

MARY ¶Elizabeth, mine own cousin,
Methought I covet always most
To speak with thee of all my kin,
Therefore I come thus in this haste.

ELIZABETH ¶Welcome, thou mild Mary,
Mine own cousin so dear;
Joyful woman am I
That I now see thee here.
Blessed may thou only
Of all women appear,
And the fruit of thy body
Be blessed far and near.
This is joyful tiding

84

That I may now here see;
The mother of my Lord king
In this wise come to me.
Soon as the voice of thy hailing
Might mine ears enter and be,
The child in my womb so young
Makes great mirth unto thee.

MARY ¶Now, Lord, blest be thou aye
For the grace thou hast me lent.
Lord, I love thee, God very,
For message thou hast me sent.
I thank thee night and day,
And pray with good intent
I may please thee by my way;
To thee my will is bent.

ELIZABETH ¶Blest be thou, goodly arrayed
To God through chastity.
Thou trowed and held thee glad
At his will for to be.
All that to thee is said
From my Lord God so free,
Such grace is for thee laid
To be fulfilled in thee.

MARY ¶To his grace I will me betake,
With chastity to deal,
That made me thus to go
Among his maidens well.
My soul shall loving make
Unto that Lord so leal;
My spirit make joy also
And my spirit make joy also
In God that is my weal.

Then she sings Magnificat.

13

THE PEWTERERS AND FOUNDERS

Maria, Josep volens dimittere eam, angelus eis loquens ut transeant usque Bethlem.

JOSEPH ¶Of great mourning may I complain,
And walk full wearily by the way,
For unto now I best have been
At ease and rest by reason aye.
For I am of great eld
And weak and all unwield,
As each man see it may.
I may neither haste nor hide,
Either in frith or field.
For shame what shall I say,
That thusgates now in my old days
Has wedded a young wench to my wife,
And may not well stride over two straws?
Now, Lord, too long I lead this life.
My bones are heavy as lead
And may not stand in stead,
As known it is full rife.
Now, Lord, teach me and guide,
Or soon drive me to death;
Thou best may stint this strife.
For bitterly then may I ban
The way I in the Temple went;
It was to me a bad bargain;
For ruth I may it aye repent.
For therein was ordained
Unwedded men should stand
All assembled at assent,
And each one a dry wand

On high held in his hand,
And I wist not what it meant.
Amongst the others one bare I . . .
It flourished fair and flowers on spread;
And they said to me thereby
That with a wife I should be wed.
The bargain I made there,
That rues me now full sore,
So am I straitly stead.
Now casts it me in care,
For well I might evermore
A single life have led.
Her works me make my cheeks to wet;
I am beguiled; how, know I not.
My young wife is with child full great;
That makes me now sorrow unsought.
That reproof near has slain me,
If any man should ask me ought,
How this thing may be wrought;
To talk of it would pain me,
The law stands hard again me;
To death must I be brought.
And loath, methinks, on the other side,
My wife with any man to defame.
And which of these two I abide,
I may not scape without some shame.
The child sure is not mine;
That reproof makes me pine
And makes me flee from home.
My life though I resign,
She is a clean virgin
For me, without all blame.
But well I wit through prophecy
A maiden clean should bear a child—
But yet it is not so, surely,
Because I wit I am beguiled.
And why would not some young man take her?
For sure, I think for to forsake her
Into some wood so wild;
Thus think I to steal from her.
God shield no wild beast slay her,

She is so meek and mild.
Of my wending none will I warn.
Nevertheless 'tis my intent
To ask her who got her her bairn—
That would I fain know ere I went.
All hail! God be herein.

I MAID   ¶Welcome, by God's dear might.

JOSEPH   ¶Where is that young virgin,
Mary, my bride so bright?

I MAID   ¶Sure, Joseph, you shall understand
That she is not full far from you;
She sits at her book fast praying
For you and us and all those too
That ought have need.
But for to tell her I will go
Of your coming, all without dread.
Have done and rise up, dame,
And to me take good heed.
Joseph, he is come home.

MARY   ¶Welcome, as God me speed.
Doubtless to me he is full dear.
Joseph, my spouse, welcome are ye.

JOSEPH   ¶Gramercy, Mary. Say, what cheer?
Tell me in sooth, how is't with thee?
Who has been here?
Thy womb is waxen great, thinks me.
Thou art with child, alas for care.
Ah maidens, woe worth ye,
That let her learn such lore.

2 MAID   ¶Joseph, you shall not trow
Ill doing she would dare.

JOSEPH   ¶Trow it not ill? Leave, wench; away!
Her sides show well she is with child.
Who's is't, Mary?

MARY   ¶Sir, God's and yours.

JOSEPH   ¶Nay, nay.
Now wit I well I am beguiled. . . .
And reason why?
With me fleshly wast thou never defiled,
And I forsake it here thereby.
Say, maidens, how is this?

Tell me the truth, say I.
Unless ye do, I wis
Bad bargains shall ye buy.

2 MAID ¶If ye threat fast as e'er you can,
There is nothing to say there, still;
For truly here came never man
To weight her body with no ill
Of this sweet wight.
For we have dwelt aye with her still,
And never from her day or night;
Her keepers have we been,
And she aye in our sight.
Came here no man between,
To touch that bride so bright.

1 MAID ¶In this house came none for the nonce,
And that ever witness will we,
Saving an angel one day once;
With bodily food her fed has he;
Other came none.
Wherefore we wit not how it should be,
But through the Holy Ghost alone,
For truly we trow this:
His grace with her is gone.
For she wrought never no miss;
We witness every one.

JOSEPH ¶Then see I well your meaning is,
The angel has made her with child;
Nay; some man in angel's likeness
With some base trick has her beguiled,
And that trow I.
For thou needest not such words so wild
To tell to me deceivingly.
Woe! Why gab ye at me so,
And feign such fantasy?
Alas, I am full woe;
For dole might I not die?
To me this is a careful case;
Reckless I rave; my peace is sped.
I dare look no man in the face;
For heavy dole would I were dead;
I loathe this life.

In Temple and in other stead
Each man to mockery will me drive.
Was ever wight so woe?
With ruth all riven I strive.
Alas, why wrought you so,
Mary, my wedded wife?

MARY ¶To my witness great God I call,
That in my mind never wrought no miss.

JOSEPH ¶Whose is the child thou art withal?

MARY ¶Yours, sir, and the king of bliss.

JOSEPH ¶Yea, and how then?
Nay, wondrous tidings then is this;
Excuse them well these women can.
But Mary, all that see thee
May wit thy works are wan;
Thy womb all ways bewrays thee
That thou hast met with man.
Whose is it, as fair might you befall?

MARY ¶Sir, it is yours, and God's own will.

JOSEPH ¶Nay, nay; I have nought to do withal;
Name it no more to me; be still.
Thou wittest as well as I
That we two same fleshly
Wrought ne'er such works with ill.
Look thou did no folly
Before me privily,
Thy maidenhead to spill.
But who is the father? Tell me his name.

MARY ¶None but yourself.

JOSEPH   Let be, for shame.
I did it never. Thou dotest, dame, by book and
    bell.
Full blameless should I bear this blame, as thou
    dost tell.
For I wrought never in word nor deed
Thing that should mar thy maidenhead
With touch of ill;
For of such work were little need.
Yet for mine own I would it feed,
Might all be still.
Therefore the father tell me, Mary.

MARY   ¶But God and you, I know right none.
JOSEPH   ¶Such sayings make me full sorry,
           With great mourning to make my moan.
           Therefore be not so bold
           That no such tales be told,
           But hold thee still at home.
           Thou art young and I am old;
           Such works if I do would,
           These games from me are gone.
           Therefore tell me in privity,
           Whose is the child thou art with now?
           Surely there shall none know but we;
           I dread the law as well as thou.
MARY   ¶Now great God of his might,
           That all may dress and dight,
           Meekly to thee I bow.
           Forgive this weary wight,
           That in his heart may light
           The truth to ken and know.
JOSEPH   ¶Who had thy maidenhead, Mary? Tell me thy
           mind.
MARY   ¶Forsooth, a maiden clean am I.
JOSEPH   ¶Nay; thou speakest now against kind.
           Such thing might no man signify—
           A maid to be with child . . .
           These words from thee are wild—
           She is not born, I ween.
MARY   ¶Joseph, you are beguiled.
           With sin was I never defiled.
           God's sending is on me seen.
JOSEPH   ¶God's sending? Yah, Mary! God help!
           But sure that child was never ours two.
           But woman kind, if they want help,
           Yet would they no man knew their woe.
MARY   ¶Sure it is God's sending;
           From that I never go.
JOSEPH   ¶Yah, Mary! Draw thy hand;
           For to ask further I intend.
           I trow it be not so.
           The truth from me to hide is vain;
           The childbearing mayest thou not hide.

But sit here till I come again;
I must an errand here beside.

MARY ¶Now great God guide in this
And mend you of your miss
Of me, whatso betide.
As he is king of bliss,
Send you some sight of this,
In truth that ye might bide.

JOSEPH ¶Now, Lord my God, that all things may
At thine own will both do and dress,
Make me to know some ready way
To walk here in this wilderness.
But ere I pass this hill,
Do with me what God will
Either of more or less,
Here must I bide full still,
Till I have slept my fill;
My heart so heavy is.

ANGEL GABRIEL ¶Waken, Joseph, and take better keep
To Mary, that is thy fellow fast.

JOSEPH ¶Ah, I am full weary. Pray let me sleep,
Forwandered, walking in this forest.

ANGEL GABRIEL ¶Rise up, and sleep no more.
Thou makest her heart full sore
That loves thee of all the best.

JOSEPH ¶Ah! Now is this a fearsome fare,
For to be caught both here and there,
And nowhere may have rest.
Say, what art thou? Tell me this thing.

ANGEL GABRIEL ¶I Gabriel am; God's angel I,
That have taken Mary to my keeping,
And sent to thee aloud to cry
In loyal wedlock lead thee;
Leave her not, I forbid thee;
No sin of her imply.
But to her fast thou speed thee;
And of her nought thou dread thee.
God's word this, from on high.
The child that shall be born of her,
It is conceived of the Holy Ghost.
All joy and bliss then shall be after,

And to mankind of all the most.
Jesus his name thou call;
Such hap shall him befall,
As thou shalt see in haste.
His people save he shall
From evils and angers all
Whereby they are now embraced.

JOSEPH   ¶And is this sooth, angel, thou says?

ANGEL GABRIEL   ¶Yea; and this to take right,
Wend forth to Mary thy wife all ways.
Bring her to Bethlehem this very night.
There shall a child born be;
God's son of heaven is he
And man the most of might.

JOSEPH   ¶Now, Lord my God, full well is me
That ever I this sight should see;
I was never ere so light.
For since I would have her refused,
And blameless blamed that aye was clear,
I must pray her hold me excused,
As some men do with full good cheer.
Say, Mary wife, how fares thou?

MARY   ¶The better, sir, for you. . . .
Why stand ye there? Come near.

JOSEPH   ¶My back fain would I bow,
And ask forgiveness now,
Wist I thou wouldst me hear.

MARY   ¶Forgiveness, sir? Let be, for shame.
Such words should all good women lack.

JOSEPH   ¶Yea, Mary. I am to blame
For words long since I to thee spake.
But gather up now all our gear,
Such poor weeds as we wear,
And press them in a pack.
To Bethlehem must I it bear,
For little things will women fear.
Help up now, on my back.

14

THE TILLE THEKERS

*Maria, Josep, obstetrix, puer natus iacens in presepio inter
bovem et asinum, et angelus loquens pastoribus, et ludentibus,
in pagina sequente.*

JOSEPH ¶All wielding God in Trinity,
I pray thee, Lord, for thy great might,
Unto thy simple servant see,
Here in this place where we are pight,
Ourselves alone.
Lord, grant us good harbour this night
Where we have gone.
For we have sought both up and down,
Through divers streets in this city;
So much people is come to town,
That we can nowhere harboured be,
There is such press.
Forsooth I can no succour see
But shelter with the beasts.
And if we here all night abide,
We shall be stormed here in this stead;
The walls are down on every side,
The roof is ruined above our head,
As I may rue.
Say, Mary, daughter, what is thy rede?
How shall we do?
For in great need now are we stead,
As thou thyself in sooth mayest see;
For here is neither clothes nor bed,
And we are weak and all weary,
And fain would rest.
Now, gracious God, for thy mercy
Guide us the best.

MARY ¶God will us guide, full well wit ye;
Therefore, Joseph, be of good cheer.
For in this place born will he be
That shall save us from sorrows here
　　Both even and morn.
Sir, wit ye well the time is near
　　He will be born.

JOSEPH ¶Then it behoves us bide here still,
Here in this same place all this night.

MARY ¶Yea, sir; forsooth it is God's will.

JOSEPH ¶Then would I fain we had some light,
　　What so befall.
It wakes right dark unto my sight,
　　And cold withal.
I will go get us light this tide,
And fuel find with me to bring.

MARY ¶All wielding God you govern and guide,
As he is sovereign of all thing,
　　For his great might,
And lend me grace to his loving
　　To wait aright.
Now in my soul great joy have I;
I am all clad in comfort clear.
Now will be born of my body
Both God and man together here.
　　Blest might he be!
Jesus! My son that is so dear,
　　Now born is he.
Hail, my Lord God! Hail, prince of peace!
Hail, my father, and hail, my son!
Hail, sovereign strong all sins to cease!
Hail, God and man on earth in one!
　　Hail, through whose might
All this world was first begun,
　　Darkness and light!
Son, as I am simple subject of thine,
Vouchsafe, sweet son, I pray to thee,
That I might take thee in these arms of mine,
And in this poor weed array thee.
　　Grant me thy bliss,
As I am thy mother chosen to be

	In truthfulness.
JOSEPH	¶Ah, Lord, what! The weather is cold,

The fellest freeze that e'er I did feel.
I pray God help them that is old,
Or find it ill their limbs to wield;
    So may I say.
Now, good God, be thou my shield.
    As thou best may.
Ah, Lord God! What light is this
That comes shining thus suddenly?
I cannot say, as I have bliss.
When I come home unto Mary,
    I will ask her.
Ah, here be good, for here come I.

MARY   You are welcome, sir.

JOSEPH ¶Say, Mary daughter, what cheer with thee?

MARY ¶Right good, Joseph, as has been aye,

JOSEPH ¶Oh, Mary—what sweet thing is that on thy knee?

MARY ¶It is my son, the sooth to say,
          So mild of mood.

JOSEPH ¶Well is me I did bide this day
          To see this good.
I marvel mickle of this light,
That thuswise shineth in this place;
Forsooth it is a wondrous sight.

MARY ¶This has he ordained of his grace,
          My son so young,
A star to be shining a space
          At his bearing.
For Balaam told full long before,
How that a star should rise full high,
And of a maiden should be born
A son that shall our saving be
          From cares so keen.
Forsooth it is my son so free
          Balaam did mean.

JOSEPH ¶Now welcome, flower fairest of hue,
I worship thee with main and might.
Hail, my Maker! Hail, Christ Jesu!
Hail, royal king, root of all right!
          Hail, Saviour!

Hail, my Lord, gleaming so light!
Hail, blessed flower!

MARY ¶Now, Lord, that all this world shall win,
To thee, my son, is what I say.
Here is no bed to lay thee in,
Therefore, my dear son, I thee pray,
Since it is so,
Here in this crib I might thee lay
Between these beasts two.
And I shall hap thee, mine own dear child,
With such poor clothes as we have here.

JOSEPH ¶O Mary, behold these beasts so mild!
They make loving in their manner,
As they were men;
Forsooth it seems well by their cheer,
Their lord they ken.

MARY ¶Their lord they ken, that wot I well;
They worship him with might and main.
The weather is cold, as ye may feel;
To hold him warm they are full fain
With their warm breath,
And breathe on him, it is certain,
To warm him with.
Now sleeps my son, blest might he be,
And lies full warm these beasts between.

JOSEPH ¶O now is fulfilled, forsooth I see
What Habakkuk in mind did mean,
And preached by prophecy;
He said our Saviour shall be seen,
Between beasts lie.
And now I see the same in sight.

MARY ¶Yea, sir; forsooth the same is he.

JOSEPH ¶Honour and worship both day and night
Aye—lasting lord, be done to thee
All way as is worthy.
Lord, to thy service I bind me,
With all my heart wholly.

MARY ¶Thou merciful Maker, most mighty,
My God, my Lord, my son so free,
Thy handmaiden forsooth am I,
And to thy service I bind me

97

THE TILLE THEKERS

With all my heart entire
Thy blessing, so beseech I thee,
Thou grant us all now here.

15

THE CHAUNDELERS

Pastores loquentes adinvicem, stella in oriente, angelus nuncians pastoribus gaudium de puero nato.

1 SHEPHERD	¶Brethren, in haste take heed and hear What I will speak and specify. Since we walk thus certain and clear, What makes my mood now move will I. Our forefathers faithful who were, Both Hosea and Ysaye, Proved that a prince without a peer Should descend down into a lady And to make mankind clearly, To heal them that are lorn, And in Bethlem here by, Shall that same bairn be born.
2 SHEPHERD	¶Ere he be born in borough hereby, Balaham foretold, I have heard say, A star should shine and signify With lightful gleams like any day. And as the text it tells clearly By witty men learned of our law With his best blood he should us buy. He should take here all of a maid. I heard my sire once say, When he of her was born She should be as clean maid As ever she was before.
3 SHEPHERD	¶Ah, merciful Maker, mickle is thy might, That thus will to thy servants see. Might we once look upon that light, Gladder brethren might no men be. I have heard say, by that same light

The children of Israel should be made free
The force of the fiend to fell in sight,
And all his power excluded be.
Wherefore, brethren, I rede that we
Flit fast over these fells,
Our flocks to find and see,
And talk of somewhat else.
(*Angels appear*)

1 SHEPHERD	¶Ah! Ooh!
2 SHEPHERD	Ah! Hoo!
1 SHEPHERD	Hearken to me!
2 SHEPHERD	¶Why man, thou maddest all out of might.
1 SHEPHERD	¶Ah, colle!
3 SHEPHERD	What care is come to thee?
1 SHEPHERD	¶Step forth, and stand by me aright,
	And tell me truly then
	If you saw ever such a sight!
3 SHEPHERD	¶I? Nay, certes, nor never no man.
2 SHEPHERD	¶Say, fellows, what? Find ye any feast?
	I ought to have my part, pardie!
1 SHEPHERD	¶Oh, oh! Behold unto the East!
	A wondrous sight then shall you see
	Upon the sky.
2 SHEPHERD	¶Why, tell me, men, among us three,
	What makes you stare so sturdily?
3 SHEPHERD	¶As long as we have herdmen been
	And kept these cattle in this clough,
	So strange a sight was never none seen.
1 SHEPHERD	¶Why, no. Now comes it new enow;
	That must we wit.
	It means some marvel, we may know;
	Full boldly do I warrant it.
3 SHEPHERD	¶What it should mean that wot not we,
	For all that ye can gape and yawn.

(*An angel sings*)

I can sing it as well as he,
And on essay it shall be soon
Proved ere we pass.
If ye will help, hold on. Let's see;
For thus it was.
(*The shepherds sing*)

2 SHEPHERD	¶Haha! This was a merry note, By the death that I shall die. I have so croaked in my throat That my lips are near dry.
3 SHEPHERD	No boasting, boys. For what it was fain wit would I, That to us made this noble noise.
I SHEPHERD	¶An angel brought us tidings new, A babe in Bethlem should be born, Of whom then spake our prophecy true, And bade us meet him there this morn, Of mood so mild. I would give him both hat and horn, If I might find that comely child.
3 SHEPHERD	¶Him for to find have we no dread; I shall tell you a reason why. Yon star to that lord shall us lead.
2 SHEPHERD	¶Yea, thou says sooth. Go we thereby Him to honour, And make we mirth and melody With song to seek our Saviour. *(Then they sing)*
I SHEPHERD	¶Brethren, be all blithe and glad; Here is the borough where we should be.
2 SHEPHERD	¶In that same steading now are we stood, Therefore I will go seek and see. Such hap of health never herdsmen had! Lo, here is the house, and here is he!
3 SHEPHERD	¶Yea, forsooth; this is the same. Lo! where that lord is laid Betwixt two beasts so tame, Right as the angel said.
I SHEPHERD	¶The angel said that he should save This world and all that dwell therein. Therefore if I should ought after crave, To worship him I will begin. Since I am but a simple knave, Although I come of courteous kin, Lo, here such harness as I have, A barren brooch with a bell of tin, At your bosom to be.

And when ye shall wield all,
Good son, forget not me,
If any advantage fall.

2 SHEPHERD ¶Son, that shall save both sea and sand,
See to me since I have thee sought.
I am over poor to make present
As my heart would and I had ought.
Two cob nuts here upon a band,
Lo, little babe, what I have brought.
And when ye shall be lord in land,
Do good again; forget me not.
For I have heard declared
Of cunning clerks and keen
That bounty asketh reward—
Now know ye what I mean.

3 SHEPHERD ¶Now look on me, my lord so dear,
Although I put me not in press.
Ye are a prince without a peer;
I have no present that may you please.
But lo, an horn spoon that have I here,
And it will harbour forty peas;
This will I give you with good cheer;
Such novelty may not displease.
Farewell, thou sweetest swain.
God grant us living long
And go we home again,
And make mirth as we gang.

16

THE MASONS

17

THE GOLDSMITHS

Tres Reges venientes ab oriente, Herodes interrogans eos de puero Jesu, et filius Herodis et duo consiliarii et nuncius. Maria cum puero, et stella desuper, et tres Reges offerentes munera.

16

HEROD ⁋The clouds clapped in clearness that their climates
    encloses,
Jupiter and Jovis, Martis et Mercurii amid,
Raking over my royalty on row me rejoices
Blustering their blasts, to blow when I bid.
Saturn my subject, that subtly is hid,
I list at my liking, and lay him full low.
The wrack of the red sky full rapidly I rid;
Thunders of my thralls by thousands I throw
        When me likes.
His voice to me Venus did owe,
That princes to play in him picks.
The prince of the planets that proudly is pight
Shall brace forth his beams that our shelter shall know;
The moon at my might, he musters his might,
And kaisers in castles great kindness me show.
Lords and ladies as lovers list, lo,
For I am fairer of face and fresher, I hold,

(The truth if I shall say) seven and six fold,
Than glorious gules that gayer is than gold
    In price.
How think ye, these tales that I told?
I am worthy, and witty, and wise.

1 KNIGHT   ¶All kings to your crown may clearly commend
Your law and your lordship as loadstone on high.
What traitor untrue that will not attend,
You shall lay him full low from gleam and from light.

2 KNIGHT   ¶The false one, in faith, that does you offend
We shall set him full sore, that sot, in your sight.

HEROD   ¶In weal shall I teach you to dwell, ere I wend,
For ye are wights full worthy, both witty and right.
But ye know well, sir knights, in counsel full cunning,
That my region so royal is ruled here by rest.
For I will that each wight in this world, truth to tell,
That forges a felony with force shall be fast.
Arrest ye these ribalds that unruly rebel;
Be they kings or knights, in care I them cast,
Yea, and wield them in woe with a vengeance to dwell.
What brat that is bawling, his brain look ye burst,
    And ding him down.

1 KNIGHT   ¶Sir, what fellow in faith will displease,
That sot full soon myself will I seize.

2 KNIGHT   ¶We shall not here doubt to do him disease;
But with countenance full cruel
We shall crack here his crown.

HEROD   ¶My son, that is seemly, how seem they, these saws?
How comely these knights they speak in this case?

SON   ¶Father, if they like not to list to your laws,
As traitors untrue ye shall teach them a trace;
For, father, unkindness ye show them no cause.

HEROD   ¶Fair fall thee, my fair son, so pretty of face.
And, knights, I command, whoso to dole draws,
Those churls as cheerless ye chastise and chase,
And dread ye no doubt.

SON   Father, I shall fell them in fight,
All rogues that would reive you your right.

1 KNIGHT   ¶With dints to his death be he dight,
That lists not to your laws to lout
    His will.

[From this point, 16 and 17 have identical texts.]

I KING   ¶Lord that lives everlasting life,
      I love thee ever with heart and hand,
      That me has made to see this sight
      Whereof my kin did covetous stand,
      They said a star with gleams all bright
      Out of the East should stably stand.
      And that it should mean mickle might,
      Of one that should be lord in land,
      That men of sin should save.
      And certes I shall say,
      God grant me hap to have
      Finding of ready way.

2 KING   ¶All wielding God, that all has wrought,
      I worship thee as is worthy,
      That with thy brightness has me brought
      Out of my realm, rich Araby.
      I shall not cease till I have sought
      What wonders it shall signify.
      God grant me hap so that I might
      Have grace to get good company,
      And my comfort increase
      With thy star shining sheen;
      For sure I will not cease
      Till I know what it mean.

3 KING   ¶Lord God, that has all good begun
      And all may end, both good and ill,
      That made for man both moon and sun,
      And set yon star to stand stone still,
      Till I the cause may clearly know
      God guide me with his worthy will.
      A hope I have these fellows will go,
      My yearning faithfully to fulfil.
      Sirs, God you save and see,
      And warn you ever from woe.

I KING   ¶Amen; so might it be;
      And save you, sir, also.

3 KING   ¶Sirs, with your will I would you pray
      To tell me some of your intent,
      Whither ye wend forth on this way,

And from what country forth ye went?

2 KING ¶Full gladly, sir, I shall you say.
A sudden sight was to us sent,
A royal star that rose ere day
Before us in the firmament.
That made us fare from home,
Some point thereof to press.

3 KING ¶Sure, sirs, I saw the same,
That makes us move no less.
For, sirs, I have heard say certain
It should be seen in wondrous wise.
Further thereof would I ask again;
That makes me move this enterprise.

1 KING ¶Of fellowship are we all fain;
Now shall we wend as one in cheer.
God grant us ere we come again
Some good enheartening to hear.
Sir, here is Jerusalem,
To guide us as we go;
And beyond is Bethleem;
There shall we seek also.

3 KING ¶Sirs, ye shall well understand,
For to be wise now were it need.
Sir Herowde is king of this land,
And has his laws here for to lead.

1 KING ¶Sirs, since we nigh now thus nearhand,
Unto his help we must take heed;
For have we his will and warrant,
Then may we wend safely with speed.

2 KING ¶To have leave of this lord,
That is reason and skill.

3 KING ¶And thereto we accord.
Wend we, and wit his will.

⌐ II

MESSENGER ¶My lord sir Herod, king with crown—
HEROD ¶Peace, dastard, in the devil's despite.
MESSENGER ¶Sir, new affair is near this town.
HEROD ¶What, false losel? List thee flight?
Go beat yon boy and ding him down.

MESSENGER ¶Lord, messengers should no man smite;
It may be for your own renown.
HEROD ¶That would I hear; tell on, then, right.
MESSENGER ¶My lord, I met at morn
Three kings talking together
Of one that is now born;
And they mean to come hither.
HEROD ¶Three kings, forsooth?
MESSENGER Sir, so I say,
For I saw them myself all clear.
I COUNCILLOR ¶My lord, examine him, we pray.
HEROD ¶Say, fellow, are they far or near?
MESSENGER ¶My lord, they will be here this day;
That wot I well; no doubt is here.
HEROD ¶Have done! Dress us in rich array,
And every man make merry cheer,
That no semblance be seen
But friendship fair and still,
Till we wot they mean,
Whether it be good or ill.
I KING ¶The lord that lends this lasting light
Which has us led out of our land,
Keep thee, Sir king and comely knight,
And all thy folk that we here find.
HEROD ¶Mahound, my God and most of might,
That has my health all in his hand,
Now save you, sirs seemly in sight;
And tell us now some new errand.
2 KING ¶Some shall we say you, sir;
A star stood us before,
Which makes us speak and enquire
Of one that is now born.
HEROD ¶Now born? That birth then hold I bad.
And sure, unwitty men ye were,
To leap o'er land to seek a lad.
Say, when lost ye him? Ought long before?
All wise men will ween ye are mad,
And therefore move it never more.
3 KING ¶Certes, such heartening have we had,
We shall not cease ere we come there.
HEROD ¶This were a wondrous thing.

Say, what bairn should that be?

1 KING ¶Sir, he shall be the king
Of Jews and of Judee.

HEROD ¶King! In the devil's way, dogs, fie!
Now I see well ye rage and rave.
By any shimmering in the sky
When should ye know or king or knave?
Nay, I am king, and none but I;
That shall ye ken, if that ye crave.
And I am judge of all Jewry,
To speak or spoil, to say or save.
Such gauds may greatly grieve,
To witness what never was.

2 KING ¶Lord, we ask nought but leave
By your power to pass.

HEROD Whither, in the devil's name?
To seek a lad here in my land?
False harlots, but ye hie ye home,
Ye shall be beaten and bound in band.

2 COUNCILLOR ¶My lord, to foil this foul diffame
Let all such wonder fall on hand,
And ask them soberly of the same.
So shall you stably understand
Their mind and their meaning,
And take good tent them to.

HEROD ¶I thank thee for this thing,
And sure, so will I do.
Now, kings, to catch all cares away,
Since ye are come out of your kith,
Look ye allege not against our law,
On pain of limb and life therewith.
And so that ye the sooth will say,
In peace both come and go ye may;
And if your point so please my way,
May be my self shall wend you with.

1 KING ¶Sir king, we all accord
And say a bairn is born,
That shall be king and lord
And heal them that are lorn.

2 KING ¶Sir King, thou needs marvel nothing
Of this affair, nor comfort lose.

For Balaham said a star should spring
Of Jacob's kind, and that is Jews.

3 KING ¶Sir, Isaie says a maiden young
Shall bear a son among Hebrews
That of all countries shall be king,
And govern all that on earth grows.
"Emmanuel" shall be his name—
That is, God's son of heaven;
And sure that is the same
That we now to you name.

1 KING ¶Sir, the approved prophet Osee
Full truly told in town and tower
That a maiden of Israel, says he,
Shall bear one like to the lily flower.
He means a bairn conceived should be
Without by seed of man succour,
And his mother a maiden free,
And he both son and saviour.

2 KING ¶What fathers told before
Has no man might to mar.

HEROD ¶Alas, then am I lorn!
This waxes worse the more.

1 COUNCILLOR ¶My lord, be ye nothing abased;
This broil shall well to end be brought.
Bid them go forth and friendly taste
The sooth of this that they have sought,
And tell it you; so shall ye test
Whether their tales be true or nought.
Then shall ye turn them with a twist,
And make all waste that they have wrought.

HEROD ¶Now sure, this was well said;
This matter makes me fain.
Sir Kings, I hold me glad
Of all your purpose plain.
Wend forth, your wishes to fulfil
To Bethlem—'tis but here at hand.
And seek the truth both good and ill
Of him that should be lord in land.
Then come again to me at will,
And tell me truly your errand.
To worship him, that is my will;

That shall we stably understand.

2 KING ❡Sure, sir, we shall you say
All the sooth of that child,
In all the haste we may.

2 COUNCILLOR ❡Farewell; ye be beguiled.

HEROD ❡Now sure this is a subtle train.
Now shall they truly take their ways
And tell me of that little swain
And of their counsel in this case.
If it be sooth, they shall be slain;
No gold shall get them better grace.
Go we now, till they come again,
To play us in some other place
This hold I good counsel;
Yet would I no man wist.
For sure we shall not fail
To use them as we list.

> *Nota. The Harrod passeth, and the iii kynges
> comyth agayn to make there offerynges.*

1 KING ❡Ah, sirs, for sight what shall I say?
Where is our sign? I see it not.

2 KING ❡No more do I. Now dare I lay
In our wending some wrong is wrought.

3 KING ❡Unto that Prince I rede we pray,
That to us sent his sign unsought,
That he guide us in ready way,
Friendly to find him as we ought.

1 KING ❡Ah sirs! I see it stand
Above where he is born.
Lo, here is the house at hand;
We have not missed this morn.

MAID ❡Whom seek ye, sirs, by ways so wild,
With talking, travelling to and fro?
Here dwells a woman with her child
And her husband; here are no mo.

1 KING ❡We seek a bairn that all shall shield;
His certain sign has said us so;
And his mother, a maiden mild.
Here hope we now to find them two.

MAID ❡Come near, good sirs, and see.
Your way to an end is brought.

3 KING ¶Behold here, sirs, here, and see
    The same that ye have sought.
I KING ¶Loved be that lord that lasteth aye,
    That us hath shown thus courteously
    To wend by many a wildsome way,
    And come to this clean company.
2 KING ¶Let us now make no more delay.
    But swift take forth our treasury
    And ordered gifts in good array,
    To worship him, as is worthy.
3 KING ¶He is worthy to wield
    All worship, and wealth to win.
    And for honour to eld,
    Brother, you shall begin.
I KING ¶Hail! fairest of free folk to find;
    From the fiend and his fellows in faith us defend.
    Hail, the best that shall be born to unbind
    All the bairns that are born and in bale bound.
    Hail! Mark us thy men and make us in mind,
    Since thy might is on mould our sins to amend.
    Hail, clean one, come of a king's kind
    Who shall be king of this kith, as all clerks have
      kenned.
    And since it shall work on this wise
    Thyself have I sought, son, I say thee;
    With gold that is greatest of price;
    Be pleased with this present, I pray thee.
2 KING ¶Hail, food that thy folk fully may feed;
    Hail, flower fairest that never shall fade;
    Hail, son that is sent of this same seed,
    That shall save us from sin that our sires made.
    Hail, mild!
    To mark us our meed thy measure is set;
    Of a maid matchless thy mother thou made.
    In that good one through grace of thy godhead
    As the gleam in the glass glad hast thou glowed.
    And since thou shalt sit to be deeming
    To hell or to heaven for to have us,
    Incense to thy service is seeming;
    Son, see to thy subjects, and save us.
3 KING ¶Hail, bairn that is best our bales to meet,

For our benefit shalt thou be bound and beat.
Hail, friend faithful! We fall at thy feet
Thy father's folk from the false fiend free shalt thou
    set.
Hail, man that is made to thy men meet,
Since thou and thy mother with mirth are met;
Hail, duke that drives death under thy feet,
But when thy deeds are done to die is thy debt.
And since thy body buried shall be,
This myrrh will I give to thy graving.
The gift is not great of degree;
Receive it, and see to our saving.

MARY   ¶Sir kings, ye travel not in vain,
As ye have thought, here may ye find.
For I conceived my son certain,
Without the miss of man in mind
And bare him here all without pain,
Where women are wont to be pined.
God's angel in his greeting plain
Said he should comfort all mankind.
Therefore doubt you no deal
Here for to have your boon.
I shall witness full well
All that is said and done.

1 KING   ¶For solace sure now may we sing;
All is performed that we have prayed.
But, good bairn, give us thy blessing,
For fair hap is before thee laid.

2 KING   ¶Wend we now to Herod the king,
For of this point will he be glad
And come himself and make offering
Unto this same, for so he said.

3 KING   ¶Let rest awhile be sought,
For to maintain our might;
And then do as we ought,
Both unto king and knight.

ANGEL   ¶Now, courteous kings, to me take tent,
And turn betime ere ye be pained.
From God himself thus am I sent,
To warn you, as your faithful friend.
Herod the king has malice meant,

And shapes with shame you for to spend.
Lest ye take harm by his intent,
By other ways God wills ye wend
Even to your own country;
And if ye ask him boon,
Your shield aye will he be,
For this that ye have done.

1 KING   ¶Ah lord! I love thee inwardly.
Sirs, God has goodly warned us three.
His angel here now heard have I,
And how he said.

2 KING   Sir, so did we.
He said Herod is our enemy,
And makes his plans our bale to be,
With falsehood feigned; and thereby,
Far from his force I rede we flee.

3 KING   ¶Sirs, fast I rede we flit,
Each one to his country.
He that is well of wit,
Us guide, and with you be.

18

THE MARSHALS

Maria cum puero et Josep fugientes in Egiptum, angelo nunciante.

JOSEPH ¶Thou maker that most is of might,
To thy mercy I make now my moan.
Lord, see unto thy simple wight,
That has no help but thee alone.
For all this world have I forsaken,
And to thy service have me taken
With wit and will
For to fulfil
Thy commandment.
Thereon my heart is set
With grace thou has me lent;
There shall none alive me let.
For all my trust, Lord, is in thee
That made me man to thy likeness;
Thou mighty maker, have mind on me,
And see unto my simpleness.
I wax as weak as any wand;
For feebleness, fail foot and hand.
Whatever it mean,
Methinks mine eyne
Heavy as lead.
Therefore I hold it best
Awhile here in this stead
To sleep and take my rest.

MARY ¶Thou lovely lord that last shall aye,
My God, my Lord, my son so dear,
To thy Godhead heartily I pray
With all my heart wholly entire.
As thou me to thy mother chose,

I do beseech thee of thy grace
For all mankind
That has in mind
To worship thee,
Thou see these souls to save.
Jesu, my son so free
This boon of thee I crave.

GABRIEL ¶Waken, Joseph, and take intent;
My sayings shall cease thy sorrows sore.
Be not heavy; thy help is meant;
Therefore I bid thee sleep no more.

JOSEPH ¶Ah, mightful lord! What ever that meant?
So sweet a voice heard I never e'er.
But what art thou with sound so still
Thus in my sleep that speaks to me?
To me appear,
And let me hear
What that thou was.

GABRIEL ¶Joseph, have thou no dread.
Thou shalt wit ere I pass;
Therefore to me take heed.
For I am sent to thee,
Gabriel, God's angel bright;
I come to bid thee flee
With Mary and her worthy wight.
For Herod the king will do to death
All boy children in every stead
That he may do,
With years two
That are of old.
Till he be dead away,
In Egipte shall ye dwell,
Till I bid you away.

JOSEPH ¶Aye lasting lord, loved might thou be
That thy sweet message to me would send.
But, lord, what ails the king at me,
For unto him I never offend?
Alas, what ails him for to spill
Small young bairns' blood that ne'er did ill
In word nor deed
Unto no seed

By night or day?
Since he would us offend,
Dear Lord, I do thee pray,
Thou would be still our friend.
For be he never so wild or wroth,
For all his force thou may us fend.
I pray thee, Lord, keep us from scathe;
Thy succour soon to us thou send.
For unto Egipte wend we will,
Thy word obedient to fulfil.
As worthy is,
Thou king of bliss,
Thy will be wrought
Mary, my daughter dear,
On thee is all my thought.

MARY   ¶Ah, Joseph, love, what cheer?
JOSEPH   ¶The cheer of me is done for aye.
MARY   ¶Alas, what tidings heard have ye?
JOSEPH   ¶Now, sure, full ill to thee to say.
There is nought else but we must flee
Out of our kith where we are known;
Full quickly must we be withdrawn,
Both thou and I.

MARY   ¶Love Joseph, why?
Conceal it nought.
To dole who has us deemed?
Or what wrong have we wrought,
Wherefor we should be blamed?

JOSEPH   ¶Wrought we him harm? Nay, nay, all wrong.
Wit thou well that it is not so.
That young page' life thou must forego,
Unless thou fast flee from his foe.

MARY   ¶His foe, alas! What is your rede?
Who would my young bairn do to death?
I cower for care.
Who may my share
Of evils end?
To flee I would full fain.
For all this world to win,
Would I not see him slain.

JOSEPH   ¶I warn thee, there is evil threat

By Herod King, hard harms to have.
With that sweet son if he be met,
There is no salve that him may save.
I warn thee well, he will slay all
Boy children, great and small,
In town and field,
Within the eld
Of a two year,
And for thy dear son's sake
Will he destroy all here.
May that traitor him take!

MARY ¶Love Joseph, who told you this?
How had you witting of this deed?

JOSEPH ¶An angel bright that came from bliss
This tiding told for sure indeed,
And wakened me out of my sleep,
That comely child from cares to keep,
And bade me flee
With him and thee
Into Egipte.
And sure I dread me sore
To make that little trip,
Or time ere I come there.

MARY ¶What ail they at my bairn
Such harms that he should meet?
Alas! Why should he yearn
To slay my son so sweet?
His heart should be full sore
On such a child to work his will,
That never did ill,
Him for to spill,
He knows not why.
Full wild in woe were I,
If my dear son should die,
And I have but him alone.

JOSEPH ¶Ah, Mary love, away; let be.
I pray thee now, leave off thy din,
And set thee forth fast for to flee,
Away with him safe for to win,
That no mischief on him betide
Nor no mishap on any side.

By way nor street
That we none meet
To slay him.

MARY   ¶Alas, Joseph, for care.
Why should I forego him,
My dear bairn that I bare?

JOSEPH   ¶That sweet swain if you'll save,
Do quick pack all our gear,
And such small harness as we have.

MARY   ¶Ah, Joseph love, I may not bear. . . .

JOSEPH   ¶Bear harm? No, no; I trow but small.
But God wot, I must care for all,
For bed and back
And all the pack
That needs now unto us.
It furthers not to feign me;
This raking bear I must,
Of all this charge I plain me.
But God grant grace I nought forget
Of tools that we should with us take.

MARY   ¶Alas, Joseph, for grieving great.
When shall my sorrows slake?
For I wot not whither to fare.

JOSEPH   ¶To Egypt told I thee long ere.

MARY   ¶Where standeth it?

JOSEPH   What wot I?
I wot not where it stands.

MARY   ¶Joseph, I ask mercy.
Help me out of this land.

JOSEPH   ¶Now sure, Mary, I would full fain
Help thee all that I may,
And at my power give pain
To win with him and thee away.

MARY   ¶Alas, what ails that fiend
By wildsome ways that makes us wend?
He does great sin;
From kith and kin
He makes us flee.

JOSEPH   ¶Love Mary, weep not yet.

MARY   ¶Joseph, full woe is me
For my dear son so sweet.

JOSEPH ¶I pray thee, Mary, hap him warm,
And set him soft and sure the while;
And if thou will ought ease thine arm,
Give him me, to bear him awhile.

MARY ¶I thank you of your great good deed.
Now, good Joseph, to him take heed;
That child so free,
To him now see,
All in this tide.

JOSEPH ¶Let him and me alone.
And if you ill can ride,
Have and hold fast by the mane.

MARY ¶Alas, Joseph, for woe.
Was never wight in world so wild.

JOSEPH ¶Away, Mary, and say not so,
For thou shalt have no cause thereto.
For wit thou well, God is our friend;
He will be with us whereso we wend.
In all our need
He will us speed;
This wot I well.
I love my Lord of all.
Such force I think I feel,
I may go where I shall.
Ere was I weak, now am I right,
My limbs to wield aye at my will.
I love my maker most of might,
That such grace granted unto me.
Now shall no noyance do no harm;
I have our help here in my arm.
He will us fend
Whereso we land;
None shall betray.
Let us go with good cheer;
Farewell, and have good day.
God bless us all three here.

MARY ¶Amen, as He best may.

41

THE HATMAKERS,
MASONS AND LABORERS

Maria cum puero, Josep, Anna, obstetrix, cum pullis columbarum. Symeon recipiens puerum in ulnas suas, et duo filii Symeonis.

PRIEST ¶Almighty God in heaven so high,
The maker of all heaven and earth,
Has ordained the things evenly;
For man, he meant to mend his mirth.
In number, weight and measure fine
God did create all things, I say.
His laws he bade men not decline,
But keep his commandments all way.
In the mount of Synay so fair
In two tables, to you to tell,
His laws to Moses took God there,
To give to the children of Israell.
That Moses shall guide them alway,
And teach them true to know God's will;
And that they should not it deny,
But keep his laws stable and still,
For pain that he had put therefore
To stone all them that keep it not
Utterly to death, both less and more;
There should no mercy for them be sought.
Therefore keep well God's commandment,
And lead your life after his laws,
Or else surely ye must repent,
Both less and more, each one in rows.
This is his will after Moyses' law,
That ye should bring your beasts good

And offer them here your God to know,
And from your sins to turn your mood,
Such beasts as God has marked here.
To Moyses spake he, as I tell,
And bade him boldly with good cheer
To say to the children of Israel
That after divers sickness severe,
And after divers sins also
Go bring your beasts to the priest even here
To offer them up in God's sight, lo.
The woman that has borne her child,
She shall come here the fortieth day,
To be purified where she was defiled,
And bring with her a lamb, I say,
And two dove birds for her offering
And take them to the priest that day,
To offer them up with his holy hand;
There should no man to this say nay.
The lamb is offered for God's honour
In sacrifice all only dight,
And the priest's prayer, purchase secure,
For her defiled then in God's sight,
And if so be that she was poor
And have no lamb to offer, then
Two turtle doves to God's honour
To bring with her for her offering.
Lo, here am I, priest present alway,
To receive offerings hither brought,
And for the folk to God to pray,
That health and life to them be wrought.

ANNA ⁊Here in this holy place I say
Is my full purpose to abide
To serve my God both night and day
With prayer and fasting every tide.
A widow I this threescore year,
And four years to, the truth to tell;
Here have I tarried with full good cheer
For the redemption of Israel.
So for my holy conversation
Great grace to me has now God sent,
To tell by prophecy for man's redemption

What shall befall by God's intent.
I tell you all here in this place,
By God's virtue in prophecy,
That one is born to our solace
Here to be present certainly
Within short space,
With his mother a maiden free,
Of all virgins most chaste soothly,
The well of meekness—blest might she be,
  Most full of grace.
And Symeon that senior
That is so seemly in God's sight,
He shall him see and do honour,
And in his arms he shall him plight,
  That worthy boy.
Of the Holy Ghost he shall soothly
Take strength, and answer when he shall hie
Forth to this Temple and place holy
  For that employ.

SYMEON ¶Ah, blessed God, be thou my shield,
And be at my bale both night and day;
In heaviness my heart I yield;
Unto myself, lo, thus I say.
For I am weak and all unwield.
My weal all wanes and passeth away;
Whereso I fare in firth or field
I fall aye down for feeble, in fay.
In fay, I fall whereso I fare;
In hair and hue and hide, I say,
Out of this world I would I were.
Thus wax I worse and worse alway;
My mischief grows in all that may.
Thou mighty God, my grief dispel,
I pray, for it should please me well,
So happy to see him if I were.
Now sure then should my game begin
If I might see him, of him to tell,
That one who is born without sin
And for mankind makes mirth to dwell—
Born of a woman and maiden free
As witness Davyd and Danyell

Without all sin or villainy
  As said also Isacheel.
That prophet keen, Melachiell.
Has told us of that babe so bright,
That he should come with us to dwell
In our Temple as gleam of light.
And other prophets prophesied
And of that blest babe did foretell
And of his mother, a maiden bright,
In prophecy the truth 'gan tell—
That he should come and harrow Hell
As a giant so strong to stride,
And fiercely the fiends' malice to quell
And put their powers all aside.
The worthiest wight in this world so wide,
His virtues' tale no tongue can tell;
He sends all succour on every side
As redemption of Israel—
      Thus say they all,
These patriarchs and prophets clear—
A babe is born, our comrade here,
Knit in our mind for all our cheer
      To great and small.
Ah, well were me for ever and aye
If I might see that babe so bright,
Ere I were buried close in clay;
Then would my corse here mend in might
      Right faithfully.
Now, Lord! Thou grant to me thy grace
To live here in this world a space,
That I might see that babe in his face
      Here ere I die.
Ah God! I think I may endure,
Trow we that babe shall find me here;
Now sure with age I am so poor
That ever it abates my cheer.
Yet if kind fail for age in me
God yet may length my life, soothly,
Till I that babe and boy so free
      Have seen in sight.
For truly, if I saw such as these,

There should no thing my heart disease.
Lord, lend me grace, if that thou please,
   And make me light.
When wilt thou come, babe? Let's see; have
   done.
Nay, come on soon, and tarry not.
For sure my life days are near done;
For aye to me great woe has wrought.
Great woe is wrought unto man's heart
When he must want what he would have.
I care no longer to have ought;
When I have seen that I for crave.
Ah! trowest thou these two eyes shall see
That blessed babe, ere they be out?
Yea, I pray God so might it be;
Then were I put all out of doubt.

ANGEL   ❡Old Symeon, God's servant right,
Bold words to thee I bring, I say.
The Holy Ghost, the most of might,
He says thou shalt not die away
   Till thou have seen
Jesus the babe that Mary bore,
For all mankind to slake their care.
He shall do comfort to less and more
   Both morn and even.

SYMEON   ❡Ah Lord, Gramercy now I say,
That thou this grace has to me plight,
Ere I be buried here in clay
To see that seemly beam so bright.
No man of mould may have more hap
To my solace and mirth alway
Than for to see in Mary's lap
Jesus my joy and Saviour aye;
   Blest be his name.
Lo, now may I see, truth to tell,
The redemption of Israel
Jesus, my Lord Emmanuell,
   Without all blame.

MARY   ¶Joseph, my husband and compeer,
Take to me now ready intent.
I will show you in this manner
What I will do; thus have I meant.
Full forty days are come and went
Since that my babe Jesus was born;
Therefore I would he were present
As Moyses' law tells us before,
Here in this Temple before God's sight,
As other women do appear,
So methinks is good skill and right
The same to do now with good cheer,
    After God's law.

JOSEPH   ¶Mary, my spouse and maiden clean,
This matter that thou moves to me
Is for all these women, I mean,
That have conceived with sin fleshly
    To bear a child.
The law is hedged for them right plain;
They must be purified again,
For in man's pleasures for certain
    They were defiled.
But, Mary bride, thou needst no so
For this cause to be purified, lo,
    In God's Temple.
For sure thou art a clean virgin
For any thought thy heart within,
Nor never wrought no fleshly sin,
    Nor never ill.

MARY   ¶That I my maidenhood have kept still
Is only through great God's own will;
    That be ye bold.
Yet to fulfil the law, I wis,
That God almighty would express,
And for example of meekness,
    Offer I would.

JOSEPH   ¶Ah, Mary! Blessed be thou aye;
Thou thinkest to do after God's will.
As thou has said, Mary, I say;

I heartily consent theretill,
　　　Without a doubt.
Therefore now dress we forth our way,
And offering make to God this day,
Even likewise as thyself did say,
　　　With hearts devout.

MARY ❡Thereto am I full ready dight;
But one thing, Joseph, I would move.

JOSEPH ❡Mary, my spouse and maiden bright,
Tell on heartily, what grieves my love?

MARY ❡Both beast and fowl must we needs have,
A lamb and two dove birds also.
Lamb have we none, nor none can crave.
Therefore, Joseph, what shall we do?
　　　What is your rede?
If we do not as custom is
We are worthy to be blamed, I wis;
I would we did nothing amiss,
　　　As God me speed.

JOSEPH ❡Ah, good Mary, the law is this—
The rich to offer both lamb and bird;
And the two turtles, as I wis,
Or two dove birds shall with good word
　　　Our offering be.
And Mary, we have done birds two,
As falls for us there where we go;
They are here in a pannier, lo,
　　　Ready to see.
And if we have not both to bear,
The lamb, the birds, as rich men have,
Think then that we must present here
Our babe Jesus as we vouchsafe
　　　Before God's sight.
He is our lamb, Mary; fear not;
For rich and poor none better sought;
Full well thou hast him hither brought,
　　　This our offering dight.
He is the lamb of God, I say,
That all our sins shall take away
Of this world here.
He is the lamb of God very

That must defend from all affray,
Born of thy womb, our joy today
And all our cheer.

MARY ❡Joseph my spouse, ye say full true;
Then let us dress us forth our way.

JOSEPH ❡Go we then, Mary, and do our due,
And make meekly offering this day.
Lo, here is the Temple on this hill
And also priest ordained by skill,
High power holding.
And, Mary, go we thither on high,
And let us both kneel devoutly,
And offer we up to God meekly
The due we bring.

MARY ❡Unto my God highest in heaven,
And to the priest ordained by skill,
Jesu my babe, I offer him
Here with my heart and my good will
Right heartily.
Pray thou for us to God in height,
Thou priest, present here in his might,
That this deed may be in his sight
Accepted goodly.

JOSEPH ❡Lo, sir, and two love birds are here;
Receive them with your holy hands.
We are no better proved of power,
For we have neither rents nor lands
Nor wealth truly.
But, good sir, pray to God of might,
To accept this that we have dight,
That we have offered as is right
Here heartily.

PRIEST ❡O God, the granter of all grace,
Blest be thy name both night and day.
Accept these offerings in this place
Presented here to thee alway.
Ah, blessed Lord, say never nay;
Let this offering be stay and shield
To all such folk living in clay
That thus to thee meekly will yield.
And this babe, Lord, present in thy sight,

127

Born of a maiden undefiled,
Accept, Lord, for their special right.
Given to mankind both man and child.
    So specially.
And this babe born and present here
May shield us that we feel no fear,
But ever ready his grace to share
    Here verily.
Ah blessed Babe, welcome thou be,
Born of a maiden in chastity;
Thou art our shield, babe, our game and our
    glee,
    Ever soothly.
Welcome, our wit and our wisdom!
Welcome, our joy both all and some!
Welcome, redemptor omnium,
    To us heartily.

ANNA   ¶Welcome, blessed Mary, Maiden aye!
Welcome, most meek in thine array!
Welcome, bright star that shines bright as day,
    All for our bliss.
Welcome, thou blessed beam so bright!
Welcome, the gleam of all our light!
Welcome, that all pleasure hast plight
    To man and wife.
Welcome, thou blessed babe so free!
Welcome, our welfare mortally!
And welcome all our bliss soothly
    To great and small.
Babe, welcome to thy shielding bower;
Babe, welcome now to our succour;
And babe, welcome with all honour
    Here in this hall.

ANGEL   ¶Old Symeon, to thee I say,
Dress thee forth in thine array.
Come to the Temple; there shall you see
Jesus, that babe that Mary bore;
    That be thou bold.

SYMEON   ¶Ah Lord! I thank thee ever and aye.
Now am I light as leaf on tree.
My age is gone, and fear, away;

Methinks, for this that is told me
        I am not old.
Now will I to yon Temple go,
To see the babe that Mary bare;
He is my health in weal and woe,
And helps me ever from great care.
Hail, blessed babe that Mary bare,
And blest be thy mother, Mary mild,
Whose womb thee girdled fresh and fair,
She a clean virgin undefiled.
Hail, babe, the Father of heaven's offspring,
Chosen to cheer us for our mischance.
No earthly tongue can tell or sing
What thy might is in every chance.
Hail, the most worthy to enhance,
Boldly thou shield us from all ill;
Without thy shield we get grievance,
And for our deeds here should we spill.
Hail, *flos campi,* flower virginal,
The odour of thy goodness blows on us all.
Hail, most happy to great and to small,
        For all our wealth.
Hail, royal rose, most ruddy of hue,
Hail, flower unfading both fresh aye and new,
Hail, kindest in comfort that ever man knew,
        For greatest health.
And meekly I beseech thee here where I kneel,
To suffer thy servant to take thee in hand,
And in mine arms for to heave thee here for my
        weal
Where I bound am in bail, to amend all my bands.
Now come to me, lord of all lands;
Come, mightiest by sea and by sands;
Come, mirth by streets and by strands
        On mould.
Come, clasp me, babe that is best born;
Come, clasp me, the mirth of our morn;
Come, clasp me, for else I am lorn
        For old.
I thank thee, Lord God, of thy great grace
That thus has spared me for a space,

This babe in mine arms to embrace,
    By prophecy plight.
I thank thee that me my life lent;
I thank thee that me thus bliss sent,
That this sweet babe take my arms bent;
    With mirth mingles my might.
Mingled are my minds aye with mirth;
Full fresh now I feel is my force;
Thy grace gave me this joy on earth,
Thus comely to catch here thy corse
    Most seemly in sight.
Of helps thus my friend never fails;
Thy mercy every man avails,
Both by downs and by dales,
    Thus marvellous and much is thy
      might.
Ah babe, be thou blessed for aye;
For thou art my saviour, I say,
And thou here rulest me in fay
    In all my life.
Now, brightest babe blest be thy name,
For thou savest us from shame,
And here thou shieldest us from blame
    And from all strife.
Now care I no more for my life.
Since I have seen this royal so rife,
My strength and my stinter of strife,
    I joyful say.
In peace, Lord, now leave thy servant,
For mine eyes have seen what is ordained,
The health for all that live on land
    Here, Lord, for aye.
That health, Lord, hast thou ordained, I say,
Here before the face of thy people aye,
And thy light hast thou shined this day
    For evermore,
To be known of thy folk that was feeble,
And the glory of thy children Israel,
That with thee in thy kingdom shall dwell,
When the damned shall be driven into hell
    Then with great care.

JOSEPH ¶Mary, my spouse and maiden mild,
In heart I marvel here greatly
How these folks speak here of this child.
They say and tell of great mastery
That he shall do.

MARY ¶Yea, sure, Joseph; I marvel also;
But I shall bear it full still in mind.

JOSEPH ¶God give him grace here well to do,
For he is come of gentle kind.

SYMEON ¶Hark, Mary. I shall say thee the truth ere I go.
This was put here to win us from woe,
In redemption of many and recovery also,
        As I thee say.
And the sword of sorrow thy heart shall thrill,
When thou shalt see soothly thy son suffer ill,
For the weal of all wretches that shall be his will
        Here in fay.
But to be comforted again right well thou may,
And in heart to be fain—the sooth I thee say—
For his might is so much there can no tongue say nay
        Here to his will.
For this babe as a giant full strongly shall stride,
And as mightiest master shall move on each side
To all the wights that dwell in this world wide
        For good or for ill.
Therefore, babe, shield us that we here not spill,
And farewell, who formedst all at thy will.
Farewell, star stablest by loud and by still
        In soothfastness.
Farewell, the royalest rose that is reigning;
Farewell, the babe best in thy bearing;
Farewell, God's Son. Grant us thy blessing,
        To end our distress.

19

THE GIRDLERS AND NAILERS

Herodes precipiens pueros occidi, iiij milites cum lanceis,
duo consiliarii Regis, et iiij mulieres deflentes occisionem
puerorum suorum.

HEROD   ¶Peace, fair sirs about,
On pain of limb and land.
Stint of your stevens stout,
And still as stones here stand,
And my speaking record.
Ye ought to dread and doubt,
And learn you low to lout
To me your lovely lord.
Ye ought in field and town
To bow to my bidding
With reverence and renown,
As falls for such a king.
The lordliest alive
Who is not ready found,
By almighty Mahound,
To death I shall him drive.
So bold look no man be
For to ask help nor shield
But of Mahound and me,
That have this world to wield,
To maintain us so well;
For well of wealth are we,
And my chief help is he.
Hereto what can you tell?

I COUNCILLOR   ¶Lord, what you like to do,
All folks will be full fain
To take intent thereto,
And none grudge there again;

That full well wit shall ye.
And if they would not so
We should soon work them woe.

HEROD   ❡Fair sirs, so should it be.

2 COUNCILLOR   ❡Then, lord, the sooth to say,
Full well we understand
Mahound is God very,
And you, lord of each land.
Therefore, I gladly tell,
I rede we watch alway
What mirth most mend you may.

HEROD   ❡Certes ye say right well,
But I am annoyed anew
That blithe I may not be;
For these kings, as ye know,
That came through this country
And said they sought a swain.

I COUNCILLOR   ❡That rule I trust they rue;
For had their tales been true,
They had come this way again.

2 COUNCILLOR   ❡We heard how they word plight,
If they might find that child,
For to have told you right;
But sure they are beguiled;
Such tales are not to trow.
Full well wots every wight,
There shall never man have might
Nor mastery unto you.

I COUNCILLOR   ❡They shame so, for certain,
They dare meet you no more.

HEROD   ❡Wherefore should they be fain
To make such fare before?
To say a boy was born
That should be most of main—
This gadling shall again,
If that the devil had sworn.
For no good thing, I know,
Whether they work well or wrong,
Made them to question so,
Or seek that gadling long
And such saying to say.

133

2 COUNCILLOR ⁋Nay, lord, they learned too late
Your bliss shall never abate;
And therefore, lord, be gay.

MESSENGER ⁋Mahound without a peer,
My lord, you save and see.

HEROD ⁋Now, messenger, come near,
And, fair sir, well be ye.
What tidings tells thou, any?

MESSENGER ⁋Yea, lord. Since I was here,
I have sought everywhere,
And seen marvels full many.

HEROD ⁋And of marvels to move,
That were most mirth to me.

MESSENGER ⁋Lord, even as I have seen,
The sooth soon shall ye see,
If you will, here in high.
I met, two towns between,
Three kings with crowns full clean,
Riding right royally.

HEROD ⁋Ah, my bliss! Boy, thou boasts too broad.

MESSENGER ⁋Sir, there may no abatement be.

[? *Some lines lost here.*]

HEROD ⁋O woe! By sun and moon,
Tales will be told tonight.
Hopes thou they will come soon
Hither, as they have plight,
For to tell me tiding?

MESSENGER ⁋Nay, lord, that dance is done.

HEROD ⁋Why, whither are they gone?

MESSENGER ⁋Each one to his own land.

HEROD ⁋How sayest thou, boy? Let be!

MESSENGER ⁋I say, for they are past.

HEROD ⁋What, forth away from me?

MESSENGER ⁋Yea, lord, in faith full fast.
For I heard and took heed
How that they went all three
Into their own country.

HEROD ⁋Ah, dogs! The devil you speed!

MESSENGER ⁋Sir, more of their meaning
Yet well I understood;
How they made offering

134

          Unto that child so good
          That now of new is born.
          They say he should be king
          And wield all earthly thing.

HEROD ¶Alas, then am I lorn.
          Fie on them, false ones, fie!
          Will they beguile me thus?

MESSENGER ¶Lord, by their prophecy
          They named his name Jesus.

HEROD ¶Fie on thee, lad! Thou lies!

2 COUNCILLOR ¶Hence, quick! But thou thee hie,
          With dole here shalt thou die,
          That bewrays him on this wise.

MESSENGER ¶Ye blame me all with wrong;
          It is thus, and well worse.

HEROD ¶Thou liest, false traitor strong!
          Look never thou nigh me near.
          Now by thy life and limb,
          May I that false one slay;
          Full high I shall him hang,
          Both thee and him this day.

MESSENGER ¶I am not worthy so to chide.
          But farewell, all the heap!

1 COUNCILLOR ¶Go, in the devil's despite,
          Or I shall make thee leap,
          And dear abide this brew.

HEROD ¶Alas, for sorrow and sight
          My woe no wight may write.
          What a devil is best to do?

2 COUNCILLOR ¶My lord, amend your cheer;
          Let nought needless annoy.
          Truly we help you here,
          That lad for to destroy—
          By counsel, if we can.

HEROD ¶That may ye not come near,
          For it is past two year
          Since that this bale began.

1 COUNCILLOR ¶Lord, therefore have no fear,
          If it were four or five.
          Now gather in great rout
          Your knights so sharp to strive,

      And bid them do death
      All boy babes they seek out
      In Bethlem and all about,
      And search in every stead.

2 COUNCILLOR ¶Lord, save none, for your weal,
      That are of two years age within.
      Then shall that foundling feel
      Full little bliss therein,
      With bale when he shall bleed.

HEROD ¶Certes ye say right well,
      And as ye deem each deal
      Shall I have done indeed.
      Sir knights courteous at hand,
      Though this need be now all new,
      Ye shall find me your friend,
      If ye this time be true.

1 COUNCILLOR ¶What say you, lord? Let see.

HEROD ¶To Bethlem must ye wend,
      With shame to make his end
      That means to master me.
      Through Bethlem borough go;
      There must you seek and spy,
      Else will wrong be done so,
      That he lose this jury.
      And sure that were great shame.

2 COUNCILLOR ¶My lord, that were us loath;
      If he escaped, 'twere shame,
      And we well worthy blame.

1 KNIGHT ¶Full soon shall he be sought;
      That make I mine avow.

2 COUNCILLOR ¶Lurk there till he be caught,
      And let me tell you how.
      Go work when ye come there,
      Because you know him not;
      To death must they be brought
      Boy children less and more.

HEROD ¶Yea, all within two year,
      That none for speech be spared.

2 KNIGHT ¶Lord, even as ye teach us here,
      Full well we take reward
      And sure we shall not rest.

II

1 KNIGHT	¶Come forth, fellows; appear!
	Wit well what must be done.
	Lo, foundlings find we here.
1 WOMAN	¶Out on you, thieves, I cry!
	Ye slay my seemly son.
2 KNIGHT	¶These brats shall dearly buy
	This bale that is begun;
	Therefore lay from thee fast.
2 WOMAN	¶Alas, for dole I die!
	To save my son shall I,
	Aye while my life shall last—
1 KNIGHT	¶Ah dame, the devil thee speed
	And me, but it be quit.
1 WOMAN	¶To die I have no dread,
	I wish thee well to wit,
	To save my son so dear.
1 KNIGHT	¶To arms, for now is need.
	Unless we do yon deed,
	These queans will quell us here.
2 WOMAN	¶Alas, this loathly strife!
	No bliss may I more get.
	The knight upon his knife
	Has slain my son so sweet—
	And I had but him alone.
1 WOMAN	¶Alas, I lose my life!
	Was never so woeful a wife,
	Nor half so woebegone.
	And sure I were full loath
	That they should harmless go.
1 KNIGHT	¶The devil might speed you both!
	False witches, rave you so?
2 WOMAN	¶Nay, false lurdans, ye lie.
1 KNIGHT	¶If ye be mad or wroth
	Ye shall not escape from scathe.
	Wend we us hence on high.
1 WOMAN	¶Alas, that we were wrought
	In world women to be.
	The bairn that we dear bought
	Thus in our sight to see

137

	Dispiteously they kill.
2 WOMAN	¶And sure, their need is nought.
	The same that they have sought,
	They shall not find for ill.
1 KNIGHT	¶Go we now to the king,
	Of all this contest keen,
	I shall let for nothing
	To say as we have seen.
2 KNIGHT	¶And sure, no more shall I.
	We have done his bidding,
	We shall say soothfastly,
	Howe'er they wrest or wring.

III

1 KNIGHT	¶Mahound, our god of might
	Save thee, Sir Herod the king.
1 COUNCILLOR	¶Sir, take heed to your knight;
	He will tell you now tiding
	Of jests where they have been.
HEROD	¶Yes; if they have gone right
	And hold us as they plight,
	Then shall solace be seen.
2 KNIGHT	¶Lord, as ye bade us we have done
	In country where we come—
HEROD	¶Then, sir, by sun and moon,
	Ye are right welcome home,
	And worthy to have reward.
	Have ye gotten us this groom?
1 KNIGHT	¶Who fared well from your doom
	Witness we well that there was none.
2 KNIGHT	¶My lord, they are dead each one.
	What would ye we did more?
HEROD	¶I ask but after one.
	The kings told of before,
	That should make great mastery?
	Tell us if he be ta'en.
1 KNIGHT	¶Lord, token had we none
	To know that same brat by.
2 KNIGHT	¶To bale we have them brought
	About all Bethlehem town.

HEROD   ¶Ye lie! Your note is nought!
The devils of hell you drown!
So may that boy be fled;
For in waste have ye wrought.
Ere that same lad be sought,
Shall I never bide in bed.

1 COUNCILLOR   ¶We will wend with you then,
To ding that dastard down.

2 COUNCILLOR   ¶Aux armes, every each man
That holds faith of Mahound!
Were they a thousand score
This bargain shall they ban.
Come after as ye can,
For we will wend before.

20

THE SPURRIERS AND LORIMERS

Doctores, Jesus puer sedens in Templo in medio eorum, interrogans eos et respondens eis, iiij Judei, Maria et Josep, querentes eum et invenientes in Templo.

JOSEPH ¶Mary, of mirths may we begin,
And truly tell betwixt us two,
Of solemn sights that we have seen
In that city where we come fro.

MARY ¶Certes, Joseph, ye will not ween
What mirths within my heart I make,
Since that our son has with us been,
And seen those solemn sights also.

JOSEPH ¶Homeward I rede we hie,
With all the might we may,
Because of company
That will wend in our way.
For good fellowship have we found,
And age henceforward shall we find.

MARY ¶Ah sir! Where is our seemly son?
I trow our wits be waste as wind.
Alas! In bale thus am I gone.
What ails us both to be so blind?
To go overfast we have begun,
And left that lovely lad behind.

JOSEPH ¶Nay, Mary, mend thy cheer,
For sure, when all is done,
He comes with folk full near,
And will overtake us soon.

MARY ¶Overtake us soon? Sir, surely nay;
Such gabbings may not me beguile,

	For we have travelled all this day
	From Jerusalem many a mile.
JOSEPH	¶I thought he had been with us aye.
	Away from us how should he wile?
MARY	¶It helps us not such saws to say.
	My bairn is lost. Alas the while,
	That ever we went out
	With him in company.
	We looked over late about;
	Full woe is me thereby,
	For he is wandered someways wrong,
	And none is worthy to blame but we.
JOSEPH	¶Againward rede I that we gang
	The right way to that same city,
	To seek and spy all men among,
	For by sure hap homeward is he.
MARY	¶Of sorrows sore shall be my song,
	My seemly son until I see.
	He is but twelve year old,
	What way some'er he wends.
JOSEPH	¶Woman, we may be bold
	To find him with our friends.

II

1 MASTER	¶Now, Masters, take to me intent
	And rank your reasons right in rows;
	And all the people here present,
	Every man, let us see his saws.
	But wit I would, ere hence we went,
	By clerkship clear if we could know,
	If any man that life has lent
	Would ought allege against our law.
	Either in more or less,
	If we default might feel,
	Duely we shall redress
	By doom every single deal.
2 MASTER	¶Well said, so might I thriving be!
	Such notes to name methinks were need,
	For masters in this land are we,
	And have the laws truly to lead,

141

And doctors also in our degree
That judgement have of every deed.
Lay forth our books; quick, let us see
What matter most were for our meed.

3 MASTER ¶We shall ordain so well,
Since we all clerkship know,
Default shall no man tell,
Neither in deed nor saw.

JESUS ¶Lordings, love be with you and good intent,
And mirth be to this company.

1 MASTER ¶Son, hence away I would thou went;
For other hefts in hand have we.

2 MASTER ¶Son, whosoever thee hither sent,
They were not wise, that warn I thee;
For we have other tales to tent
Than now with bairns babbling to be.

3 MASTER ¶Son, if ye list ought to learn
To live by Moses' law,
Come hither, and thou shalt hear
The saws that we shall say.
For in some mind it may thee bring
To hear our reasons read by rows.

JESUS ¶To learn of you I need nothing,
For I know both your deeds and saws.

1 MASTER ¶Now hear yon bairn with his bragging!
He weens he knows more than we know.
Nay, certes, son; thou art over young
In clerkship yet to know our laws.

JESUS ¶I wot as well as ye
How that your laws were wrought.

2 MASTER ¶Come, sit; soon shall we see;
For sure, so seems it nought.
Wonder it were that any wight
Unto our reasons right should reach.
And thou sayst that thou hast insight,
Our laws truly to tell and teach?

JESUS ¶The Holy Ghost has on me light,
And has anointed me as a leech,
And given me full power and might,
The Kingdom of heaven for to preach.

1 MASTER ¶Whence e'er may this bairn be

That shows these novels now?

JESUS ❡Certes, I was ere ye,
And shall be after you.

I MASTER ❡Son, of thy saws, as I have weal,
And of thy wit is wonder thing,
But nevertheless fully I feel
It may fall well in the working,
For David deems of every deal,
And says thus of the children young
  Ex ore infancium et lactancium perfecisti laudem.
Of their months, saith David well,
Our Lord he has performed loving.
But yet, son, thou shouldest let
Here for to speak over large;
For where masters are met,
Child's words are not to charge.
And if thou wouldst ever so fain
Give all thy list to learn the law.
Thou art neither of might nor main
To know it as a clerk may know.

JESUS ❡Sirs, I say you for certain
That soothfast shall be all my saw,
And power have I plenary and plain
To say and answer as I owe.

I DOCTOR ❡Masters, what may this mean?
Marvel methinks have I
Whence ever this bairn has been
To talk thus cunningly.

2 DOCTOR ❡As wide in world as ever I went,
Yet found I never such wondrous lore.
For sure, I trow this barin be sent
Full sovereignly to salve our sore.

JESUS ❡Sirs, I shall prove to you present
All the sayings that I said ere.

3 DOCTOR ❡Which callest thou the first commandment
And most of might in Moses' lore?

JESUS ❡Sirs, since ye are set in rows,
And have your books abroad,
Let's see, sirs, in your saws,
How rightly ye can read.

I DOCTOR ❡I read this is the first bidding

143

That Moyses taught us to keep still—
To honour God over all thing
With all thy wit and all thy will,
And all thine heart on him shall hang,
Early and late, both loud and still.

JESUS ❡Ye need no other books to bring,
But find ye this for to fulfil.
The second may men prove
And clearly know, whereby
Your neighbours shall ye love
As yourself certainly.
These commanded Moses to all men
In his commandments clear.
In these two biddings, shall ye ken,
Hangs all the lore we ought to fear.
Whoso these two fulfilleth, then,
With main and might in good manner,
He truly fulfils all the ten
That follow after these two here.
Then should ye God honour
With all your might and main,
And love well each neighbour
Right as yourself certain.

I DOCTOR ❡Now, son, since thou hast told us two,
Which are the eight, can you ought say?

JESUS ❡The third biddeth whereas ye go
That ye shall hallow the holy day.
Then is the fourth for friend or foe
That father and mother honour aye.
The fifth then bids you not to slay
No man nor woman by any way.
The sixth, soothly to see,
Commands all mankind's kin
That they shall seek to flee
All filths of fleshly sin.
The seventh forbiddeth you to steal ,
Your neighbour's goods or more or less—
Which faults now may we find such deal
Among all folks that marvel 'tis.
The eighth learneth you to be leal,
Here for to bear no false witness.

Your neighbour's house, while ye have heal,
The ninth bids take not by distress.
His wife nor his women
The tenth bids not covet.
These are the biddings ten,
Whoso will truly set.

2 DOCTOR ¶Behold how he alleges our law,
And never learned on book to read.
Full subtle saws methink he says,
And also true, if we take heed.

3 DOCTOR ¶Bah! Let him wend forth on his ways;
For if he dwell, as I may dread,
The people shall full soon him praise
Well more than us, for all our deed.

1 DOCTOR ¶Nay, nay; then were we wrong;
Such speaking will we spare.
As he came, let him gang,
And move us now no more.

MARY ¶Ah, dear Joseph, what is your rede?
Of our great harm no help may be.
My heart is heavy as any lead,
My seemly son until I see.
Now have we sought in every stead
Both up and down these long days three;
And whether he be quick or dead,
That wot we not, so woe is me.

JOSEPH ¶Keen cares had never man more,
But mourning may not mend.
I rede further we fare,
Till God some succour send.
About yon Temple if he be ought
I would we wist, this weary night.

MARY ¶Ah, sir! I see him we have sought!
In world was never so seemly a sight!
Lo, where he sits—see ye him not?—
Among yon masters mickle of might.

JOSEPH ¶Now blest be he us hither brought!
In land was never none so light.

MARY ¶Ah, dear Joseph, as we have weal,
Go forth and fetch your son and mine.
This day is gone near every deal,

145

	And we have need hence for to go.
JOSEPH	¶With men of might I meddle ill;
	All my travail must I lose so.
	I cannot with them, wot you well;
	They are so gay in furs so fine.
MARY	¶To them your errand for to say
	Soothly ye need not dread no deal.
	They will take regard to you alway
	Because of eld; this wot you well.
JOSEPH	¶When I come there, what shall I say?
	I wot never, as I have weal.
	Sure, Mary, you will have me shamed for aye,
	For I can neither crook nor kneel.
MARY	¶Go we together, I hold it best,
	Unto yon wights worthy in weed;
	And if I see, as I have rest,
	That ye will not, then must I need.
JOSEPH	¶Gang on, Mary; tell thy tale first;
	Thy son to thee will take good heed.
	Wend forth, Mary, and do thy best;
	I come behind, as God me speed.
MARY	¶Ah, dearest son Jesus!
	Since we love thee alone,
	Why dost thou thus to us,
	And make us move such moan?
	Thy father and I betwixt us two,
	Son, for thy love have liked full ill;
	We have sought thee both to and fro,
	Weeping full sore as sad wights will.
JESUS	¶Yet whereto should ye seek me so?
	Oft times it hath been told to you,
	My Father's works, for weal or woe,
	Thus am I sent in all to do.
MARY	¶Those sayings, as I have weal,
	Can I not understand
	I shall think on them well,
	To find what follows on.
JOSEPH	¶Now soothly, son, the sight of thee
	Has salved us of all our sore.
	Come forth, son, with thy mother and me;
	At Nazareth I would we were.

JESUS ❡Now live ye well, my lords so free;
For with my friends now will I fare.

I DOCTOR ❡Now, son, where thou shalt bide or be,
God make thee good man evermore.
No wonder if yon wife
Of his finding be fain;
He shall, if he have life,
Prove to a pretty swain.
Son, look thou hide for good or ill
The matters that we have named here now;
And if thou like to live here still
And dwell with us, welcome art thou.

JESUS ❡Gramercy, sirs, of your good will;
No longer may I linger now.
My friends' thoughts thus will I fulfil
And as they bid, obedient bow.

MARY ❡Full well is us this tide;
Now may we make good cheer.

JOSEPH ❡No longer will we bide.
Farewell, all folk now here.

21

THE BARBOURS

Jesus, Johannes Baptista baptizans eum, et Ij angeli ministrantes.

JOHN BAPTIST ¶Almighty God, Lord verily,
How wonderful is man's lying.
For though I preach them day by day,
And tell them, Lord, of thy coming
    That all has wrought,
Men are so dull that my preaching
    Serves all for nought.
When I have, Lord, in name of thee
Baptised the folk in water clear,
Then have I said that after me
Shall he come that has more power
    Than I at most;
He shall give baptism more entire
    In fire and Holy Ghost.
Thus am I come in message right
To be forerunner in certain,
In witness-bearing of that light,
The which shall lighten every man
    That comes at hand
Into this world; now whoso can
    May understand.
These folk made marvel of my fare,
And what I was full fast they spied.
They asked if I a prophet were,
And I said "nay", but certified
    All openly;
I said I was a voice that cried
    In desert high.
"Look thou make thee ready," aye said I,

"Unto our Lord God most of might;
That is, that thou be clean wholly
In word, in work, aye ready dight
    Against our Lord,
With perfect life, that every wight
    Be well restored.
For if we be clean in living,
Our bodies are God's temple then,
In the which he will make his dwelling;
Therefore be clean, both wife and man;
    This is my rede.
God will make in you wholly then
    His dwelling-stead.
And if you set all your delight
In lust and liking of this life,
Then will he turn from you in flight,
Because of sin, both man and wife,
    And from you flee.
For with all those whose sin is rife
    God will not be."

ANGEL   ¶Thou John, take tent what I shall say.
I bring thee tidings wondrous good.
My Lord Jesus shall come this day
From Galilee unto this flood
    Ye Jordan call,
Baptism to take mildly with mood,
    This day he shall.
John, of his sending then be glad,
And thank him heartily, both loud and still.

JOHN BAPTIST   ¶I thank him ever, but I dread;
I am not able to fulfil
    This deed certain.

2 ANGEL   ¶Nay, John; you ought with heart and will
    To be full fain
To do his bidding swift and plain.
But in his baptism . . . John, take tent . . . .
The heavens shall be open seen;
The Holy Ghost shall down be sent
    To see in sight,
The Father's voice with great talent
    Be heard full right,

That shall say thus to him thereby . . .
[*Perhaps two stanzas lost, and the context confused.*]

JOHN BAPTIST ... ¶With words full few,
I will be subject night and day,
As well I owe,
To serve my Lord in pleasing way
In deed and saw.
But well I wot, baptism is ta'en
To wash and cleanse a man of sin;
And well I wot that sin is not
In him, without him or within.
What needs he then
To be baptised for any sin,
Like sinful men?

JESUS ¶John, kind of man is frail,
To which I have me knit.
But I shall show thee reasons two,
That thou shalt know by kindly wit
The cause why I have ordained so;
And one is this—
Mankind may not unbaptised go
To endless bliss.
And since myself have taken mankind,
Men shall me for their mirror make.
I have my doing in their mind,
And also I do this baptism take.
I will thereby
Myself be baptised for their sake
Full openly.
Another reason I shall thee tell.
My will is this, that from this day
The virtue of my baptism dwell
In baptism water ever and aye,
That man may taste
Through my grace there to take alway
The Holy Ghost.

JOHN BAPTIST ¶Almighty Lord, great is thy grace;
I thank thee for thy great foredeed.

JESUS ¶Come, baptise me, John, in this place.

JOHN BAPTIST ¶Lord, save thy grace if I forbid
That it so be;

For, Lord, methinks it were more need
    Thou baptised me.
That place I long for most of all,
From thence thou comes, Lord, as I guess.
How should I, then, that am a thrall,
Give thee baptism that righteous is,
    And hast been ever?
For thou art root of righteousness
    That forfeits never.
What rich man goes from door to door,
To beg from him that has right nought?
Lord, thou art rich and I full poor;
Thou mayest bless all, since thou all wrought.
    From heaven comes all
That helps on earth, if sooth be sought;
    From earth but small.

JESUS   ¶Thou sayest full well, John, certainly,
But suffer now, for heavenly need,
That righteousness be not only
Fulfilled in word, but also in deed,
    Through baptism clear.
Come, baptise me in my manhood
    Openly here.
First shall I take, then shall I preach;
For so behoves man to fulfill
All righteousness, as very leech.

JOHN BAPTIST   ¶Lord, I am ready at thy will,
    And will be aye;
Thy subject, Lord, in loud and still,
    In what I may.
Ah, lord; I tremble where I stand,
So am I averse to do that deed.
But save me, Lord that all ordained,
For thee to touch have I great dread,
    For doings dark.
Now help me, Lord, through thy godhead,
    To do this work.
Jesu, my lord of mights the most,
I baptise thee here in the name
Of the Father and of the Son and Holy Ghost.
But in this deed, Lord, set no blame

This day by me,
And bring all those unto thy home
That trust in thee.
Then the two angels sing Veni creator Spiritus.

JESUS ¶John, for man's profit, wit thou well,
I take this baptism certainly.
The dragon's power every deal
Through my baptism destroyed have I;
This is certain;
And saved mankind, soul and body,
From endless pain.
Men that believe and baptised be
Shall saved be and come to bliss;
Whoso trusts not, to pain endless
He shall be damned soon, trow well this.
But wend we now
Where most need folk to guide there is,
Both I and thou.

JOHN BAPTIST ¶I love thee, Lord, as sovereign leech
That comes to salve men of their sore.
As thou commandest, I shall preach,
And learn to every man that lore
That ere was thrall.
Now, sirs, that bairn that Mary bore
Be with you all.

22

THE LOKK SMYTHYS

Jesus super Pynaculum templi, et diabolus tempians eum, cum lapidibus, et ij angeli administrantes etc.

DEVIL ¶Make room! Be alive! And let me gang.
What makes here all this madding throng ?
Hie you all hence! High might you hang,
    Right with a rope.
I dread me that I dwell too long
    To do a jape.
For since the first time that I fell
For my high pride from heaven to hell,
Ever have I mustered me to tell
    Among mankind
How I in dole might make them dwell,
    There to be pined.
And sure, all that have since been born
Have come to me, mid-day and morn;
I have ordained so therefor;
    None may them fend,
That from all liking they are lorn
    Without an end.
And now some men speak of a swain,
How he shall come and suffer pain,
And with his death to bliss again
    They should be bought.
But sure, this tale's but a trick and vain;
    I trust it nought.
For I know every deal, I ween,
Of this same minion that men mean,
How he has in great trouble been
    Since he was born,
And suffered mickle plots and pain,

Both even and morn.
And now it is brought so about,
That lurdan that they love and lout,
To wilderness he is gone out,
    He and no mo.
To hurt him now I have no doubt,
    Betwixt us two.
Before this time he has been intent,
That I might get him with no glint;
But now since he so alone went,
    I shall essay,
And make him to some sin assent,
    If that I may.
He has fasted—that mars his mood—
These forty days now without food.
If he be man in bone and blood
    He hungers ill.
In gluttony then hold I good
    To wit his will.
For so it shall be known indeed
If the Godhead in him be hid.
If he will do as I him bid,
    When I come near—
There was never deed that ever he did
    To grieve him more.
Thou witty man and wise of rede,
If thou can ought of godhead,
Bid now that these stones be made bread
    Betwixt us two.
Then may they stand thyself in stead
    And others too.
For thou hast fasted long, I ween;
I would now that some meat were seen,
For old acquaintance us between;
    Thyself knows how.
There shall no man know what I mean,
    But I and thou.

JESUS ¶My Father, that all sorrow may slake,
Honour evermore I to thee make,
And gladly suffer for thy sake
    Such villainy.

154

And thus temptation for to take
    Of mine enemy.
Thou wicked wight, thy wits are gone.
For written it is, whoso has undertsood,
A man lives not in main and mood
    With bread alone,
But God's own words are ghostly food
    To men each one.
If I have fasted, 'tis of skill.
Wit thou, I hunger not so ill
That I work not my Father's will
    In all degree.
Thy bidding will I not fulfil;
    That I warn thee.

DEVIL ¶Away! Such talking never I kenned.
He hungers not so as I weened.
Now since thy Father may thee fend
    By subtle sleight,
Let see if thou alone may land
    There upon height,
Upon the pinnacle perfectly—
Aha! Now go we well thereby.
I shall essay in vainglory
    To make him fall.
And if he be God's Son mighty,
    Surely I shall.
Now list to me a little space.
If thou be God's Son full of grace,
Show some affair here in this place,
    To prove thy might.
Let's see . . . Fall down upon thy face,
    Here in my sight.
For it is written, as well is kenned,
How God shall angels to thee send,
And they shall keep thee in their hand
    Whereso thou goes,
That thou shall on no stone descend
    To hurt thy toes.
Since thou may with no danger, i'faith,
Fall so and do thyself no scathe,
Then tumble down to ease us both,

Here to my feet.
If thou do not, I shall be wroth;
That shalt thou see.

JESUS ¶Let be, warlock, thy words all vain.
For written it is full clear and plain,
"Thy God thou shalt not tempt with pain
Nor with discord,
Nor quarrel shalt thou none maintain
Against thy Lord."
And therefore trow thou yet again
That all thy gauds shall nothing gain.
Be subject to thy sovereign
Early and late.

DEVIL ¶What! All this travail is in vain,
By ought I wot.
He proves that he is mickle of price;
There it is good I me advise;
And since I may not in this wise
Make him my thrall,
I shall essay in covetise
To make him fall.
For sure, I shall not leave him yet.
Who is my sovereign, I would wit?
Myself ordained thee there to sit;
This wot you well.
And right even as I ordained it
Is done each deal.
Then mayest thou see, since it is so,
That I am sovereign of us two.
And yet I grant thee ere I go,
And without fail,
That if thou wilt assent me to,
It shall avail.
For I have all this world to wield,
Tower and town, forest and field;
If thou thine heart will to me yield
With word full kind,
Yet will I surely be thy shield
And faithful friend.
Behold now, sir, and you shall see
Many a kingdom, many a country;

All this here will i give to thee
    For evermore,
If thou wilt fall and honour me,
    As I said ere.

JESUS   ¶Cease of thy saws, thou Sathanas.
I grant no thing that you me ask.
To pine of hell I bid thee pass
    And swiftly wend,
And dwell in woe, as thou ere was,
    Without an end.
No other might shall be thy meed.
For written it is, who right can read,
The Lord thy God thou ought to dread
    And honour aye,
And serve him in thy word and deed,
    Both night and day.
And since thou does not as I thee tell,
No longer will I let thee dwell.
I command thee, thou hie to hell,
    And hold thee there,
With fellowship of fiends fell
    For evermore.

DEVIL   ¶Out! I dare not look, alas!
It is worse than ever it was.
He musters all the might he has.
    High might he hang!
It follows fast, for I must pass
    To torments strong.

I ANGEL   ¶Ah, mercy, Lord. What may this mean?
I marvel that you bear this pain
Of this foul fiend artful and keen
    Talking to you.
And you his wickedness, I ween,
    May waste at will.
Methinks that you were straitly stead,
Lord, with this fiend that now is fled.

JESUS   ¶Mine angel dear, be not adread;
    He may not grieve.
The Holy Ghost aye has me led;
    Thus now believe.
For when the fiend shall my folk see

Assailing them in sore degree,
Their mirror may they make of me,
For to stand still.
For overcome they shall not be,
But if they will.

2 ANGEL ❡Ah, Lord, this is a great meekness
In you in whom all mercy is,
And at your will may doom or dress,
As is worthy;
And three temptations takes express
Thus sovereignly.

JESUS ❡My blessing have they with my hand
That with such grief grudge not nor bend,
And also that will stiffly stand
Against the fiend.
I know my time is fast at hand.
Now will I wend.

23

THE CURRIERS

Petrus, Jacobus et Johannes; Jesus ascendens in montem et transfigurans se ante eos. Moyses et Elyas apparentes et vox loquentis in nube.

JESUS ¶Peter, mine own disciple dear,
And James and John, my cousins two,
Take heartily heed, for ye shall hear
What I will tell unto no mo.
And also ye shall see sights here
Which none shall see but ye also.
Therefore come forth with me to appear,
For to yon mountain will I go;
There shall ye see a sight
Which ye have yearned for long.

PETER ¶My lord, we are full light
And glad with thee to gang.

JESUS ¶Long did ye covet for to ken
My Father, for I set him before;
And well ye wot time and when
In Galylee going, we were.
"Show us the Father," said ye then;
"That sufficeth us without more."
I said to you and to all men,
"Who sees me sees my Father there."
Such words to you I spake
In truth to make you bold;
Ye could not undertake
The tales that I you told.
Another time for to increase
Your faith, and worldly you to wis,
I said, "Quem dicunt homines
Esse filium hominis?"

I asked you whom the people chose
To be man's son, without amiss.
Ye answered and said, "Some, Moyses;"
And some said then "Hely it is,"
And some said "John Baptist."
Then more I asked you yet;
I asked if ye ought wist
Who I was, by your wit.
You answered, Peter, profit to know,
And said that I was Christ, God's Son.
But of thyself that had not thou;
My Father had that grace begun.
Therefore obey and bide ye now
To the time ye have my Father seen.

JAMES ¶Lord, to thy bidding will we bow
Full buxomly, as we are bound.

JOHN ¶Lord, we will work thy will
All way with true intent.
We love God, loud and still,
That us this loan has lent.

PETER ¶Full blithe and glad ought we to be,
And thank our Master mickle of main,
That says we shall such good sights see,
The which none other shall see certain.

JAMES ¶He told us of his Father free;
Of that faring would we be fain.

JOHN ¶All that he promised hold will he;
Therefore we will no further strain,
But as he shall vouchsafe,
So shall we understand.

. . . . . .
Behold, here we have now in haste
Some new tidings
. . . . . . [A passage lost here.]

HELYAS ¶Lord God, I love thee lastingly
And highly, both with heart and hand,
That me, thy poor prophet Hely.
Has summoned in this stead to stand.
In Paradise dwelling am I,
Aye since I left that earthly land.
I come Christ's name to clarify,

And God his Father has me ordained
Now for to bear witness
In word to man and wife
That this His own son is
And lord of lasting life.

MOYSES ¶Lord God, that of all wealth is weal,
With wit and will we worship thee,
That unto me Moses would tell
This great point of thy privity,
And kindly caught me out of Hell
This solemn sight that I should see,
When thy dear darlings that there dwell
Have not thy grace in such degree.
Our forefathers full fain
Would see this solemn sight,
That in this place thus plain
Is mustered through thy might.

PETER ¶Brethren, what may yon brightness be?
No blaze before so bright has been.
It mars my might; I may not see;
So wondrous thing was never seen.

JAMES ¶What will it work, that wot not we;
How weak I wax ye will not ween.
Ere was there one, now there is three;
We think our Master is between.

JOHN ¶That our Master is there,
That we may truly trow.
He was full fair before,
But never as he is now.

PETER ¶His clothing is white as the snow
His face shines as the sun.
To speak with him I have great awe;
Such doing before was never done.

JAMES ¶The other two fain would I know,
And wit what work them here has won.

JOHN ¶I rede we ask them all on row,
And ask them how this game's begun.

PETER ¶My brethren, if that ye be come
To make more clear Christ's name,
Tell here unto us three,
For we seek to the same.

ELIAS ¶It is God's will we make you wise
Of his works, as is worthy.
I have my place in Paradise,
Enoch my brother is near by.
As messenger without amiss
Am I called to this company,
To witness that God's son is this,
Even with him measured almighty.
To death we were not dight
But quick shall we soon come
With Antichrist to fight,
Before the day of doom.

MOYSES ¶My friend, if that ye ask my name,
Moyses then may ye read by row.
Two thousand year after Adam
Then gave God unto me his law.
And since in hell has been our home.
Alas, Adam's kin, this shall ye know
Unto Christ come. This is the same
That us shall from that dungeon draw,
He shall bring them to bliss
That now in bale are bound;
This mirth we may not miss.
For this same is God's son.

JESUS ¶My dear disciple, dread thou nought,
I am thy sovereign certainly.
This wondrous work that here is wrought
Is of my Father almighty.
These both are hither brought,
The one Moyses, the tother Ely,
And for your sakes thus are they sought
To tell you that his Son am I.
So shall both heaven and hell
Be deemers of this deed,
And ye in earth shall tell
My name where it is need.

PETER ¶Loved be thou ever, Lord Jesus,
That all this solemn sight hast sent,
That vouchest safe to show us thus,
So that thy might be evident.
Here is full fair dwelling for us,

A liking place in which to land.
Ah, lord, let us no further truss,
For we will make with heart and hand
A tabernacle unto thee
At once if thou shalt abide;
One shall to Moyses be
And to Ely the third.

JAMES ¶Yea surely, sir, that were well done,
But we ought not such case to crave,
They need but say and have it soon,
Such services if he vouchsafe.
He promises his men, morn and noon,
Their harbour high in heaven to have;
Therefore is best we bide his boon;
Who other rédes, rudely they rave.

JOHN ¶Such sending as he sends
May mend all our mischief,
And were he likes to land
We will land, with his leave.
 (*Here a cloud descends, and the Father in the cloud.*)

GOD THE FATHER ¶Ye feeble of faith and folk afraid;
Be not afeared that I appear.
I am your God that goodly made
Both earth and air with high clouds clear.
This is my Son, as ye have said,
As he has shown you by signs here.
With all his works I am well pleased,
Therefore to him take heed and hear.
Where he is, there am I;
He is mine, I am his;
Who trows this steadfastly
Shall bide in endless bliss.

JESUS ¶Peter, peace be unto thee,
And to you also, James and John.
Rise up, and tell me what you see,
And be no more so woe begone.

PETER ¶Ah, lord! What may this marvel be?
Where is this glorious gleam all gone?
We saw here plainly persons three,
And now is our Lord left alone.
This marvel moves my mind,

163

And makes my flesh afraid.

JAMES ¶This brightness made me blind;
Such sudden start I never made.

JOHN ¶Lord God, our maker almighty,
Tell what this matter may have meant.
We saw two bodies stand thee by,
Who said the Father had them sent.

PETER ¶There came a cloud out of the sky,
Light as the gleams that on them bent,
And now fares all as fantasy,
For wot we not what way they went.

JAMES ¶That cloud confused us clean,
That came shining so clear.
Such sight was never seen,
To seek on all sides near.

JOHN ¶Nay, nay. That noise annoyed us more
That here was heard so hideously.

JESUS ¶Friends, be ye not afeared therefor;
I shall you say a reason why.
My Father wist how that ye were
In your faith failing, and thereby,
He came to witness everywhere,
And said that his true Son am I.
And also in this stead
To witness of the same,
A quick man and a dead
Came to make clear my name.

PETER ¶Ah, lord, why lettest thou not us see
Thy Father's face in his fairness?

JESUS ¶Peter, you ask overgreat degree;
That grace may not be given, I guess.
In his Godhead so high he is
As all your prophets can express,
That longer alive he shall not be
That sees his Godhead as it is.
Here have ye seen in sight
Points of his privacy,
As much as earthly wight
May suffer on earth to see.
And therefore wend we now again
To our company, and mend their cheer.

JAMES   ¶Our fellows to ask will be full fain
       How we have fared while we were here.

JESUS   ¶This vision hide with might and main;
       To no man living it declare,
       Till time man's Son have suffered pain
       And risen from death. Know it then clear.
       For all that trows that thing
       Of my Father and me
       They shall have his blessing
       And mine. So mote it be.

24

THE CAPPEMAKERS ETC.

(The PLUMMERS, PATENMAKERS, POUCHEMAKERS, and BOTELLERS)

Jesus, duo apostoli, mulier deprehensa in adulterio, iiij Judei accusantes eam.

1 JEW	¶Leap forth; let us no longer stand,
	But smartly let our gear be arrayed.
	This filly that we with folly found,
	Let's haste fast that she be afraid.
2 JEW	¶We will bear witness and warrant
	How we roused her all unarrayed,
	Against the laws of this our land,
	Where she was with her leman laid.
1 JEW	¶Yea, and he a wedded man;
	That was a wicked sin.
2 JEW	¶That bargain shall she ban
	With bale when we begin.
1 JEW	¶Ah, false stud-mare and stinking stray,
	How durst thou steal so still away,
	To do so vile adultery,
	That is so greatly against our law?
2 JEW	¶Her bawdry shall she dearly buy;
	For as we saw, so shall we say;
	And also her working is worthy
	That she be doomed to death this day.
1 JEW	¶The masters of the law
	Are here even at our hand.
2 JEW	¶Go we, rehearse by row
	Her faults as we them found.
1 JEW	¶God save you, masters mickle of main,
	That clerkship great and counsel can.
3 JEW	¶Welcome, friends; but tell me again,

How fare ye with that fair woman?
2 JEW   ¶Ah sirs, we shall tell you certain
Of much sorrow since she began.
We have her taken with whoredom plain;
Herself may not gainsay it then.
4 JEW   ¶What hath she done? Folly,
In fornication and sin?
1 JEW   ¶Nay, nay, adultery
Full bold, and stands therein.
3 JEW   ¶Adultery! Name it not, for shame.
It is so foul; openly I say Fye.
Is it sooth they say of thee, dame?
2 JEW   ¶What, sir? She may it not deny.
We then were worthy for to blame
To grieve her, save she were guilty.
4 JEW   ¶Now sure, this is a foul diffame,
And mickle bale must be thereby.
3 JEW   ¶Yea, sir; ye said well there.
By law and righteous rede
There falls nought else therefore
But to be stoned to death.
1 JEW   ¶Sirs, since ye tell the law this tide,
And know its course in this country,
Doom her on high; no longer bide;
And after your words work shall we.
4 JEW   ¶Be not so fierce, fair sirs; abide;
A new matter now moveth me. . . .

> [*A leaf is lost here from the MS., containing upwards
> of 60 lines or more. The sense of the missing passages
> may perhaps be supplied tentatively as follows* ★-★:
★That prophet from the country side,
He now draws near to us, I see.

. . . . . .

Let be, and bid him say
What judgment in her case.
Will he the law obey,
Or its good force efface?
Jesus   ¶Full well I know your hidden thought,
And what your meaning is in mind.
Ye learned long the law have taught,
Be not to its true meaning blind

My judgment now hear ye;
I say this word alone—
He that from sin is free,
He first shall cast a stone.*]

3 JEW ¶He shows me my misdeeds and sin.
I leave you here; let him alone.

4 JEW ¶Out, out! Here will new gauds begin;
Yea, greet all well; say that I am gone.

1 JEW ¶And since ye are not bold,
No longer bide will I.

2 JEW ¶Peace! Let no tales be told,
But pass forth privily.

JESUS ¶Woman, say now where those men went,
That keenly here accused thee?
Who has condemned thee, took thou intent?

WOMAN ¶Lord, no man has condemned me.

JESUS ¶Neither do I condemn. Repent.
Of all thy miss I make thee free.
Look thou no more to sin assent.

WOMAN ¶Ah, lord, aye loved might thou be.
All earthly folk now here,
Love him and his high name,
That me on this manner
Has saved from sin and shame.

1 APOSTLE ¶Ah, lord, we love thee inwardly,
And all thy lore both loud and still,
That grants thy grace to the guilty,
And spares them that thy folk would spill.

JESUS ¶I shall say you a reason why.
I know it is my Father's will,
And to make them aware thereby,
To know themselves have done more ill.
And evermore of this same
Example shall be seen;
Whoso shall others blame,
Look first themselves be clean.

2 APOSTLE ¶Ah, master, here may men see also
How meekness makes full mickle amend,
To forgive gladly where we go
All folk that may us ought offend.

JESUS He that will not forgive his foe,

And use meekness with heart and hand,
That kingdom may he not come to
That is ordained without an end.
And more soon shall we see
Here ere we further fare,
How that my Father free
Will muster might yet more.

MESSENGER ¶Jesu, that prophet is very,
My ladies Martha and Mary,
If you vouchsafe, they would you pray
For to come unto Bethany.
He whom you love full well alway
Is sick, and like, lord, for to die.
If you would come, mend him you may,
And comfort all that company.

JESUS ¶I say you that sickness
Is not only to death,
But joy of God's goodness
Shall be shewed in that stead,
And God's Son shall be glorified
By that sickness and signs so clear.
Therefore, brethren, no longer bide;
Two days fully have we been here.
We will go sojourn here beside
In the Jewry where friends appear.

I APOSTLE ¶Ah, lord, you know well every tide
The Jews they seek thee far and near
To stone thee unto death,
Or put to peerless pain;
And thou to that same stead
Covet to come again.

JESUS ¶Ye wot by course well for to cast.
The day is now of twelve hours long;
And while light of the day may last
It is good that we readily gang.
For when daylight is plainly past,
Full soon then may we wend all wrong.
Therefore take heed and travail fast,
While light of life is you among.
And to you say I more,
How that Lazar your friend

Sleeps now, and I therefore
With you to him will wend.

2 APOSTLE ¶We will be ruled after thy rede.
But if he sleeps, he shall be safe.

JESUS ¶I say to you, Lazar is dead,
And for you all great joy I have.
Ye know I was not in that stead
What time that he was graved in grave.
His sisters pray with humble bede,
And for comfort they call and crave.
Therefore go we together,
To make for them mirth more.

1 APOSTLE ¶Since he will needs wend thither,
Go we, and die with him there.

MARY ¶Alas! Out on God's will alone,
That I should sit to see this sight.
For I may mourn and make my moan;
So woe in world was never wight.
Him I loved most is from me gone,
My dear brother that Lazar hight.
And I durst say I would be slain,
For now fail both my mind and might.
My weal is gone for ever;
No medicine mend me may.
Ah, death, do thou thy devoir,
And have me hence away.

MARTHA ¶Alas! for ruth now may I rave,
And feebly fare by frith and field.
Would God in ground I had my grave,
That death had covered and concealed.
For health in heart may I not have,
Unless he help that all may wield,
Of Christ I will some comfort crave,
For he may be my help and shield.
To seek I shall not cease,
Till I my sovereign see.
Hail, peerless prince of peace,
Jesu, Master so free.

JESUS ¶Martha, what means thou to make such cheer?

[*A leaf is missing here, and therefore about 60 lines lost.*]

? MARTHA ¶This stone we shall full soon

Remove and set aside.

JESUS ¶Father, that is in heaven in height,
I thank thee ever for all thing,
That hastes to hear me day and night,
And takes heed unto my asking.
Wherefore vouchsafe of thy great might,
So that this people, old and young,
That stand and bide to see this sight,
May truly trow and have knowing
This time here ere I pass,
How that thou hast me sent.
LAZARE, VENI FORAS:
Come from thy monument.

LAZARUS ¶Ah, peerless prince, full of pity,
Worshipped be thou in world alway,
That thus has shewed thy might in me
Both dead and buried this fourth day.
By certain signs here may men see
How that thou art God's Son very.
All those that truly trust in thee
Shall never die; that dare I say.
Therefore, ye folk now here,
Serve him with main and might;
His laws look that ye hear;
Then will he lead you to his light.

MARY ¶Here men may find a faithful friend,
That thus recovered us from our care.

MARTHA ¶Jesu, my lord and master kind,
For this we thank thee evermore.

JESUS ¶Sisters, I may no longer spend;
To other folk now must I fare,
And to Jerusalem will I wend,
For things that must be fulfilled there.
Therefore tell I you right,
My men, to wend with me.
Ye that have seen this sight,
My blessing with you be.

25

THE SKYNNERS

Jesus super asinum cum pullo suo, xij apostoli sequentes Jesum, sex divites et sex pauperes, vij pueri cum ramis palmarum cantantes Benedictus etc., et Zacchaeus ascendens in arborem sicamorum.

JESUS   ¶To me take tent and give good heed,
My dear disciples that be here.
I shall tell you that shall be indeed.
My time to pass hence draweth near,
    And by this skill,
Man's soul to save from sorrows sore,
    That lost was ill.
From heaven to earth when I descend,
Ransom to make I made promise.
The prophecy now draws to an end;
My Father's will forsooth it is
    That sent me hither.
Peter, Philip, I shall you bless,
    And go together
Unto yon castle that is you again.
Go with good heart and tarry not.
My commandment to do be ye fain;
As I charge you, look it be wrought.
    There shall ye find
An ass, there fast as you had sought;
    Then her unbind
With her foal, and to me them bring,
That I on her may sit a space;
So the prophecy clear meaning
May be fulfilled here in this place:
    "Daughter of Sion,
Lo, thy lord comes riding on an ass,

Thee to open."
If any man will you gainsay,
Say that your lord has need of them,
And shall restore them this same day
Unto what man will then them claim.
Do thus this thing.
Go forth ye both, and aye remain
In my blessing.

PETER ¶Jesu, Master, even at thy will
And at thy list we like to do.
Yon beast which thou desirest still
Even at thy will shall come thee to,
Unto thine ease.
Surely, Lord, we will thither, all
Thee for to please.

PHILIP ¶Lord, thee to please we are full fain,
Both night and day to do thy will.
Go we, brother, with all our main,
My Lord's desire for to fulfil.
For prophecy,
We must it do to him by skill
To do duly.

PETER ¶Yea, brother Philip. Behold, surely!
For as he said we soon should find,
Methinks yon beasts before mine eye,
They are the same we should unbind.
Therefore freely
Go we to him that did them bind,
And ask meekly.

PHILIP ¶The beasts are common, well I know,
Therefore we need to ask less leave,
And our Master shall keep the law.
We may take them straight, I believe,
For nought we let.
Full well I wit our time is brief;
Go we them get.

PORTER ¶Say,
What are ye makes here mastery,
To loose these beasts sans livery?
You seem too bold, for nothing ye
Have here to do; therefore rede I

173

Such things to cease,
Or else ye may fall in folly
And great disease.

PETER ¶Sir, with your leave heartily we pray
This beast that we might have.

PORTER ¶To what intent, first shall ye say,
And then I grant what you will crave
By good reason.

PHILIP ¶Our master, sir, that all may save
Asks for this one.

PORTER ¶What man is't that ye master call?
Such privilege how dare he claim?

PETER ¶Jesus, who of Jews is king and ever shall,
Prophet of Nazareth by name,
This same is he;
Both God and man without all blame,
That trust well we.

PORTER ¶Sirs, of that prophet heard I have;
But tell me first plain, where is he?

PHILIP ¶He comes at hand, so God me save;
That lord we left at Bethphage,
He bides us there.

PORTER ¶Sir, take this beast, with heart full free,
And forth now fare.
And if thou think it should be done,
I shall declare plain his coming
To the chief of the Jews, that they may soon
Assemble them to his meeting.
What is your rede?

PETER ¶Thou sayest full well in thy meaning;
Do forth thy deed.
And soon this beast we shall thee bring,
And it restore, as reason will.

PORTER ¶These tidings shall have no hiding,
But to the citizens declare I still
Of this city;
I suppose freely that they will
Meet him with me.
And since I will they warned be,
Both young and old, of every state,
For his coming I will them meet,

> To let them know, without debate—
>> Lo, where they stand,
> These citizens chief in their estate
>> Of all this land.
> He that is ruler of all right
> And freely shaped both sand and sea
> Save you now, lordlings gaily dight,
> And keep you in your seemlity,
>> And all honour.

I BURGESS ¶Welcome, Porter. What novelty,
>> Tell us, this hour?

PORTER ¶Sir, novelty I can you tell,
> And trust that fully as for true.
> Here comes of kin of Israel
> At hand the prophet called Jesu,
>> Lo, this same day,
> Riding on an ass; this tidings true
>> Conceive ye may.

2 BURGESS ¶And is that prophet Jesus near?
> Of him I have heard great marvels told.
> He does great wonders, as I hear;
> He heals the sick, both young and old;
>> The blind—gives them their sight;
> Both dumb and deaf, as himself would,
>> He cures them right.

3 BURGESS ¶Yea,
> Five thousand men with loaves but five
> He fed, and each one had enow;
> Water to wine he turned rife;
> He made corn grow without a plough,
>> Where ere was none.
> To dead men also he gave life—
>> Lazar was one.

4 BURGESS ¶Oft in our Temple has he preached
> Against the people that lived wrong,
> And also new laws has he teached
> Against our laws we used so long,
>> And said plainly,
> The old shall waste, the new shall gang—
>> That we shall see.

5 BURGESS ¶Yea, Moyses' law he know each deal,

And all the prophets in a row;
He tells them so each man may feel
And that they may entirely know,
    If ought were dim;
What prophets have said in their saw
    Belongs to him.

6 BURGESS ¶Emmanuel also by right
They call that prophet, as cause will;
He is the same that once was hight
By Ysaye before, who still
    Thus said full clear,
"Lo, a maiden that knew never ill
    A child should bear."

7 BURGESS ¶King David spoke of him, I ween,
And left witness, ye know each one.
He said the fruit of his flesh clean
Should royal reign upon his throne,
    And therefore he
Of David's kin and other none
    Our king shall be.

8 BURGESS ¶Methinks, good sirs, ye say right well,
And good examples forth ye bring.
And since we thus this matter feel,
Go we, meet him as our own king,
    And king him call.
What is your counsel in this thing?
    Now say ye all.

I BURGESS ¶Against reason I will not plead,
For well I wot our king he is.
Whoso against his king will threat,
He is not wise; he does amiss.
    Porter, come near.
What knowledge hast thou of his coming?
    Tell us all here,
And then we will go meet him free,
And him honour, as well we owe,
    Worthily to our city,
And for our sovereign lord him know,
    In whom we trust.

PORTER ¶Sir, I will tell you all on row,
    If ye will list.

Of his disciples two this day
Where that I stood, they fair me greet,
And on their lord's behalf did pray
Our common ass that they might get
    But for a while,
Whereon their master soft might sit,
    Space of a mile.
And all this matter they me told
Right wholly as I say to you,
And the ass they have right as they would,
And soon will bring again, I trow;
    So they professed.
What ye will do, advise you now;
    Thus think I best.

2 BURGESS   ¶Truly then as for me I say,
I rede we make us ready anon;
Him to greet goodly go this day,
And him receive with great renown,
    As worthy is;
And therefore, sirs, in field and town
    Fulfil ye this.

PORTER   ¶Yea, and your children with you take,
Though all in age they be full young;
Ye may fare better for their sake,
Through blessing of so good a king.
    This is no doubt.

3 BURGESS   ¶I give thee thank for thy saying.
    We will him lout.
And him to meet I am right fain,
In the best manner that I can;
For I desire to see him plain
And honour him as his own man,
    Since sooth I see.
King of Jews will we call him then;
    Our king is he.

4 BURGESS   ¶Our king is he; that is no lies.
Our law to it accords full well.
The prophets all bear full witness,
Who of his secret truth could tell,
    And thus would say,
"Amongst ourselves shall come great weal,

Through God's own way."

5 BURGESS ¶This same is he—there is none other—
Was promised us full long before.
For Moses said, who is our brother,
A new prophet God should restore.
Therefore look ye
What ye will do. Delay no more.
Our king is he.

6 BURGESS ¶Of Juda comes our king so free,
Of Jesse, David, Salamon.
Also by his mother's kin, see ye,
The genealogy bears witness on;
This is right plain.
Him to honour right as I can
I am full fain.

7 BURGESS ¶Of this conceit of your clean wit
I am full glad in heart and thought,
And to meet him I will not let;
I am ready, and will feign nought,
But with you come
To him who bliss again has brought
With mirth and game.

8 BURGESS ¶Your arguments, they are so clear,
I gainsay not, but grant you still.
For when I of that counsel hear,
I covet him with fervent will
Once for to see.
I trow I from henceforward shall
Better man be.

1 BURGESS ¶Go we then with procession
To meet him comely, as we owe,
With branches, flowers and unison,
And mighty songs here in a row.
Our children shall
Go sing before, that men may know
This grant we all.

PETER ¶Jesu, my lord and master free,
As thy command, so have we done.
This ass here we have brought to thee.
What is thy will? Now show us soon,
And tarry not;

	And then we shall, delay to shun, Fulfil thy thought.
JESUS	¶I thank you, brethren mild of mood. Do on this ass your clothes now lay, And lift me up with hearts right good, That I on her may sit this day In my blessing.
PHILIP	¶Lord, thy will to do alway We grant all thing.
JESUS	¶And now, my brethren, with good cheer Give good intent, for ride I will Unto yon city ye see so near; Ye shall me follow together still, As I ere said.
PHILIP	¶Lord, on our life, with all good will We hold us glad.

BLIND MAN	¶Ah lord, that all this world has made,
	Both sun and moon and night and day,
	What noise is this that makes me glad?
	From whence it comes I cannot say,
	    Or what it mean.
	If any man walk in this way,
	    Say what is seen.

POOR MAN	¶Why, man, what ails thee so to cry? Where would thou be? Now tell me here.

BLIND MAN	¶Ah, sir, a poor blind man am I,
	And aye have been from tender year,
	    Since I was born.
	I heard a voice of noble cheer,
	    Here me before.

POOR MAN	¶Man, wilt thou ought that I can do?
BLIND MAN	¶Yea, sir; for gladly would I wit, If thou would ought declare me to— This mirth I heard, what mean may it To understand?
POOR MAN	¶Jesus the prophet full of grace Comes here at hand, And all the citizens from town Go him to meet with melody, With the fairest procession That was ever seen in this Jewry.

He is right near.

BLIND MAN ¶Sir, help me to the street hastily,
That I may hear
That noise, and that I might through grace—
My sight of him to crave I would.

POOR MAN ¶Lo, he is here at this same place.
Cry fast on him; look thou be bold,
With voice right high.

BLIND MAN ¶Jesu, Thou Son of David called,
Have thou mercy.
Alas! I cry, he hears me not;
He has no ruth for my misfare.
He turns his ear. Where is his thought?

POOR MAN ¶Cry somewhat louder; do not spare.
So may you speed.

BLIND MAN ¶Jesu, thou salver of all sore,
To me give good heed.

PHILIP ¶Cease, man, and cry not so.
The prince of the people goes thee by.
Thou should sit still and attend thereto.
Here passes the prophet of mercy;
Thou dost amiss.

BLIND MAN ¶Ah, David's son, to thee I cry,
The king of bliss.

PETER ¶Lord, have mercy and let him go;
He cannot cease of his crying.
He follows us both to and fro;
Grant him his boon and his asking,
And let him wend.
We get no rest until this thing
Be brought to end.

JESUS ¶What wouldst thou, man, I to thee did?
In this presence, tell openly.

BLIND MAN ¶Lord, mine eyesight from me is hid;
Grant it to me, I cry mercy.
This would I have.

JESUS ¶Look up now with cheer blithely.
Thy faith can save.

BLIND MAN ¶Worship and honour aye to thee,
With all service that can be done!
The king of bliss, loved might he be,

That thus my sight has sent me soon,
 And by great skill.
I was as blind as any stone;
 I see at will.

LAME MAN ¶Ah, well were them that ever had life,
Old or young, which ever it were,
Might wield their limbs free without strife,
Go with this mirth which I see here,
 And continue;
For I am set in sorrows sore
 That aye are new.
Thou Lord that shaped both night and day,
Of thy mercy have mind on me,
And help me, lord, as well you may.
 I may not gang;
For I am lame, as men may see,
 And have been long.
For well I know, as known is rife,
Both dumb and deaf, thou grantest them grace;
And to the dead thou hast given life.
Therefore grant me, lord, in this place
 My limbs to wield.

JESUS ¶Man, rise; cast thy crutches forth good space,
 Here in the field.
And look in truth thou steadfast be,
And follow me forth with good meaning.

LAME MAN ¶Lord, lo, my crutches, where they flee
As far as I may let them fling
 With both my hands.
That ever again we have meeting,
 That now is banned.
For I was halt of limb and lame,
And I suffered pain and sorrows enow.
Everlasting Lord, loved by thy name.
I am as light as bird on bough.
 Aye be thou blest!
Such grace hast thou showed unto me,
 Lord, as thou list.

ZACHEUS ¶Since first this world was made of nought,
And all things set in equity,
Such wondrous thing was never wrought

As men this time may see with eye.
    What may it mean?
I cannot say what it may be,
    Comfort or pain.
And chiefly of a prophet new
That makes much profit, and of late
Both day and night to him they sue,
Our people all, through street and gate,
    New laws to hear.
Our old laws outworn now they hate,
    But hold his dear.
From death to life men will he raise,
To blind and dumb give speech and sight;
Greatly therefore our folk him praise,
And follow him both day and night
    From town to town.
They call him prophet by good right,
    As of renown.
And yet I marvel of that thing,
Since prince of publicans am I,
Of him I could have no knowing,
For all I would have come him nigh,
    Early and late.
Yet I am low, and of my height
    Full is the gate.
But since no better may befall,
I think what best is for to do.
I am so short, ye know well all,
Therefore yon tree I will go to,
    And in it climb.
Whether he come or pass me fro,
    I shall see him.
Ah, noble tree, thou sycamore,
I bless him that thee on earth brought.
Now may I see both here and there,
That under me it may be nought.
    Therefore in thee
Will I bide high in heart and thought,
    Till I him see.
Until the prophet come to town,
Here will I bide, whatso befall.

JESUS   ¶Zacheus, do thou fast come down.
ZACHEUS   ¶Lord, at thy will in haste I shall,
          And tarry not.
      To thee on knees, Lord, here I fall,
          For sin I wrought.
      And welcome, prophet trusty and true,
      With all those that to thee belong.
JESUS   ¶Zachee, thy service new
      Shall make thee clear of all the wrong
         That thou has done.
ZACHEUS   ¶Lord, I spare not for all this throng
         Here to say soon,
      My sin shames me, but not to repent.
      I sin forsake; therefore I will
      Have all my good that is unspent
      Unto poor folk to give them still;
         This will I fain.
      Whom I beguiled, to them I will
         Make right again.
JESUS   ¶Thy clear confession shall thee cleanse;
      Thou mayest be sure of lasting life.
      Unto thy house, without offence,
      Is granted peace all without strife.
         Farewell, Zachee.
ZACHEUS   ¶Lord, worship thee aye man and wife.
         Blest might thou be.
JESUS   ¶My dear disciples, behold and see.
      Unto Jerusalem we shall ascend.
      Man's son shall there betrayed be,
      And given into his enemies' hand
         With great despite.
      Their spitting on him shall they spend,
         And smartly smite.
      Peter, take thou this ass me fro,
      And lead it where thou first it took.
      I mourn, I sigh, I weep also,
      Jerusalem, on thee to look,
         And so may you,
      That ever you your king forsook
         And was untrue.
      For stone on stone shall none be left;

Down to the ground shall all be cast;
Thy game, thy glee, all from thee reft,
And all for sin that thou done hast.
      Thou art unkind.
Against thy king thou hast trespassed.
      Have this in mind.

PETER   ¶Porter, take here thine ass again;
At hand my lord comes on his feet.

PORTER   ¶Behold, where all the burghers's train
Come now with worship him to meet.
      Therefore I will
Let him abide here in this street,
      And lout him still.

1 BURGESS   ¶Hail, prophet proved without a peer!
Hail, prince of peace shall ever endure!
Hail, king comely, courteous and clear!
Hail, sovereign seemly to sinful sore!
      To thee all bows.
Hail, lord lovely our cares to cure!
      Hail, King of Jews!

2 BURGESS   ¶Hail, flourishing flower that ne'er shall fade!
Hail, violet vernal with sweet odour!
Hail, mark of mirth, our medecine made!
Hail, blossom bright; hail, our succour;
      Hail, king comely!
Hail, worshipful! We thee honour
      With heart freely.

3 BURGESS   ¶Hail, David's son, doughty in deed!
Hail, rose ruddy; hail, beryl clear!
Hail, well of wealth that makes our meed!
Hail, salver of our sores severe!
      We worship thee.
Hail, gentle one with solace sure!
      Welcome thou be.

4 BURGESS   ¶Hail, blissful babe in Bethleme born!
Hail, help of all our bitter bales!
Hail, lord that shaped both even and morn!
Hail, talker trustful of true tales!
      Hail, comely knight!
Hail, man of mood that most prevails
      To save aright!

5 BURGESS ¶Hail, diamond with jewels dight!
Hail, jasper gentle of Jewry!
Hail, lily lovesome, gleaming light!
Hail, balm of healing moist and dry
　　To all in need!
Hail, bairn most blest of mild Mary!
　　Hail, all our meed!

6 BURGESS ¶Hail, conqueror; hail, most of might!
Hail, ransomer of sinners all!
Hail, pitiful! Hail, lovely light!
Hail! Welcome of us shall on thee fall.
　　Hail, royal Jew!
Hail, comely corse that we thee call,
　　With mirth still new!

7 BURGESS ¶Hail, sun aye shining with bright beams!
Hail, lamp of life that ne'er shall waste!
Hail, lucid lantern's lovely gleams!
Hail, text of truth so true to taste!
　　Hail, king and sire!
Hail, maiden's child that graced her most!
　　We thee desire.

8 BURGESS ¶Hail, doomsman dread that all shall doom!
Hail, that all quick and dead shall lout!
Hail, whom worship shall most beseem!
Hail, whom all things shall dread and doubt!
　　We welcome thee
Hail and welcome of all about,
　　To our city!

26

THE CUTLERS

Pylatus, Cayphas, duo milites, tres Judei, Judas vendens Jesum.

PILATE   ¶Under the royalest ruler of rank and renown,
          Now am I regent to rule this region in rest.
          Obey unto bidding must bishops be bound,
          And bold men that in battle meet breast to breast.
          In my charge is the care of this tower-builded town;
          For traitors straight I attaint, the truth for to trust.
          The dressing of my dignity may not be done down
          Neither with dukes nor doughty peers, my deeds are so
              drest.
          My desire must daily be done
          By them that are greatest of game,
          And there again find I but few
          Wherefore I shall better their boon;
          But he that me grieves, full soon
          Be he ware, for furious I am.
          Pounce Pilate of three parts That is my proper name
          I am a perilous prince To prove where I appear.
          Among the philosophers first, There found I my fame,
          Wherefore I fall to affect I find not my peer;
          If all my bloom be as bright As blossom on briar.
          He shall full bitterly ban That shall bide my blame,
          For soon his life shall he lose Or be left for lame,
          That lowts not to me low, Nor lists not to learn.
          And since we thus stand in our state,
          As lords with all liking in land,
          Come now, let us wit if ye wot
          Either, sirs, of blight or debate,
          That needs to be handled full hot,
          Since all your help hangs in my hand.

CAYPHAS ¶Sir, for to certify the sooth in your sight,
To you as our sovereign seemly we seek.

PILATE ¶Why, is there any mischief That musters his might,
Or malice through mean men us musters to make?

ANNAS ¶Yea, sir; There is a rank swain
Whose rule is not right,
For through his rumour in this realm
Has raised mickle reek.

PILATE ¶I hear well ye hate him;
Your hearts are on height;
And else if I help would,
His harms for to eke—
But why are we wildly thus wroth?
Be ruly; array forth your reason.

CAYPHAS ¶To us, sir, his lore is full loath.

PILATE ¶Beware that ye wax not too wroth.

ANNAS ¶Why, sir, to shift from his scathe
We seek for your succour this season.

PILATE ¶If that wretch in our ward
Have wrought any wrong,
Since we are warned we would wit,
And will ere we wend.
But if his saw be lawful,
Allege not too long,
For we shall leave him if we list
With love here to live.

I DOCTOR ¶And if that false fellow
Your furtherance may find,
Then feel I well that our folk
May fail of a friend.
Sir, the strength of his speaking aye still is so strong,
Save he shortly be spent he shapes us to end.
For he teaches folk him for to call
Great God's son; Thus grieves he us all,
And says that be sitting he shall
In high heaven, for there is his hall.

PILATE ¶And, friends, if that force to him fall,
It seems not ye shall him consume,
But that he himself is the same
Ye said should descend,
Your seed and you all for to succour.

CAYPHAS   ¶Ah, soft, sir, and cease.
For of Christ when he comes
No kin shall be kenned,
But of this caitiff's kindred
We know the increase.
He likens him to be like God
Dwelling world without end,
To lift up this looby to loose or release.

PILATE   ¶His masteries should move you
Your mood to amend.

ANNAS   ¶Nay, for such miss from malice
We may not release.
For he says he shall doom us, that dote,
Which to us is disdain or despite.

PILATE   ¶To annoy him your need is all now;
But yet the law lies in my lot.

I DOCTOR   ¶And if ye will wit, sir, ye wot
That he is blameworthy, I vow.
For in our Temple he has taught
By times more than ten,
Where tables full of treasure lay
To tell and to try
Of our chief money-changers,
But, curstly to ken,
He cast them over, that caitiff,
And counted not thereby.

CAYPHAS   ¶Lo, sir, this is perjury to print under pen
Wherefore make ye that apostate, we pray you, to
ply.

PILATE   ¶How mean ye?

CAYPHAS   Sir, to mar him for moving of men.

PILATE   ¶Then should ye make him to mourn
But through your mastery.
Let be, sirs, and move that no more.
But what in your Temple betide?

I KNIGHT   ¶Eh! There, sir, he skelped out a score,
That stately stood selling their store.

PILATE   ¶Then felt he them faulty before,
And made the cause well known beside.
But what taught he that time,
Such tales as you tell?

I KNIGHT   ¶Sir, that our Temple is the tower
       Of his throned sire,
       And thus to praise in that place
       Our prophets compel,
       To him that has power
       Of prince and empire.
       And they make *domus domini*
       That ill-doing there dwell
       The den of their daring,
       And oft that they desire.

PILATE   ¶Lo! Is he not mad
       That meddles to do well,
       Since ye imagine all bad,
       Him matchless to quell?
       Your rancour is raking full raw.

CAYPHAS   ¶Nay, nay, sir; we rule us but right.

PILATE   ¶Forsooth, ye are over cruel to know.

CAYPHAS   ¶Why, sir? Because he would loose our law,
       Heartily we hate him, as we owe,
       And thereto should you maintain our might.
       For why? Upon the Sabbath day
       The sick will he save,
       And will not cease for our saws
       To sink so in sin.

2 KNIGHT   ¶He recovers all who come
       Recovery to crave,
       But in a short continuance;
       That kens all our kin.
       But he holds not our holy days,
       Hard hap might he have!
       Therefore hanged let him be
       By the neck; that we crave.

PILATE   ¶Ah, how now, sir? Hold in.
       For though ye go thus giddy
       Him guiltless to grave,
       Without ground you gain nought,
       Such grief to begin.
       And look your alleging be true,
       Without any trifles to tell.

ANNAS   ¶Our sayings for sure dare we seal.

PILATE   ¶And then may we profit full well.

CAYPHAS ¶If his faults were not many to tell,
We meant not with him for to deal.
For he perverts our people
That approve his preaching
And for that point you should press
His power to impair.

2 DOCTOR ¶Yea, sir; and also this caitiff,
He calls him our king;
For that cause our commons are cast into care.

PILATE ¶If so be, that boast to bale will him bring,
And make him to ban the bones that him bare.
For that wretch from our vengeance shall not wring
Ere there be on him woe.

1 DOCTOR   So would we it were,
For so should you sustain your weal,
And mildly have mind for to teach you.

PILATE ¶Well, wit ye this work shall be well,
For taught shall that knave be to kneel.

2 DOCTOR ¶And so that our force he may feel,
All together for the same we beseech you.

JUDAS ¶*Ingenti pro injuria*—That Jesus, that Jew,
Unjust to me Judas, I judge I may loathe.
For at supper as we sat, the sooth to pursue,
With Simon the Leper (full soon) My shift came to
scathe.
To him one brought a box, My bale for to brew,
That near to his bare feet Bowed low, by my troth.
She anointed him with ointment That noble was and
new.
But for that work that she wrought I waxed wondrous
wroth;
And this to discover was my skill;
For of his pence purser was I,
And this trick was taught me thereby—
The tenth part thence would I steal still.
But now since I want of my will,
That bargain with bale shall he buy.
That same ointment I said Might sure have been sold
For silver pennies in a sum Three hundred, and then
Have been shared to poor men, As plain pity would.
But for the poor nor their part There pricked me no pain ;

'Twas all pain for my tenth part, The truth to behold,
That thirty pence of three hundred So lightly I should
    lose.
And since I miss this money I mourn in my heart.
Wherefore for to mischief This master of mine,
Now therefore fast forth will I flit
The princes and high priests unto,
And sell him full soon ere I sit
For thirty pence in a knot knit.
Thusgates full well shall he wit
That of my wrath wreak me I will.
Now open, porter, the port of this proud place,
That I may pass to your princes, Your profit to prove.

PORTER   ¶Go hence, thou glowering gadling; God give thee ill
    grace.
Thou glancest so grimly Thou givest me heart pain.

JUDAS   ¶Good sir, be toward this time, And tarry not my trace,
For I have tidings to tell.

PORTER   Yea, some treason I trow.
For I feel by a figure in your false face
It is but folly to fasten affection on you.
For Mars he has morticed his mark,
After all lines of my lore,
And says ye are wicked of work,
And both a strong thief and a stark.

JUDAS   ¶Sir, thus at my beard if ye bark,
It seems it shall set you full sore.

PORTER   ¶Say, beetle-browed briber, Why blows thou such
    boast?
Full false in thy face in faith can I find.
Thou are cumbered in curstness And cares to this coast.
To mar men of might Hast thou marked in thy mind.

JUDAS   ¶Sir, I mean you no malice, But mirth move I must.

PORTER   ¶Say on then, hanged harlot; I hold thee unkind,
Thou lookest like a lurdan His livelihood who has lost.
Woe shall I work thee, away but thou wend.

JUDAS   ¶Ah, good sir, take tent to my talking this tide,
For tidings full true can I tell.

PORTER   ¶Say, brawler, I bid thee abide;
Thou chatterest like a churl that can chide.

JUDAS   ¶Yea, sir; but the truth should be tried;

Of mirth are these matters I tell.

For through my deeds your doughty peers From dread
    may be drawn.

PORTER   ❡What! Deemest thou to our dukes some dole may be
    dight?

JUDAS   ❡Nay, sir; so said I not.

If I be called to counsel That cause shall be known,
Among that comely company, To clerk and to knight.

PORTER   ❡Bide me here, fair sir, Ere more boast be blown,
And I shall busk to the bench Where banners are bright,
And say unto our sovereigns, Ere more seed be sown,
That such a fellow as thyself Sues here to their sight.
My lord now, of wit that is well, I come that a case be
    not hid.

PILATE   ❡Well, speak on, and spare not thy spell.

CAYPHAS   ❡Yea, and we need meddle as well,
Since you bear of beauty the bell,
Blithely shall we bow as you bid.

PORTER   ❡Sir, without this abating, there hangs as I hope
A man hilt full of ire, for hasty he is.

PILATE   ❡What comes he for?

PORTER   I ken him not, but he is clad in a cape.
He comes with a keen face uncomely to kiss.

PILATE   ❡Go get him, that his grief We may straitly grope,
So no open language be going amiss.

PORTER   ❡Come on lively now to my lord, If ye list for to leap;
But utter so thy language That thou bar not their bliss.

JUDAS   ❡May that lord, sirs, sustain your weal
That flower is of fortune and fame.

PILATE   ❡Welcome; thy words we hear well.

CAYPHAS   ❡Say, hearest thou, knave? Canst thou not kneel?

PILATE   ❡Lo, here may men fault in you feel.
Let be, sir, your scorning, for shame.
But, fair sir, be not abashed to bide at the bar.

JUDAS   ❡Before you, sirs, to be brought About have I been,
And alway for your worship.

ANNAS   ❡Say, wot you any war?

JUDAS   ❡Of work that makes you wrathful—I wot what I mean.
But I would make a merchandise Your mischief to mar.

PILATE   ❡And mayest thou so?

JUDAS   Else mad I am such masteries to name.

ANNAS ⁋Thou knowest of some cumbrance, Our charge for to
cheer?
For, cousin, thou art cruel.

JUDAS My cause, sir, is keen.
For if ye will bargain or buy,
Jesus this time will I sell you.

I DOCTOR ⁋My blessing, son, have thou thereby.
Lo, here is a sport for to spy!

JUDAS ⁋And him dare I promise you on high,
If you will be toward as I tell you.

PILATE ⁋What hightest thou?

JUDAS Judas Iscariot.

PILATE Thou art a just man.
Then will Jesus be justified by our judgment.

ANNAS ⁋But howgates bought shall he be? Bring forth thy
bargain.

JUDAS ⁋But for a little amends To bear hence again.

PILATE ⁋Now, what shall we pay?

JUDAS Sir, thirty pence, flat; no more then.

PILATE ⁋Say, are ye pleased of this price He presses to present?

2 DOCTOR ⁋Else contrary were our conscience, Conceive since we
can
That Judas knows him culpable.

PILATE ⁋I call you consent. But, Judas, a knot for to knit,
Wilt thou to this convenant accord?

JUDAS ⁋Yea, at a word.

PILATE Welcome is it.

2 KNIGHT ⁋Take thee off, traitor, quick!

I KNIGHT ⁋Now leave, sir. Let no man wit
How this losel larks with his lord.

PILATE ⁋Why, dwells he with that dotard Whose deeds do us
dread?

I KNIGHT ⁋That has he done, sir, and does; No doubt is this day.

PILATE ⁋Then would we know why this knave Has cursedly
contrived.

2 KNIGHT ⁋Enquire of him, since ye can best Know if he false play.

PILATE ⁋Say, man, to sell thy master—What amiss has he
moved?

JUDAS ⁋Of as mickle money he made me delay
As of you I receive, shall but right be reproved.

ANNAS ⁋I tell thee now, think not Our rule so to array;

193

	For that the false fiend shall thee hang.
1 KNIGHT	¶Then deal in devices we must.
1 DOCTOR	¶To whom work we wittingly wrong?
2 DOCTOR	¶To him, save he hastily hang.
3 DOCTOR	¶Your language you lay out too long.

But, Judas, we truly thee trust.
But truly thou must teach us That caitiff to catch,
Or away through a trick That lurdan may leap.

JUDAS ¶I shall teach you a token Him quick for to take,
Where he is ringed in the throng; My word will I keep.

1 KNIGHT ¶We know him not.

JUDAS   Take care then that caitiff to catch
Whom there I shall kiss.

2 KNIGHT   That becomes thee well, cunning and deep.
But yet to warn us wisely All ways must you watch.
When thou shalt wend forthwith A wild walk we shall
    keep.
And therefore look busy thou be.

JUDAS ¶Yes, yes; a space shall I spy us,
As soon as the sun is set, as ye see.

1 KNIGHT ¶Go forth, for a traitor are ye.

2 KNIGHT ¶Yea, and a wicked man.

1 DOCTOR   Why, what is he?

2 DOCTOR ¶A losel, unless loyalty belie us.
He is top full of tricks, the truth for to trust.
I hold it but folly his faith for to trow.

PILATE ¶Abide in my blessing, And bring what is best;
For it is best for our boot In trouble to bow.
And, Judas for our profit We pray thee make haste.

JUDAS ¶Yet have I not a penny, My profit to show.

PILATE ¶Thou shalt have deliverance Full soon at thy list;
So shall you have liking Our lordship to love.
And therefore, Judas, mend thou thy moan,
And take here thy silver all told.

JUDAS ¶Yea; now is my great grief overgone.

1 KNIGHT ¶Be light, then.

JUDAS   Yea, let me alone,
For quick shall that traitor be gone,
And thereto jocund and jolly am I.

PILATE ¶Judas, to hold thy behest, Be handy for our hap,
And our help and uphold We promise thee to have.

JUDAS ¶I shall counsel you his corse In care for to clap.

ANNAS ¶And more comfort in this case We covet not to crave.

1 KNIGHT ¶When we may reach that reckless His ribs shall we rap,
And make that rogue ere we rest For running to rave.

PILATE ¶Nay, sirs, if ye scourge him Yet spoil not his shape.
For if the sot be sinless, It behoves us to save.
Wherefore when ye go forth to get him,
Unto his body brew ye no bale.

2 KNIGHT ¶Our list is from leaping to let him;
But in your sight sound shall we set him.

PILATE ¶Do flit now forth till ye get him,
With solace all sure to your soul.

27

THE BAKSTERES

Agnus Paschalis, Cena Domini, xij apostoli, Jesus percinctus lintheo lavans pedes eorum; institucio sacramenti corporis Cristi in nova lege, communio apostolorum.

JESUS ¶Peace be both by day and night
Unto this house, and to all that are here.
Here will I hold, by promise plight,
The feast of Pasch with friends full dear.

MARCELLUS ¶Master, we have arrayed full right
Service that beseems for your supper.
Our lamb is roast and ready dight,
As Moyses' law declares full clear.

JESUS ¶That is, each man that has
People in his own family
Shall roast a lamb at Pasch
For all his company.

ANDREW ¶Master, the custom well we know,
That with our elders ever has been,
How every man with his folk owe
To roast a lamb and eat it clean.

JESUS ¶I thank you soothly of your saw,
For as you say, yourself has seen.
Therefore array you all in row;
Myself shall part it you between.
Wherefore I will that ye
Eat thereof every one;
The remnant parted shall be
To the poor that purvey none.
Of Moyses' law here make I an end
In some party, but not in all.
My command shall otherwise be kenned
With them that men shall craftily call.

But the lamb of Pasch that here we spend,
While Jews use it both great and small,
Henceforward now I do defend
From Christian folks, whatso befall.
In that stead shall be set
A new law us between;
But who thereof shall eat
Behoves to be washed clean.
For that new law whoso shall learn,
In heart they must be clean and chaste.
Marcell, my own disciple dear,
Do bring us water here in haste.

MARCELLUS ¶Master, it is already here,
And here a towel clean to taste.

JESUS ¶Come forth with me together here;
My words shall not be wrought in waste.
Set your feet forth; let's see.
They shall be washen soon.

PETER ¶Lord, with thy leave, by thee
That deed shall not be done.
Never shall I make my members meet
Of my sovereign's service to me.

JESUS ¶Peter,
Unless thou let me wash thy feet,
Thou gets no part in bliss with me.

PETER ¶Ah mercy, lord and master sweet!
Out of that bliss that I not be,
Wash on, my lord, till all be wet,
Both head and hand, I beseech thee.

JESUS ¶Peter, thou wottest not yet
What this my work may mean.
Hereafter shalt thou wit;
So shall ye all, I ween.   *Tunc lavat manus.*
Your lord and master ye me call;
And so I am, all weal to wield.
Here have I kneeled unto you all,
To wash your feet, as ye did feel.
Example of me take ye shall,
Ever for to guard in youth and eld:
Meek for to be in bower and hall,
Each one for to be each other's shield.

197

If all of you be true,
And loyal of love each one,
Ye shall find other aye new
To grieve for when I am gone.

JAMES   ¶Now since our master says he shall
Wend, and will not yet tell us whither,
Which of us shall be principal?
Let's look now while we dwell together.

JESUS   ¶I know your will, both great and small,
And your high hearts I hear them hither,
To which of you such affair should fall,
That ye might tell when ye come thither,
Where it so should betide
Such matters may befall.
But first behoves you bide
Trials full fierce and fell.
Here shall I set for you to see
This young child for example clear.
Both meek and mild of heart is he,
And from all malice merry of cheer.
So meek and mild but if ye be. . . .

      [*A whole leaf is lost here, some 65 or 70 lines at
      least, including the central part of the Last Supper.*]

QUOD FACIS FAC CICIUS.

That thou shalt do, do soon.

THOMAS   ¶Alas, so wandering wights as we
Was never in world walking indeed.
Our master says his own company
Has betrayed him to sinful seed.

JAMES   ¶John, I think that thou sittest next his knee;
We pray thee, ask him for our speed.

JOHN   ¶*Domine, quis est qui tradit te?*
Lord, who shall do that doleful deed?
Alas, our play is past;
This false fortune is fast.
I may no longer last;
For bale my heart may burst.

JUDAS   ¶Now is it time for me to gang,
For here begins annoy all new.

My fellows mutter them among,
That I should all this bargain brew.
And sure they shall not ween it wrong;
To the prince of priests I shall pursue,
And they shall teach him other ere long,
That all his saws sore shall he rue.
I know where he removes
With his fellows each one;
I shall tell to the Jews,
And swift he shall be ta'en.

JESUS   ¶I warn you now, my friends so free;
See to these sayings that I say.
The fiend is wroth with you and me,
And will you mar, if that he may.
But Peter, I have prayed for thee,
So that thou shalt not fear his affray;
And comfort thou this company
And guide them, when I am gone away.

PETER   ¶Ah, lord, where thou wilt stay
I shall stay in that stead,
And with thee make my way
Evermore, alive or dead.

ANDREW   ¶No worldly dread shall me withdraw,
But I shall with thee live and die.

THOMAS   ¶Certes, so shall we all on row,
Else mickle woe were we worthy.

JESUS   ¶Peter, I say to you this saw,
Which you shall find no fantasy.
This very night ere the cock crow,
Shalt thou three times my name deny,
And say ye knew me never,
Nor company of mine.

PETER   ¶Alas, lord, I would liever
Be put to endless pine.

JESUS   ¶As I tell you, so shall it be.
You need no other recourse to crave.
All that in world is written of me
Shall be fulfilled, for knight or knave.
I am the herd, the sheep are ye;
And when the shepherd harms shall have,
The flock shall be full fain to flee

And succour seek, themselves to save.
Ye shall, when I am alone.
In great misliking be;
But when I rise again,
Then shall your mirth be free.
My grief to amend were ye ready,
Therefore your shield aye shall I be.
And since ye did in wet and dry
My commandments in each country,
The kingdom of heaven promise I,
Even as my Father has to me.
With ghostly measure there shall ye mete,
And on twelve seats there sit shall ye.
For true care took ye yet
In world with me to dwell;
To judge shall ye be set
Twelve tribes of Israel.
But first ye shall bewildered be
In woes that pass now your belief;
From time shall come that they take me,
Then shall ye turn away with grief.
And look that ye have swords each one;
And whoso has none you among,
Shall sell his coat and buy him one;
Thus bid I that you do ere long.
Satchels I will ye have,
And staves to stint all strife,
Your selves so for to save,
In lengthening of your life.

ANDREW   ¶Master, we have here swords now two,
To save us with on all sides here.

JESUS   ¶It is enough; ye need no mo,
For from all woes I shall keep you clear.
But rise up now, for we will go.
By this our enemies ordered are.
My Father said it shall be so;
His bidding will I not forbear.
Look ye learn forth this law,
As ye have heard of me.
All that will well it know,
Aye blessed shall they be.

28

THE CORDWANERS

Pilatus Cayphas Annas, xiii milites armati, Malcus Petrus
Jacobus Johannes Jesus et Judas osculans et tradens eum.

JESUS   ¶Behold, my disciples in dignity dear,
            My flesh shudders and shrinks for doubt of my deed.
            Mine enemies will newly be nighing full near,
            With all the might if they may to mar my manhood.
            But since ye are forwatching and wandered in fear,
            Look ye set ye down And rest you, I rede.
            Be not heavy in your hearts, But hold you even here,
            And bide me a brief while Still in this same stead.
            Be witty and wise in your resting,
            So that ye be waking alway;
            And look now that promptly ye pray
            To my Father that ye fail in no testing.

PETER   ¶Yea, Lord, at thy bidding
            Full obedient we abide;
            For thou are boot of our bale,
            And biddest for the best.

JOHANNES   ¶Lord, all our help and our hale,
            That is not to hide,
            In thee, our faith and our food,
            All wholly is fast.

JACOBUS   ¶What way is he wandered
            In this world wide?
            Whither is he walked,
            Eastward or west?

PETER   ¶Yea, sirs, I shall tell you;
            Sit we down on each side.
            And let us now readily here take our rest.
            My limbs are as heavy as lead.

JOHANNES   ¶And I must sleep; down must I lie.

JAMES   ¶In faith, fellows, right so fare I;
           I may no longer hold up my head.

PETER   ¶Our life, by his loyalty His life shall he lose.
           Unkindly be crucified And nailed to a tree.

JESUS   ¶I bid by my blessing
           Your eyes ye unclose,
           That ye fall in no testing,
           For ought that may be;
               But pray fast.

JOHANNES   ¶Lord, some prayer do thou learn us,
           That somewhat might mirth us or mend us.

JAMES   ¶From all finding unfaithful defend us,
           Here in this world alive while we last.

JESUS   ¶I shall teach you and comfort you
           And keep you from your care.
           Ye shall be brought, wit ye well,
           From bale unto bliss.

PETER   ¶Yea, but, Lord, if your will were,
           Wit would we more;
           Of this prayer so precious let us not miss,
               We beseech thee.

JOHANNES   ¶For my fellows and me, give us here
           Some prayer that is precious in lore.

JAMES   ¶Unto thy Father that most is of power
           Some solace of succour to send thee.
           ... [A page is lost here.]

JESUS   ¶The hurts that have nighed me
           It needs not to name;
           For all wot ye well
           In what ways I went.
           Renew me and strengthen
           With voice still and calm.
           I pray thee entirely thou take intent;
           Maintain now my manhood with mood.
           My flesh is full dreading for dread;
           For my days' work of my manhood
           I sweat now both water and blood.
           These Jews, they mean in their mind full of malice
           And pretend me to take Without any trespass.
           But, Father, as thou wots well, I meant never amiss.
           In word nor in work I never worthy was.

As thou art help of all sorrow and shielder of bliss
And all help and health in thy hands has,
Maintain now my manhood, Who mends what is amiss.
If it possible were, This pain might I overpass.
But, Father, if thou see it may not,
Be it worthily wrought,
Even at thine own will.
Evermore both mildly and still
With worship always be it wrought.
Unto my disciples will I go again,
Kindly to comfort them That caught are in care.
What? Are ye fallen asleep Now every each one?
And the passion of me in mind have no more?
What? Will ye leave me thus lightly And let me alone
In sorrow and sighing that settle full sore?
To whom may I move me And make now my moan?
I would that ye wakened, if your will were.
Do, Peter, sit up; now let's see.
Thou art strongly oppressed by this power.
Might ye not the space of one hour
Have waked now mildly with me?

PETER   ⁋Yes, Lord. With your leave now will we learn
Full warily to ward you, that failing appal not.

JESUS   ⁋Be waking and pray fast, all ye here,
To my Father, that tempted ye fall not.
For evil spirits are drawing full near
That will tarry you at this time with their tempting.
But I will wend where I was without any fear;
Bide ye here obedient in my blessing.
Again to the mount will I gang
Till soon I come where I was ere.
But look that you catch you no care,
For truly I shall not dwell long.
Thou Father that formed all with food for to fill,
I feel by my fearing my flesh would full fain
Be turned from this torment and turned unto thee,
For mazed is my manhood in mood and in main.
But if thou see soothly that thy Son shall
Without surfeit if sin be so innocent slain,
Be it worthily wrought even at thine own will.
For, Father, at thy bidding I bowing obedient remain.

Now quickly again will I wend
Unto my disciples so dear.
What? Sleep ye so fast all here?
I fear ye are failing your friend.
But yet will I leave you and let you alone,
And soon where I was again will I wend.
Unto my Father of might now make I my moan,
As thou art salver of all sore some succour to send.
The passion they purpose to put me upon,
My flesh fears it fell, and fain would defend.
At thy will be it wrought, and worthily won.
Have mind of my manhood, my mood for to mend.
Some comfort be mine in this case.
And, Father, if I shall death taste,
I will it not defend;
Yet, if thy will be,
Spare me a space.

ANGEL   ¶Unto the Maker unmade That most is of might
Be love everlasting in light that is lent.
Thy Father that in heaven Is most high in height
Thy sorrow to sober, To thee has me sent.
For deeds that mankind did Thy death shall be dight
And thou with torments be toiled. But take now intent.
Thy bale shall be all for the best;
Through that shall man's sin be amend.
Then shalt thou without any end
Right royally reign full of rest.

JESUS   ¶Now if my flesh feared be, Father, I am fain
That mine anguish and noyance Be near at an end.
Unto my disciples will I go again
Kindly to comfort them That are mazed in their mind.
Sleep ye now safely now. Soon shall I say,
Waken up quickly And let us hence wend
For full soon must I be taken With treason and pain.
My flesh is full feared And fain would defend.
Full dreadful my death shall be dight.
And as soon as I am taken,
Then by each of you am I forsaken;
Ye'll say ye ne'er saw me with sight.

PETER   ¶Nay, soothly, I'll never my sovereign forsake,
If here for the deed I should dreadfully die.

JOHANNES   ¶Nay, such mean louts shall never man us make;
            First would we die all at once.
JAMES   Now in faith, fellows, so should I.
JESUS   ¶Yea,
            But when that time befals That men shall me take,
            For all your hearty pledges Fast flight shall ye make;
            Like sheep that were scared Away shall ye shake.
            There shall none of you be bold To bide me then by.
PETER   ¶Nay, soothly, while I may avail thee,
            I shall watch thee and wake thee;
            And if all men other forsake thee,
            I shall never for fainting defail thee.
JESUS   ¶Ah, Peter, of such boasting I warn thee let be.
            For all thy keen crying Full keenly I know
            For fear of mine enemies Thou soon shalt deny me
            Thrice yet full throughly Before the cock crow,
            For fear of my foemen Full fain be to flee,
            And for great doubt of death Thee fast to withdraw.

II

ANNAS   ¶Sir Cayphas, of your counsel Do soon let us see,
            For truly it belongs to us To look to our law.
            And therefore, sir, presently I pray you,
            Since that we are of counsel each one,
            That Jesus that traitor were taken,
            Do soon let us see now, I pray you.
CAYPHAS   ¶In certain, sir, and soon shall I say you.
            I would ween by my wit This work would be well.
            Let us justly us join To Judas' intent.
            For he knows his dignities Full duly each deal;
            Yea, and best knows, I warrant, What way that he went.
ANNAS   ¶Now this was wisely said, And that I see well;
            And sir, to your saying I seriously assent.
            Therefore take we of our knights That are stedfast as
              steel,
            And let Judas go lead them Where that he last went.
CAYPHAS   ¶Full well, sir. Now, Judas, dear neighbour, draw near
             us.
            Lo, Judas, thus in mind have we meant;
            To take Jesus is our intent,

And 'tis thou that must teach us and lead us.
And also beware That he will not away.

JUDAS ¶Sirs, I shall show you the way, Even at your own will.
But look that ye have Many mighty men
That are both strong and stirring And stay them stone
still.

ANNAS ¶Yea, Judas, but by what knowledge Shall we that corse
ken?

JUDAS ¶Sir, a token in this time Now tell you I will.
But look by your loyalty No life ye him lend.
What man soe'er I kiss, That corse shall ye kill.

CAYPHAS ¶Why, nay, Judas, beshrew you again.
We purpose the page shall not pass.
Sir knights, in haste.

I KNIGHT Lord, we are here.

CAYPHAS ¶Call forth your fellows to appear,
And go justly with gentle Judas.

I KNIGHT ¶Come, fellows, by your faith, Come forth all fast,
And talk with Sir Cayphas; he commands me to call.

2 KNIGHT ¶Beshrew him all his life That loves to be last.

3 KNIGHT ¶Go we hence then, I say, And haste us to the hall.

4 KNIGHT ¶Lord, of your will worthily Would I wit what was't.

CAYPHAS ¶To take Jesus, that stroller, All same that ye shall.

I KNIGHT ¶Lord, to that purpose I would that we passed.

ANNAS ¶Yea, but look that ye be armed well all.
The most gentle of Jewry shall guide you.

CAYPHAS ¶Yea, and every knight each in degree
Both armed and harnessed be ye,
To shield you and promptly provide you.

ANNAS ¶Yea, and therefore, Sir Cayphas, go hie you,
Your worship to win in this case.
As ye are a lord most lovesome to view
Under Sir Pilate that lives in this empire,
Yon sayer that calls himself a sire
With trouble and toil shall we taste him.
Of yon losel, his bale shall we brew.
Trot on now for that traitor apace.

CAYPHAS ¶Now, sirs, since ye say my power is most best,
And I have all this work Thus to work at my will,
Now certain right soon I think not to rest
But solemnly in haste your will to fulfil.

206

Full fast shall this traitor be ta'en.
Sir knights, now hie you each one,
For in certain that slave shall be slain.
Sir Anna, I pray you have done.

ANNAS   ¶Full ready soon shall I be bound
To this journey work for to go still.
As ye are a lord of great renown,
Spare not to speed him to ill.
May the devil him speed. Go we with our knights here.
Lo, they are arrayed and armed clear.
Sir knights, look ye be of full good cheer;
Where ye see him, of him take good heed.

1 JEW   ¶Good heed to him, lord, shall we take.
He shall ban the time that he was born.
All his kin shall come looking too late;
He shall not escape without scorn
    From us all here.

2 JEW   ¶We shall seek him both even and morn,
Early and late, with full good cheer;
    'Tis our intent.
Step nor street, we shall spare none,
Field nor town, thus we intend
    With one accord.

MALCUS   ¶Aye, aye, and I should have reward,
And rightly, as full worthy were,
For lo, I bring light for my lord.

CAYPHAS   ¶Ah, sir, of your speech let, and let us speed
A space, and of our speeches spare.
And, Judas, go guide thou before,
And wisely go show them the way.
For soothly soon shall we assay
To make him to mar us no more.

III

JESUS   ¶Now will this hour be nighing full near
That will certify all the sooth that I have said.

JUDAS   ¶All hail, Master, in faith, And fellows all here.
With gracious greeting This ground be arrayed.
I would ask you a kiss, Master, if your will were,
For all my love and my liking Is wholly upon you laid.

JESUS	¶Full heartily, Judas, have it even here.
	With this kissing is Man's Son betrayed.
1 KNIGHT	¶Ha! stand, traitor. I tell thee for ta'en.
CAYPHAS	¶On, on, knights. Go fall on before.
2 KNIGHT	¶Yes, master. Now move thou no more,
	But lightly let us alone.

A brilliant light shines from Jesus.

3 KNIGHT	¶Alas! we are lost for gleam of this light.
JESUS	¶Say ye here, whom seek ye? Do tell me; let's see.
1 JEW	¶One Jesus of Nazareth; I think that name right.
JESUS	¶Behold ye all hitherward. Lo, here; I am he.
1 KNIGHT	¶Stand, dastard. So dreadful Thy death shall be dight.
	I will be no more abashed Thy shining to see.
1 JEW	¶Ah, out! I am mazed almost In main and in might.
2 JEW	¶And I fear, by my faith, and fain would I flee;
	For such a sight have I not seen.
3 JEW	¶This gleam, it gleamed so light,
	I saw never such a sight.
	I marvel much what it may mean.
JESUS	¶Come, whom seek ye assembled, yet I say?
1 JEW	¶One Jesus of Nazareth; him would we be nigh now.
JESUS	¶And I am he soothly, And that shall I say.
MALCUS	¶For that shalt thou die, dastard, Since it is thou.
PETER	¶And I shall try by my faith thee for to flay.
	Here with a slash, lurdan, I shall thee allow.
MALCUS	¶Ah, out! All my devoirs are done.
PETER	¶Nay, traitor, but truly I shall trap thee, I trow.
JESUS	¶Peace, Peter, I bid thee;
	Meddle thee nor move thee no more.
	For wit you well, if my will were,
	I might have power in great plenty,
	Of angels full many To muster my might.
	Wherefore put up thy sword Full goodly again.
	For he that takes vengeance All ruled shall be right;
	For vengeance with vengeance To void is in vain.
	Thou man thus in dread And doefully dight,
	Come here to me safely And be salved of thy pain.
	In the name of my Father That in heaven is most in height,
	Of thy hurts be thou whole In hide and in bone,
	As this virtue in thy veins shall avail.

MALCUS   ¶What? Ill hail! I believe that I be whole!
           Now beshrew him this time that gives tale
           To touch thee for thy travail.

1 JEW   ¶Do, fellows, by your faith, Let us hang on all here.
           For I have on this hind Firm hold as I can.

2 KNIGHT   ¶And I have a lock on him now. How, fellows, draw
           near.

3 KNIGHT   ¶Yea,
           By the bones that him bare This jest shall he ban.

JESUS   ¶Even like a thief heinously Hurl ye me here.
           I taught in your Temple; Why took ye me not then?
           Now has darkness on earth All his power.

1 JEW   ¶Do, do! Look alive, lay your hands on this lurdan.

3 JEW   ¶We have hold of this hawk in our hands.

MALCUS   ¶Why, yes, fellows; by my faith he is fast.

4 JEW   ¶Unto Sir Cayphas I would that he passed.
           Farewell, for I guess we will wend.

29

THE BOWERS AND FLECCHERS

Jesus, Anna, Cayphas, et iiii Judei percucientes et colaphizantes Jesum; Petrus, mulier accusans Petrum, et Malchus.

CAYPHAS ¶Peace, fair sirs; I bid no jangling ye make,
And cease soon of your saws, and see what I say,
And true tent to me this time that ye take,
For I am a lord learned truly in your law.
By cunning of clerkship and casting of wit
Full wisely my words I wield at my will;
So seemly in seat it beseems me to sit,
The law for to learn you and lead it by skill.
What wight so will ought with me, Full friendly in faith
    am I found right soon.
Come now; no delay; let me see
How graciously I shall grant him his boon.
There is neither lord nor lady learned in the law,
Nor bishop nor prelate that proved is for price,
Nor clerk in court that cunning will know,
With wisdom to ward him in world is so wise.
I have the rank and the rule of all the royalty,
To rule it by right as reason it is.
All doomsmen on dais ought for to dread me,
That has them in subjection in bale or in bliss.
Wherefore take tent to my tales and lout unto me.
And therefore, sir knights,
I charge you, challenge your rights
To wait both by days and by nights
For the bringing of a boy into bail.

1 KNIGHT ¶Yes, lord; we shall wait if any wanderers walk,
And ask how your folk fare that are forth run.

2 KNIGHT ¶We shall be obedient to your bidding and will not balk,
If they present you that boy in a band bound.

ANNAS   ¶Why, sir, and is there a boy that will not lout to your
bidding?

CAYPHAS   ¶Yea, sir; and of the cleverness of that churl there is
talking.
But I have sent for that fellow for mocking.

ANNAS   ¶What wonderful works works that wight?

CAYPHAS   ¶To sick men and sorry he sends sure healing,
And to lame men and blind he sends their sight;
Of crooked cripples that we know. . . .
Great wonder it is for the hearing,
How he heals them all in a row,
And all through his false fortune, I trow.
I am sorry of a sight
That eggs me to ire.
Our law he breaks with all his might;
That is most his desire
Our Sabbath day will he not save,
But goes about bringing it down;
And therefore sorrow must he have.
May he be caught in field or town
For his false steven!
He defames foully the Godhead,
And calls himself God's Son of heaven.

ANNAS   ¶I have good knowledge of that knave;
Mary I mean, his mother hight . . .
And Joseph his father, as God me save,
Was called and known well for a wright.
But one thing I marvel much over all,
Of divers deeds that he has done.

CAYPHAS   ¶With witchcraft he fares withal;
Sirs, that same shall ye see full soon.
Our knights, all forth they went
To take him and betray;
By this I hold him spent;
He cannot wend away.

ANNAS   ¶Would ye, sir, take your rest—
The day is come at hand—
And with wine slake your thirst?
Then durst I well warrant
Ye should have tidings soon
Of the knights that are gone,

And how they yet have done,
To trap and take him anon.
Now put all thought away,
And let your matters rest.

CAYPHAS ¶I will do as ye say;
Do get us wine of the best.
For be we once well wet,
The better will we rest.

1 KNIGHT ¶My lord, here is wine That will make you to wink;
It is liquor delicious, My lord, if you like.
Wherefore I rede deeply A draught that ye drink,
For in this country that we know I vow is none like.
Wherefore we counsel you
This cup savourly for to kiss.

CAYPHAS ¶Come now daintily, and dress me on dais,
And handily heap on me happing;
And warn all wights to be in peace,
For I am laid late unto napping.

ANNAS ¶My lord, with your leave,
If it like you, I pass.

CAYPHAS ¶Adieu be unto you,
As the manner is.

WOMAN ¶Sir knights, do keep this boy so bound,
For I will go wit what it may mean,
Why that yon wight was following found
Early and late, morning and even.
He will come near, he will not let;
He is a spy, I warrant, full bold.

3 KNIGHT ¶It seems by his semblance he'd liever be set
By the fervent fire, to flee from the cold.

WOMAN ¶Yea, but ye wist as well as I
What wonders that this wight has wrought;
And for his master sorcery
Full fiercely should his death be bought.

3 KNIGHT ¶Dame, we have him now at will
That we have long time sought;
If others go by us still,
For them we have no thought.

WOMAN ¶It were great scorn if he should 'scape,
Without he had reason and skill;
He looketh lurking like an ape;

I think in haste to take him still.
Thou caitiff, what moves thee to stand
So stable and still in thy thought?
Thou has wrought mickle wrong in land,
Ah, lubber! A leader of law,
To set him and sue him hast thou sought.
Stand forth and thrust in yon throng.
Thy mastery brings thee unto nought.
Wait now! He looks like a brock,
Were he in a band bound for to bait;
Or else like an owl on a stock,
Full privily his prey for to wait.

PETER ¶Woman, thy words and thy wind do not waste.
Of his company never was I kenned.
Thou hast mismarked me, truly me trust;
Wherefore of thy miss do thou mend.

WOMAN ¶Then gainsay you here the saws that you said,
That he should claim to be called God's Son,
And with the works that he wrought Whilst he walked
in this wold
Briskly at our bidding Always to be done.

PETER ¶I will consent to your saws; What should I say more?
For women are crabbed; That comes of their kind.
But I say as I first said, I ne'er saw him e'er.
But as a friend of your fellowship Shall ye me aye
find.

MALCUS ¶Hearken, knights that are known In this country as we
ken,
How yon boy with his boast Has brewed mickle bale.
He has forsaken his master Before yon women.
But I shall prove to you openly And tell you my tale.
I was present with people When press was full pressed,
To meet with his master With main and with might,
And hurled him hardily And hasted his arrest,
And in bonds full bitterly Bound him sore all that night
And for token of truth I shall tell you
How yon boy with a brand brayed me full near—
To move of these matters avail you—
For he swiftly swapped off mine ear.
His master by his might healed me all whole
By no sign I could see no man could it wit;

And then bade him bear peace in every such bale,
For he that smites with a sword shall be smit.
Let's see whether grantest thou guilt.
Come, speak on and spare not to tell us,
Or full fast I shall force thee to flit,
The sooth if thou say not all free now.
Come quickly, I say; let us see now,
In saving of thyself from shame,
Yea, and also for bearing of blame.

PETER ¶I was never with him in work that he wrought,
In word nor in work, in will nor in deed.
I know none that ye have hither brought,
In no court of this kith, if I should right rede.

MALCUS ¶Hear, sirs, how he says and has forsaken
His master to this woman here twice;
And newly our law has he taken.
Thus hath he denied him this thrice.

JESUS ¶Peter, Peter, thus said I ere,
When you said you would abide with me
In weal and in woe, in sorrow and care,
Whilst I should thrice forsaken be.

PETER ¶Alas the while that I came here,
Or e'er denied my Lord apart.
The look of his fair face so clear
With full sad sorrow shears my heart.

3 KNIGHT ¶Sir knights, take care of this churl; let cunning be there,
Because of Sir Cayphas we know well the thought.
He will reward us full well, that warrant I dare,
When he knows of our works, how well we have
wrought.

4 KNIGHT ¶Sir, this is Sir Cayphas' hall here at hand;
Go we boldly with this boy that we have here brought.

2 KNIGHT ¶Nay, sirs, we must stalk to that stead and full still stand,
For it is now in the night, if they nap ought.

1 KNIGHT ¶Say, who is here? Say, who is here?

3 KNIGHT   I, a friend,
Well known in this country for a knight.

2 KNIGHT ¶Go forth; on your ways may ye wend,
For we have harboured enough for tonight.

1 KNIGHT ¶Go back, fair sirs; ye both are to blame,
To brawl when our Bishop is gone to his bed.

4 KNIGHT	¶Why, sir, it were worthy to welcome us home;
	We have gone for this warlock, and we have well sped.
2 KNIGHT	¶Why, who is that?
3 KNIGHT	The Jew's King, Jesus by name.
1 KNIGHT	¶Ah, ye be welcome, I dare wager my head.
	My lord has sent for to seek him.
4 KNIGHT	¶Lo, see here the same.
2 KNIGHT	¶Abide as I bid, and be not adread.
	My lord! My lord! My lord! Here is lark, if ye list.
CAYPHAS	¶Peace, losels; it is good advice.
1 KNIGHT	¶My lord, it is well if ye wist.
CAYPHAS	¶Well, name us no more, for it is twice.
	Thou takest no heed to the haste That we have here on hand.
	Go find how our folk fare That are forth run.
2 KNIGHT	¶My lord, your knights have fared As ye gave them command,
	And they have fallen full fair.
CAYPHAS	¶Why, and is the fool found?
1 KNIGHT	¶Yea, lord, they have brought a boy in a band bound.
CAYPHAS	¶Where now? Sir Anna! That is one that is able to be near.
ANNAS	¶My lord, with your leave, it behoves me to be here.
CAYPHAS	¶Ah sir, come near, and sit we in company here.
ANNAS	¶Do, sir, bid them bring in that boy that is bound.
CAYPHAS	¶Peace, now, Sir Anna; be still, and let him stand,
	And let us grope if this game be goodly begun.
ANNAS	¶Sir, this game is begun of the best.
	Now had he no force for to flee them.
CAYPHAS	¶Now in faith I am fain he is fast.
	Do lead in that lad; let me see, then.
2 KNIGHT	¶Lo, sir, we have said to our sovereign;
	Go now and sue to himself for the same thing.
3 KNIGHT	¶My lord, to your bidding we have obeyed not in vain.
	Lo, here is this fair sir brought that ye bade bring.
4 KNIGHT	¶My lord, frame now for to fright him.
CAYPHAS	Now am I fain;
	And fellows, fair might ye fall for your finding.
ANNAS	¶Sir, if ye trow them be true. Nor tricksters and vain,
	Bid them tell you the time of the taking.
CAYPHAS	¶Say, fellows, how went you so nimbly by night?

3 KNIGHT	¶My lord, there was no man to mar us nor mend us.
4 KNIGHT	¶My lord, we had lanterns and light,
	And some of his company kenned us.
ANNAS	¶But say, how did he, Judas?
3 KNIGHT	Ah, sir, full wisely and well.
	He marked us his master among all his men,
	And kissed him full kindly his comfort to cool,
	Because of a countenance that churl for to ken.
CAYPHAS	¶And thus did he his devoir?
4 KNIGHT	Yea, lord, every deal.
	He taught us to take him; the time, after ten.
ANNAS	¶Now, by my faith, a faint friend might he there find.
3 KNIGHT	¶Sir, ye might so have said, Had ye seen him then.
4 KNIGHT	¶He set us to the same that he sold us,
	And feigned to be his friend and no hater;
	This was the token before that he told us.
CAYPHAS	¶Now truly, this was the trick of a traitor.
ANNAS	¶Yea, be he traitor or true give we never tale,
	But take tent at this time and hear what he tells.
CAYPHAS	¶Now see that our household be holden here whole,
	So that none speak in case but he that in court dwells.
3 KNIGHT	¶Ah lord, this brawler has brewed much bale.
CAYPHAS	¶Therefore shall we speed us to sift of his spells.
	Sir Anna, take heed now and hear him.
ANNAS	¶Say, lad, list ye not lout to a lord?
4 KNIGHT	¶No, sir; with your leave we shall learn him.
CAYPHAS	¶Nay, sir; not so; no haste.
	It is no jest to beat beasts that are bound.
	And therefore with fairness will we him taste,
	And then further him forth as we have found.
ANNAS	¶Sir, we might as well talk To an empty tun.
	I warrant him witless or wrested to wrong,
	Or else waits to work ill, As by wont he has done.
3 KNIGHT	¶His wont was to work mickle woe,
	And make many masteries among us.
CAYPHAS	¶And some shall he grant ere he go,
	Or you must attend him and tell us.
4 KNIGHT	¶My lord, to wit the wonders that he has wrought,
	To tell you the tenth would wear our tongues bare.
CAYPHAS	¶Since the boy for his boast is into bale brought,
	We will wit, ere we wend, how his works were.

3 KNIGHT ¶Our Sabbath Day we say Saves he right nought,
That he should hallow and hold Full worthy and full
dear.

4 KNIGHT ¶No, sir; in the same feast As we the sot sought,
He salved them of sickness On many sides here.

CAYPHAS ¶What then? Makes he them goodly to gang?

3 KNIGHT ¶Yea, lord; even forth in every one town
He will doctor to life after long.

CAYPHAS ¶Ah, this maketh he by the might of Mahound.

4 KNIGHT ¶Sir, our stiff Temple that made is of stone,
That passes any palace for price to appraise,
If it were down to the earth and to the ground gone,
This ribald he boasts him it rapidly to raise.

3 KNIGHT ¶Yea, lord; other wonders he works many a one,
And with his loud lying he looses our laws.

CAYPHAS ¶Go loose him and leave him, and let me alone;
For myself I will search him and hear what he says.

ANNAS ¶Hearken! Jesus of Jews shall have joy,
To spill all thy sport for thy spells.

[*A 16th-century note marks a loss of some lines here.*]

CAYPHAS ¶Do move, fellow, of thy friends that fed thee before,
Then further of thy faring to ask am I fain.
Now name us this lightly. . . . His language is lorn.

3 KNIGHT ¶My lord, with your leave, he likes not to be plain;
But should he scape scatheless it were a foul scorn,
For he has mustered among us full much of his main.

4 KNIGHT ¶Malkus, your man, lord, that had his ear shorn,
This harlot full hastily healed it again.

CAYPHAS ¶What? If he list to be nice for the nonce,
Hear then how we haste to re-heat him.

ANNAS ¶Now by Belial's blood and his bones,
I hold it were better to beat him.

CAYPHAS ¶Nay, nay, sir, no haste; we shall have game ere we go.
Boy, be not aghast if we seem gay.
I conjure thee kindly, and command thee also,
By great God that is living and last shall aye,
If thou be Christ, God's son, tell it to us two.

JESUS ¶Sir, thou sayest it thyself. And soothly I say,
That I shall go to my Father as I came fro,
And dwell with him joyful in weal alway.

CAYPHAS ¶Why, fie on thee, traitor, untrue!

217

The father hast thou foully defamed.
Now need we no notices new;
Himself with his saws he has shamed.

ANNAS ¶Now needs neither witness not counsel to call,
But take his saws as he sayeth in the same stead.
He slanders the Godhead and so grieves us all,
Wherefore he is well worthy to be dead.
And therefore, sir, tell him the truth.

CAYPHAS Surely, so I shall.
Hearest thou not, harlot? Ill hap on thy head.
Answer here directly to great and to small,
And reach us out rapidly some reason, I rede.

JESUS ¶My reasons are not to rehearse,
Nor they that might help me are not here now.

ANNAS ¶Say, lad, if ye list to make verse,
Say on now or stay; let us hear now.

JESUS ¶Sir, if I say thee sooth, thou shalt not assent,
But hinder, or haste me to hang.
I preached where people were most present,
And no point in privity to old nor young.
And also in your Temple I told my intent;
Ye might have taken me then for my telling,
Much better than bring me with brands unburnt,
Thus to annoy me by night, and all for nothing.

CAYPHAS ¶For nothing! Losel, thou liest.
Thy words and thy works a vengeance will bring.

JESUS ¶Sir, since thou with wrong so turnest me awry,
Go ask them that heard of my speaking.

CAYPHAS ¶Ah, this traitor has grieved me With tales that he has
told,
Yet had I never such scorn Of a harlot as he.

I KNIGHT ¶What, fie on thee, beggar! Who made thee so bold
To boast with our Bishop? Thy bane shall I be.

JESUS ¶Sir, if my words be wrong, or worse than ye would,
A wrong witness I wot now are ye.
If my sayings be sooth they must be sore sold;
Wherefore ye boast too broad when you beat me.

2 KNIGHT ¶My lord, will ye hear? By Mahound,
No more now to name that it needs.

CAYPHAS ¶Go dress you and ding you him down,
And deafen us no more with his deeds.

ANNAS ¶Nay, sir; then blemish ye prelates' estates;
You ought to doom no man, to death for to bring.
CAYPHAS ¶Why, sir, better so than to be in debate;
Ye see the boy will not bow for our bidding,
ANNAS ¶Now, sir, ye must present this boy unto Sir Pilate,
For he is the doomsman near and next to the king;
And let him hear the whole, how ye him hate,
And whether he will help him or haste him to hang.
1 KNIGHT ¶My lord, let men lead him by night;
So shall ye best scape out of scorning.
2 KNIGHT ¶My lord, it is now in the night;
I rede ye abide till the morning.
CAYPHAS ¶Fair sir, ye say best, and so shall it be.
But learn yon boy better to bend and to bow.
1 KNIGHT ¶We shall learn yon lad, by my loyalty,
To lout unto every lord like unto you.
CAYPHAS ¶Yea; and, fellows, watch that he be aye waking.
2 KNIGHT ¶Yes, lord; that warrant will we;
It were a full needless note to bid us nap now.
3 KNIGHT ¶Certes, will ye sit, and soon shall ye see
How we shall play Papse for his profit enow.
4 KNIGHT ¶Let's see—who starts for a stool?
For I have here a hood for to hide him.
1 KNIGHT ¶Lo, here's one full fit for a fool;
Go get it, and set thee beside him.
2 KNIGHT ¶Nay, I shall set it myself, and strike him also.
Lo, here a shroud for a shrew, and of sheen shape.
3 KNIGHT ¶Play fair, then, all here. And there's one; and there's
two.
I shall find how to fix it, with a fair flap.
2 KNIGHT ¶And there's three; and there's four.
3 KNIGHT ¶Say now, with an evil hap,
Who is near thee now? Not a word, no?
4 KNIGHT ¶Come, noddle on him with knuckles, That he nought
nap.
1 KNIGHT ¶Nay now, to nap is no need.
Wassail, wassail! I warrant him waking.
2 KNIGHT ¶Yea, and but he can better jests bide,
Such buffets shall he still be taking.
3 KNIGHT ¶Prophet Ysaie, to be out of debate,
"*Injuste percussit*" . . . man, read if ye may.

4 KNIGHT	❡These words are in waste. Thou seest his state.
	It seems by his working His wits are away.
1 KNIGHT	❡Now let him stand as he stood in a fool's state;
	For he likes not this lark, my life dare I lay.
2 KNIGHT	❡Sirs, we must present this page to Sir Pilate.
	But go we first to our sovereign And see what he says.
3 KNIGHT	❡My lord, we have bandied with this boy,
	And held him full hot here among us.
CAYPHAS	❡Then heard ye some japes of his joy?
4 KNIGHT	❡The devil of a song, lord, he sung us.
ANNAS	❡Sir, bid quickly they go and bind him again,
	So that he scape not, for that were a scorn.
CAYPHAS	❡Go, tell to Sir Pilate our plaints all plain,
	And say, this lad with his lying has our laws lorn;
	And say, this same day must he be slain,
	Because of the Sabbath which is in the morn;
	And say that we come ourselves for certain,
	For to further the affair. Now fare ye before.
1 KNIGHT	❡My lord, with your leave we must wend,
	Our message to make as we may.
ANNAS	❡Sir, your fair fellowship we commend to the fiend.
CAYPHAS	❡Go on, now; dance forth in the devil's way.

30

THE TAPITERS AND COUCHERS

Jesus, Pilatus, Anna, Cayphas, duo consiliarii, et iiii Judei accusantes Jesum.

PILATE   ¶Ye cursed creatures that cruelly are crying,
Restrain you for striving For strength of my strokes.
Your plaints in my presence Use plainly applying,
Or this brand in your brains Soon bursts and soon breaks.
What brawler with brawling me brews,
That wretch may not writhe from my rage,
Nor his sleights so slyly assuage.
Let that traitor not trust in my truce.
For Sir Sesar was my sire, And I soothly his son,
That excellent Emperor exalted in height,
Who all this wide world with his wits had won;
And my mother named Pila that proudly was plight.
Of Pila the proud was Atus the father once hight.
This Pila was added to Atus——
Now, sir knights, rede ye it right?
For thus shortly I have shewn you in sight
How I am proudly proved Pilatus.
Lo, Pilate am I, proved a prince of great pride.
I was put into Pontus, the people to press;
And then Caesar himself, with senators by his side,
Remitted me to these realms, all ranks to redress.
And thus am I granted on ground, as I guess,
To justify and judge all the Jews.
Ah, love! Here's my lady, no less.
Lo, sirs, my wife, how worthy she is,
So seemly, lo, certain she shows.

WIFE   ¶Was never judge in this Jewry of so jocund generation
(Percula) Nor of so joyful genealogy to gentry adjoined,
As you, my duke doughty, doomer of damnation

To princes and prelates That your precepts purloined.
For whoso your precepts has pertly purloined,
With dread to his death shall ye drive him.
By my troth, he is stoned as untrue
That is slow your behests to pursue;
All to rags shall ye rend him and rive him.
I am Dame Precious Percula, of princes the prize,
Wife to Sir Pilate here, prince without peer.
All well of all womanhood am I, witty and wise;
Conceive now my countenance so comely and clear.
The colour of my corse is full clear,
And in richness of robes I am arrayed.
There is no lord in land far or near,
In faith, that hath friendlier dear
Than you, my lord, myself though I say it.

PILATE ¶Now say may ye safely; I will certify the same.

PERCULA ¶Gracious lord, gramercy; your good will is gain.

PILATE ¶Yet to comfort my corse I must kiss you, madame.

PERCULA ¶To fulfil your forward, my fair lord, I am fain.

PILATE ¶How, how, fellows! now in faith I am fain
Of these lips that so lovely are lapped.
In bed 'tis full blithe to remain.

PERCULA ¶Yea, sir; it needs must be plain,
All ladies, we covet then Both to be kissed and to be
clapped.

BEADLE ¶My liberal lord, O leader of laws,
O shining show that all shames eschews,
I beseech you, my sovereign, assent to my saws,
As you are gentle judge and justice of Jews. . . .

PERCULA ¶How now? Hearken, jawing and jangling of Jews!
Why, begone, whoreson boy, when I bid thee.

BEADLE ¶Madame, I do but what due is.

PERCULA ¶But if thou rest on thy reason, thou rues.
Away, cursed churl; haste and hide thee.

PILATE ¶Do mend you, madame, and your mood be amending,
For meseems it were fitting to hear what he says.

PERCULA ¶My lord,
He told never tale that to me was attending,
But with twists and with turns to wend me my ways.

BEADLE ¶I know well of your ways to be wending Belongs to
our laws.

222

PERCULA ¶Lo, lord, this lad with his laws, How think ye it profits well
His preaching to praise?

PILATE ¶Yea, love; he knows what becomes best our ways;
All our customs he rightly can tell.

BEADLE ¶My lord, will ye see now the sun in your sight?
For his stately strength he stems in his streams.
Behold over your head how he holds from height,
And glides to the ground with his glittering gleams;
To the ground he goes with his beams,
And the night draws nearer anon.
Ye may doom after no dreams.
But let my lady here With her light gleams
Blithely now to her bower be gone.
For ye must sit, sir, this same night of life and of limb.
It is not lawful for my lady, By the law of this land,
In doom hall for to dwell After day waxes dim.
Let her then take her leave while the light is.

PILATE ¶Now, wife, be you blithely preparing.

PERCULA ¶I am here, sir, handily faring.

PILATE ¶This boy for the best has given rede as right is.

PERCULA ¶Your commandment to keep, to fare forth I cast me.
My lord, with your leave, no longer I let you.

PILATE ¶It were approved to my person That privily ye passed me;
And went not forth this once Ere with wine you had wet you.
Get drink. What dost thou? Have done.
Come seemly beside me, and set you.
Lo, now it is even here that I ere met you.
Ha! Essay it now serious and soon.

PERCULA ¶It would glad me, my lord, would you goodly begin.

PILATE ¶I assent to your counsel so comely and clean.
Now drink ye, madame. To death all this din.

PERCULA ¶If it like you, my good lord, your good health be here.
No need for to learn me this lore.

PILATE ¶Give after to your damsel, madame.

PERCULA ¶In thy hand hold now, and have here.

MAID ¶Gramercy, my lady so dear.

PILATE ¶Now farewell, and walk on your way.

PERCULA ¶Now farewell, my friendliest, your foemen to fend.

PILATE ¶Now farewell, fairest figure that e'er did food feed.
And fare ye well, damsel, fair featured indeed.
MAID ¶My lord, I commend me to your royalty.
PILATE ¶Fair lady, this son shall you lead.
Sir, go with this worthy indeed,
And whatever she bids, look obedient you be.
SON ¶I am proud and prepared to pass on a pace,
To go with this gracious, her goodly to guide.
PILATE ¶Take tent to thy tale; turn thou on no trace;
Come quickly and tell me if tidings betide.
SON ¶Sir, if any tidings my lady betide,
I shall full soon, sir, speed you to say.
Thus seemly shall I show by her side.
At once, sir; no longer we bide.
PILATE ¶Now farewell, and walk on your way.
Now gone is my wife, if it were not her will,
And she rakes to her rest as she recked now of nought.
Tis time now, I tell thee, to attend unto me,
And busk thee brisk, belamy, to bed were I brought.
And look I be richly arrayed.
With comfort and care be all made.
BEADLE ¶As your servant, that seriously I sought;
And this night, sir, annoy you shall nought,
I dare lay, once ye lovely are laid.
PILATE ¶I command thee, come near; I will go to my couch.
Have me in your hands handily, and heave me from
here.
But look thou hurt me not with handling, but tenderly
touch.
BEADLE ¶Ah sir, ye weigh well.
PILATE   Yea, I have wet me with wine.
Yet heave down; lap me evenly here.
For I will lay me to sleep for a while.
Look that no man or minion of mine
With no noise may come nigh me or near.
BEADLE ¶Sir, what warlock you wakens With words full wild,
That boy for his brawling Were better unborn,
PILATE ¶Yea, who chatters, him chastise, Be he churl or child;
For if he scape scatheless, It were a great scorn.
If scatheless he scape, 'twere a scorn;
The ribald that readily will roar,

THE TAPITERS AND COUCHERS

I shall meet with that minion to-morn,
And for his loose lewdness him learn to be lorn.
BEADLE ¶Why, so, sir; sleep ye, and say ye no more.

PERCULA ¶Now are we at home; come, help if you may;
For I will make me ready, and run to my rest.
MAID ¶Ye are weary, madame, and forspent of your way;
Go briskly to bed, for that I hold best.
SON ¶Here now is a bed arrayed of the best.
PERCULA ¶Then hap me, and fast hence ye hie.
MAID ¶Madame, anon all duly is dressed.
SON ¶With no stepping or strife be distressed.
PERCULA ¶Now be ye in peace, with your chatter and cry.
SATAN ¶Out, out, haro!
Into bale am I brought, This bargain may I ban.
Unless some wile I work Into woe am I gone.
This gentleman Jesus, of cursedness he can. . . .
By any sign that I see, this same is God's son.
If he shall be slain, our solace shall cease.
He will save man's soul from our hand,
And rive us the realms all round.
I will on stiffly as I am bound,
Unto Sir Pilate's wife openly, and put me in press.
O woman, be wise and wary, and waken thy wit.
There shall a gentleman Jesus unjustly be judged
Before thy husband in haste, and by harlots be hit,
And this doughty today to his death thus be dight.
Sir Pilate for his preaching and thou
Needs must you of all men be annoyed,
Your strife and your strength be destroyed,
Your riches shall be reft you full rude
With vengeance; that dare I avow.
PERCULA ¶Ah! I am drawn with a dream too dreadful to doubt.
Say, child; rise up readily, and rest thee not now.
Thou must launch to my lord, and lowly him lout;
Command me to his reverence, as right well I do.
SON ¶O what! Shall I travel untimely this tide?
Madame, for the mercy of heaven,
Such need is noisome to name,
And it nighs unto midnight full even.
PERCULA ¶Begone, boy; I bid thee no longer thou bide;

225

And say to my sovereign this same
Is sooth that I send him this tide.
All naked this night as I napped,
With trouble and tricks was I trapped
With a dream that swiftly me lapped,
Of one Jesus, the just man the Jews will undo.
Attend to that true man; With tricks be not trapped,
But as a doomsman duly be dressing,
And loyally deliver him at need.

SON ⁊Madame, I am addressed to that deed.
But first will I nap in this need;
For he has need of a morn sleep that midnight is
   missing.

ANNAS ⁊Sir Cayphas, ye ken well, This caitiff we have catched,
That ofttimes in our Temple Was teaching untrue,
Our meyny with might At midnight him matched,
And drove him to his dooming For his deeds undue.
Wherefore I counsel that this boy we bore
To Sir Pilate our prince and there pray him,
That he for our right will array him,
This fraud for his falsehood to flay him.
For after we say him the sooth I shall set him full sore.

CAYPHAS ⁊Sir Anna, this sport have ye speedily spied.
As I am pontifical prince of all priests,
We will press to Sir Pilate, and present him with pride
With this harlot that has hewed our hearts from our
   breasts
Through talking of tales untrue. And therefore, sir
   knights. . . .

I KNIGHT ⁊My lord?
CAYPHAS ⁊Sir knights that are courteous and kind,
We charge you that churl be well chained.
Come, briskly and readily him bind,
And rig him in ropes, his race till he rue.

I KNIGHT ⁊Sir, your sayings shall be served both shortly and soon.
Come on, fellow.
By my faith, let us fasten this liar full fast.

2 KNIGHT ⁊I am doughty for this deed; deliver; have done.
Let us pull on with pride till his power be past.

I KNIGHT ⁊Have him fast, now, and hold by his hands.

2 KNIGHT	¶For this same is he so lightly that vaunted,
	And God's Son he hath himself granted.
I KNIGHT	¶He is hurled from the height that he haunted.
	Lo, astonished at us he stares where he stands.
2 KNIGHT	¶Now is the boor bound for all the boast he has blown,
	And the last day he lied no lordings might law him.
ANNAS	¶Yea; he thought that this world had been wholly his own.
	As you are doughtiest this day To his dooming now draw him,
	And then we shall ken How he can excuse him.
I KNIGHT	¶Here, fellows, give us room, give us gate;
	We must step to yon star of estate.
2 KNIGHT	¶We must merrily wend in at this gate.
	He that cometh to Court, to courtesy must use him.
I KNIGHT	¶Come, rap on the rails, That we may pass on before.
	Come forth there, sir coward. Why cower ye behind?
BEADLE	¶What wranglers are these that rush and that roar?
I KNIGHT	¶Ah, good sir, be not wroth, for words are as wind.
BEADLE	¶I say, gadlings, go back with your gauds.
2 KNIGHT	¶Have sufferance, sir, I beseech you;
	More mild in this matter now make you.
BEADLE	¶Why, uncunning knaves, if I click you,
	I shall fell you, by my faith, for all your false frauds.
PILATE	¶Say, child—ill chase you—what churls are so clattering?
BEADLE	¶My lord, uncunning knaves they cry and they call.
PILATE	¶Go boldly, be lively, and those brawlers be beating,
	And put them in prison, on pain that may fall. . . .
	Yea, speedily ask them if any sport they can spell. . . .
	Yea, and look what lordings they be.
BEADLE	¶My lord that is lovely to see,
	Obedient and blithe to your bidding I be.
PILATE	¶And if they can talk any tidings, Come quick and me tell.
BEADLE	¶Can ye tell any tidings, by your faith, my fellows?
I KNIGHT	¶Yea.
	Sir Cayphas and Anna are come both together
	To Sir Pilate of Pontus the prince of our law.
	And they have caught a caitiff That is lawless and lither.
BEADLE	¶My lord, my lord!
PILATE	How?

BEADLE	¶My lord, unlap you lively where you lie.
	Sir Cayphas to your Court now is carried,
	And Sir Anna, but a traitor them tarried;
	Many wights of that warlock have wearied;
	They have brought him in a band, his bale to abide.
PILATE	¶But are these saws certain in sooth as thou says?
BEADLE	¶Yea, lord; the estates yonder stand——
	For strife, I'll be bound.
PILATE	¶Now then am I light as a roe And easy to raise.
	Go bid them come in both, And the boy they have bound.
BEADLE	¶Sirs, my lord gives you leave To come in your ways.
CAYPHAS	¶Hail, prince that is peerless in price.
	Ye are leader of laws in this land.
	Your help is full handily at hand.
ANNAS	¶Hail, strong in your state for to stand;
	All this doom must be dressed as you duly devise.
PILATE	¶Who are they? My prelates?
BEADLE	Yea, lord.
PILATE	Now be ye welcome, I wis.
CAYPHAS	¶Gramercy, my sovereign. We beseech, all the same,
	Because of waking you unwarily Be not wroth with this.
	For we have brought here a lewd lad Who looks like a lamb.
PILATE	¶Come in, you both, and to the bench haste you.
CAYPHAS	¶Nay, good sir; lower is lawful for us.
PILATE	¶Ah, sir Cayphas, be courteous ye must.
ANNAS	¶Nay, good sir, it may not be thus.
PILATE	¶Say no more, but come sit you beside me,
	In soberness as I bid you.
SON	¶Hail, thou seemliest seat under sun sought.
	Hail, dearest duke and doughtiest in deed.
PILATE	¶Now bienvenu, beausire; what bidding has you brought?
	Has any langour my lady new caught in this need?
SON	¶That comely commends her to you,
	And says, all naked this night as she napped,
	With trouble and toil was she trapped
	With a vision that swiftly her snapped,
	Of one Jesus the just man the Jews will undo.

She beseeches you as her sovereign that simple one to
   save;
Doom him not to death, for dread of vengeance.

PILATE   ❡What?
I hope this is he that hither hauled ye have.

CAYPHAS   ❡Yea, sir.
The same and the self; but this is but a chance.
With his witchcraft this wile has he wrought;
Some fiend on his message has he sent,
Who wrought on your wife ere he went.
That servant to shame should be sent;
This is sure and certain, and sooth should be sought.

ANNAS   ❡Yea,
Through his phantom and falsehood and fiend's craft
He has worked many wonders Where he walked full
   wide;
Wherefore, my lord, it were lawful His life were him
   reft.

PILATE   ❡Be ye never so fierce, ye both must abide,
Unless this same traitor be taught for untrue.
And therefore make sermons no more.
I will certainly send himself for,
And see what he says, less and more.
Beadle, go bring him. For of that man have I ruth.

BEADLE   ❡This forward to fulfil Am I fain moved in my heart.
Say, Jesus, the judges and the Jews Have me enjoined
To bring thee before them Even bound as thou art.
Yon lordings to lose thee Full long have they mind.
But first shall I worship thee With wit and with will.
This reverence I do thee thereby
For wights that were wiser than I,
They worshipped thee full holy on high,
And with solemnity sang Hosanna to thee.

I KNIGHT   ❡My lord, that is leader of laws in this land,
All bedells to your bidding should be obedient and fain.
And yet this boy here before you Full boldly was
   bowing.
To worship this warlock. Methinks we work all in vain.

2 KNIGHT   ❡Yea, and in your presence he prayed him for peace,
In kneeling on knees to this knave;
He besought him his servant to save.

CAYPHAS ¶Lo, lord, such error among them they have,
It is great sorrow to see; none may make it cease.
It is no honour to your manhood that mickle is of might
To forbear such forfeits that falsely are feigned.
Such spites in especial should be eschewed in your sight.

PILATE ¶Sirs,
Move you not in this matter But be mildly demeaned,
For your courtesy I ken had some cause.

ANNAS ¶In your sight, sir, the sooth shall I say.
As you are prince, take heed, I you pray.
Such a lurdan unloyal, I dare lay,
Many lords of our lands Might lead from our laws.

PILATE ¶Say, losel, who gave thee leave So to lout to yon lad?
And solace him in my sight So seemly as I saw?

BEADLE ¶Ah, gracious lord, grieve not, For good cause I had.
You commanded me to go, As you knew well and know,
To Jerusalem on a journey for you.
Then this seemly one was on an ass set,
And many men mildly him met;
As a god in that ground they him greet,
To welcome him on his way with worship true.
Osanna they sang, the Son of David.
Rich men with their robes, they ran to his feet,
And poor folk fetched flowers of the field,
And made mirth and melody this man for to meet.

PILATE ¶Now, good sir, by thy faith, What is Osanna to say?

BEADLE ¶Sir, construe it we may, By language of this land as I
believe,
—It is as much to me for to move—
(Your prelates in this place can it prove)
As "Our Saviour and Sovereign, Now save us, we
pray."

PILATE ¶Lo, seigneurs, how seems you? The sooth has he said?

CAYPHAS ¶Ah, lord, this lad is full lewd, by this light.
If his sayings were searched and seriously assayed,
Save your reverence, His reason they reckon not with
right.

BEADLE ¶Sir, truly the truth have I told
Of this wight whom with such might ye hold.

ANNAS ¶I say, harlot, thy tongue shouldest thou hold,
And not against thy masters to move thus.

230

PILATE	¶Cease now of your saying; I'll search him full sore.
ANNAS	¶Sir, doom him to death, or do him away.
PILATE	¶Sir, have you said?
ANNAS	¶Yea, lord.
PILATE	¶Then go sit you down with sorrow and care.
	For I will lose no lad that is loyal to our law.
	But step forth and stand up on high,
	And busk to my bidding, thou boy.
	For the nonce name us here no annoy.
BEADLE	¶I am here at your hand to haloo Ahoy.
	Come, move of your mastery, for I shall mix it with might.
PILATE	¶Cry, Oyez.
BEADLE	Oyez.
PILATE	Yet again, by my faith.
BEADLE	Oyez.
PILATE	¶Yet louder, that each man may hear right.
	Cry peace in this press, upon pain thereupon.
	Bid them assuage of their shouting both swiftly and soon,
	And stint of their striving and stand still as a stone.
	Call "Jesus, the kinsman of Jacob the Jew,
	Come swift and appear;
	To the bar draw thou near
	To thy judgment here,
	To be doomed for thy deeds undue."
I KNIGHT	¶Hark how this harlot all movement will mar.
	This loathly lad lists not my lord for to lout.
2 KNIGHT	¶Say, beggar, why brawlest thou? Go brisk to the bar.
I KNIGHT	¶Step on thy standing so stern and so stout.
2 KNIGHT	¶Step on thy standing so still.
I KNIGHT	¶Sir coward, to court must ye go,
2 KNIGHT	¶A lesson to learn of our law.
I KNIGHT	¶Flit forth, foul mightest thou fare.
2 KNIGHT	¶Say, warlock, thou wantest of thy will.
2 SON	¶O Jesus ungentle, thy joy is in japes.
	Thou canst not be courteous, thou catiff I call thee.
	No ruth were it to rig thee and rive thee in ropes.
	Why falls thou not flat here, foul fall thee,
	For fear of my father so free?
	Thou wottest not his wisdom, I wis;
	All thy help in his hand that it is,

231

	How soon might he save thee from this.
	Obey him, thou brawler, I bid thee.
PILATE	¶Now Jesus, thou art welcome all ways, as I ween.
	Be not abashed, but boldy bring thee to the bar.
	These seigneurs will sue for thee sore, I have seen——
	To work on this warlock . . . his wits wander far.
	Come presently, on pain, and appear.
	And, sir prelates, your points be ye proving.
	What cause can ye cast of accusing?
	This matter ye mark to be moving,
	And handily in haste let us hear.
CAYPHAS	¶Sir Pilate of Pontus, and prince of great price,
	We trust you will trow our tales to be true,
	To death for to doom him with all due device.
	The cursedness yon knave has in case if you knew,
	In heart would ye hate him on high.
	For unless it were so——
	We meant not to misdo;
	Trust, sir, shall ye thereto——
	We had not him taken to thee.
PILATE	¶Sir, your tales would I trow, But they touch no intent.
	What cause can ye find Now this fellow to fell?
ANNAS	¶Our Sabbath he saves not, but sure gives assent
	To work full unwisely; that wot I right well.
	He works when he will, well I wot;
	And therefore in heart we him hate.
	It suits you, to strenghten your state,
	Yon lewd one for loose life to slay.
PILATE	¶Every loose lad to slay if his life is not well,
	Your laws are lawful; and to your laws belongs it
	This pretender to punish with scourging full fell,
	And woe may ye work him by law, when he wrongs it.
	Therefore now take him to you with speed,
	And like as your laws will you lead,
	Now doom him to death for his deed.
CAYPHAS	¶Nay, nay, sir; that doom must we dread.
	In our land now there lies no such law.
	It belongs not to us no lad to destroy.
PILATE	¶What would you I did, then? May the devil you draw!
	Full few are his friends, but fell are his foes.
	His life for to lose, there belongeth no law,

Nor no cause can I kindly contrive
For why he should lose thus his life.

ANNAS ❡Ah, good sir, it goeth full rife,
In steads where he stirred mickle strife,
Of lads that are loyal to your life.

CAYPHAS ❡Sir, halt men and hurt he has healed in haste;
The deaf and the dumb he delivered from dole.
By witchcraft, I warrant, his wits shall he waste.
For the wonders he works, how they follow that fool.
Our folk thus he frights in great fear.

ANNAS ❡The dead men he raiseth anon.
That Lazarus that low lay alone,
He granted him his gate to be gone,
And openly proved thus his power.

PILATE ❡Now, good sirs, I say then, what would ye today?

CAYPHAS ❡Sir, to death you should doom him, or put him away.

PILATE ❡Yea, because he does well must I doom him, ye say?
Go, go; ye lark lightly. Where learned you such law?
This touches no treason, I tell you.
Ye prelates approved of great price,
Ye should be both witty and wise,
To allege the true law where it lies.
Your matters then move thus, I tell you.

ANNAS ❡Misplease not your person, thou prince without peer,
It touches to treason, this tale I shall tell.
Yon briber, fall boldly he bade to forbear.
The tribute to the Emperor. Thus would he compel
Our people his points to apply.

CAYPHAS ❡The people he says he shall save,
And Christ makes them call him, yon knave,
And says the high kingdom he'll have.
Look whether then he deserves to die.

PILATE ❡To die he deserves, if he do so indeed.
But I will see for myself what he says.
Speak, Jesu; and spend now thy space for to speed.
These lordings allege thou livest not by our laws;
They accuse thee full cruelly and keen.
And therefore as a chieftain I charge thee,
If thou be the Christ that thou tell me,
And God's Son thou grudge not to grant thee;
For this is the matter that I mean.

JESUS ¶Thou sayest so thyself; I am soothly the same,
Here dwelling in world to work willingly.
My Father is faithful to fell all thy fame.
Without trespass or trouble they take me to thee.

PILATE ¶Lo, bishops, why blame ye this boy?
Meseems it is truth that he says.
Ye move all the malice ye may,
With your wrenches and wiles to writhe him away,
Unjustly to judge him from joy.

CAYPHAS ¶Not so, sir; his saying is full soothly sooth.
It bringeth our bairns in bale for to bind.

ANNAS ¶Sir, doubtless we deem him as due of the death.
This fool that you favour, great faults can we find
This day for to deem him to die.

PILATE ¶Say, losel, thou liest, by this light!
Say, thou ribald, thou reckonest unright.

CAYPHAS ¶Advise you sir, with main and with might,
And wreak not your wrath now thereby.

PILATE ¶I like not this language so largely to lie.

CAYPHAS ¶Ah, mercy, lord, meekly! No malice we meant.

PILATE ¶Now done is it doubtless; be bold and be blithe;
Talk of that traitor, and tell your intent.
His saying is subtle, ye say.
Good sirs, then where learned he that lore?

ANNAS ¶In faith, sir, we cannot find where.

PILATE ¶Yes; his father with some wonders did fare,
And hath learned this lad of his lore.

ANNAS ¶Nay, nay, sir; we wist that he was but a wright;
No subtlety showed he that any man saw.

PILATE ¶Then mean ye of malice to mar him by might;
Of cursedness convict no cause can ye know.
I marvel you malign him amiss.

CAYPHAS ¶Sir, from Galely hither also
The greatest against him can go
Yon warlock to watch unto woe,
And of his work witness, I wis.

PILATE ¶Why, and has he gone in Galely, this gadling again?

ANNAS ¶Yea, lord; there was he born, this brawler, and bred.

PILATE ¶Now without deceiving, my friends, in faith I am fain,
For now shall our strife full sternly be sped.
Sir Herod is king there, ye ken;

<table>
<tbody>
</tbody>
</table>

His power is proved of the best
To rid him or reive him of rest.
And therefore, to go with yon guest
Mark out of our manliest men.

CAYPHAS ¶As wit and as wisdom your will shall be wrought.
Here are knights full keen to the king for to fare.

ANNAS ¶Now, seigniours, I tell you, since sooth shall be sought,
If he be not soon sent it will suit us full sore.

PILATE ¶Sir knights that are cruel and keen,
That warlock now bind and woefully wrest,
And look that he bitterly be braced.
And therefore, sir knights, now in haste
Take that traitor away you between.
To Herod in haste with that harlot now hie;
Commend me full meekly to his most might;
Say, the doom of this boy to deem him to die
Is done upon him duly, to dress or to dight,
Or alive for to leave, as he list.
Say, in ought I may do him in deed
His own am I worthily at need.

I KNIGHT ¶My lord, we shall spring on a-speed.
Come then, doom this traitor outright.

PILATE ¶Fair sirs, I bid you ye be not too bold;
Take tent for our tribute full truly to treat.

2 KNIGHT ¶My lord, we shall try this behest for to hold,
And work it full wisely in will and in wit.

PILATE ¶So to me, sirs, it seems to be fitting.

I KNIGHT ¶May Mahound, sirs, defend you with might.

2 KNIGHT ¶And save you, sirs, seemly in sight.

PILATE ¶Now with a wild vengeance, walk off with that wight,
And freshly be found to be flitting.

31

THE LYTSTERES

Herodes, duo consiliarii, iiii milites, Jesus et iii Judaei.

HEROD ⁋Peace, ye beggars and brats so broad and so bold,
Brave braggarts so bravely your boldness to boast;
From treating of trifles put reins on your tongues,
Or this brand that is bright shall burst in your brain.
Push not for places, but sit ye down plain;
Draw in no draffing, but dress you to dread
With dashes.
Travail not as traitors in treason that trust,
Or by the blood that Mahound bled, with this blade
shall you bleed.
Thus shall I brittle all your bones abroad,
Yea,
And slash all your limbs with lashes.
Dragons that are dreadful shall droop in their dens,
In wrath when we writhe or are wrathfully wrapped;
Against giants ungentle we make war with machines;
And swans that are swimming to our sweetness shall be
snapped,
And jogged down their jolliness our gentries engender-
ing.
Whoso reproves our estate we shall clap them in chains;
All ranks that run to us respect shall receive.
Therefore I bid you cease ere any bale be,
That no beggar be bold his boast for to blow.
Ye that love well your lives, listen loyally to me,
As a lord that is learned to lead you by laws;
And ye that are of my men and of my meinie,
Since we come of one kindred, as ye well know,
Assembled all here in this same city,
It suits us in serious style to say all.

I DUKE	¶Yea, lord, we shall take heed to your call,
	And press to no place but you summon us.
	No grievance too great nor too small.
HEROD	¶Yea, but look that no fault shall befall.
2 DUKE	¶Loyally, my lord, so we shall.
	You need not no more to remind us.
I DUKE	¶Monseigneur,
	Demean you in honour to mind what I mean;
	We bow to your bidword, for so I hold best.
	For all the commons of this Court have avoided clean,
	And all men, as reason is, are gone to their rest.
	Wherefore I counsel, my lord, ye command you a drink.
HEROD	¶Now, sure, I assent as thou says,
	Since every man went on his ways.
	Lightly, without any delays,
	Give us wine gaily, and let us go wink,
	And see that no dinning be done.
I DUKE	¶My lord, now unlace you to lie;
	Here shall none come for to cry.
HEROD	¶Now speedily look that thou spy
	That no noise be nigh us this noon.
I DUKE	¶My lord, your bed is new made;
	You need not for to bide it.
HEROD	¶Yea, but as thou lovest me heartily,
	Lay me down softly,
	For thou wottest full well
	That I am full tenderly hided.
I DUKE	¶How lie ye, my good lord?
HEROD	¶Right well, by this light,
	All wholly at my desire.
	Wherefore I pray Sir Satan our sire
	And Lucifer most lovely of lure,
	Save you all, sirs, and give you good night.
I KNIGHT	¶Sir knight, ye know we are warned to wend,
	To wit of this warlock what is the king's will.
2 KNIGHT	¶Sir, here is Herod even here at your hand,
	And all your intent you may tell as you will.
I KNIGHT	¶Who is here?
I DUKE	Who is there?
I KNIGHT	¶Sir, here we knights stand,
	Who come to your counsel this churl for to kill.

1 DUKE	¶Unless, sirs, your message our mirth may amend,
	Stalk forth by yon streets, or stand stone still.
2 KNIGHT	¶Yea, sure, sirs, of mirths do we mean.
	The king shall have matters to deal him.
	We bring here a boy us between;
	Wherefore to have worship we ween.
1 DUKE	¶Well, sirs, if no trouble be seen,
	Hold him there, and we will go tell him.
	My lord,
	Yonder is a boy bound that brought is in blame.
	Haste you to hie; they hover at your gates.
HEROD	¶What, and shall I rise now, in the devil's name?
	To stickle among strangers in tricks of estate?
	But have here my hand; hold now;
	And see that my smock be well sitting.
1 DUKE	¶My lord, all good will I would wish you;
	No wrong would I work by my witting.
	My lord, we can tell you strange tidings.
HEROD	¶Yea, but look ye tell us no tales but are true.
2 DUKE	¶My lord, they bring you yonder a boy bound in band,
	That bodes either boasting or bales for to brew.
HEROD	¶Then have we some uproar full hastily at hand.
1 DUKE	¶My lord,
	There is work that is needful to name you anew.
HEROD	¶Why, hopest thou they haste him to hang?
2 DUKE	¶We wot not their will nor their meaning,
	But bidding full blithely they bring.
HEROD	¶Then come now, let us hear of their saying.
2 DUKE	¶Lo sirs, ye shall talk with the king,
	And tell to him manly your meaning.
1 KNIGHT	¶My lord, wealth and worship be with you alway.
HEROD	¶Well, what would you?
1 KNIGHT	A word, lord, if that were your will.
HEROD	¶Well, say on then.
1 KNIGHT	¶My lord, we would fright foolish men
	Who transgress against you.
HEROD	Fair befall you then.
1 KNIGHT	¶My lord, when ye hear what we say,
	It will heave up your heart every way.
HEROD	¶Yea, but say, what hind have ye there?
1 KNIGHT	¶A present from Pilate, the prince of our law.

HEROD	¶Peace in our presence, and name him not here.
I KNIGHT	¶My lord, he would worship you fain.
HEROD	¶Ye are foes foul as ever I saw.
2 KNIGHT	¶My lord,
	He offers you honour amain,
	And so he has sent you this swain.
HEROD	¶Go back quick with that gadling again,
	And say that a borrowed bean for him I care not.
I DUKE	¶Nay, my lord, with your leave they have fared far,
	And to taste of their fare no folly would be.
2 DUKE	¶My lord,
	If this gadling go thus it may grieve many more,
	For he grows on this ground of villainy store.
HEROD	¶This midget, you mean, may my might mar?
I DUKE	¶Nay, lord; but on this mould such mastery he makes.
HEROD	¶Go on; let us hear what they say, then.
	But if they have boasted, they both shall abide.
2 KNIGHT	¶My lord, we were worthy to blame,
	To bring you a message amiss.
HEROD	¶Why, then; can you name us his name?
I KNIGHT	¶Sir, Christ we have called him at home.
HEROD	¶Why, the self and the same one is this?
	Now, sirs, ye be welcome, I wis.
	And in faith I am fain he is found, His marvels to test and to tell.
	Now these games are goodly begun.
2 KNIGHT	My lord, loyally that likes us well.
HEROD	¶Yea, but dare ye say surely that harlot is he?
I KNIGHT	¶My lord, take heed, and soon you shall hear how.
HEROD	¶But what means that this message was made unto me?
2 KNIGHT	¶My lord, for it touches to treason, I trow.
I KNIGHT	¶He is culpable called in all our country,
	Of many parlous points, as Pilate proves now.
2 KNIGHT	¶When Pilate perceived he went through Galilee,
	He learned us that lordship to you doth belong;
	And before he might learn what your will might be,
	No further would speak, lest he do wrong.
HEROD	¶He admits, then our might is the more?
I KNIGHT	¶Yea, certes, sir; so we agree.
HEROD	¶Now surely, our friendship therefore
	We grant him, no grievance to hold long.

And, sirs, a warm welcome to you I well owe;
You may wend at your will, that I warrant.
For I coveted kindly that caitiff to know;
His cunning, men say, is apparent.

2 KNIGHT ¶My lord, would he say you sooth here to your face,
You never saw such strangeness by sea or by sand.

HEROD ¶Stand back now, and give him for breathing a space,
For I hope we get some high thing hastily at hand.

1 KNIGHT ¶Jerusalem town and the Jews may have joy
And hail in their heart for to hear him.

HEROD ¶Say, bien venu en bon foi,
Plait-il que vous parliez a moi?

2 KNIGHT ¶Nay, he joins not in jesting, this boy.

HEROD ¶No, sir? By your leave, we shall learn him.

1 SON ¶My lord, see these knights, that know and are keen,
How they come to your court without any call.

HEROD ¶Yea, son; and muster great masteries. What may this
mean?

1 DUKE ¶My lord, yet your might is more than they all;
They seek you as sovereign, and sure that is seen.

HEROD ¶Now sure, since ye say so, assay him I shall,
For I am fainer of that fellow than other fifteen.
Yea, and he that first found him, fair may he fall.

1 KNIGHT ¶Lord, truly we tell you no lie;
This life that he leads will sure waste him.

HEROD ¶Well, sirs, draw you aside;
And beausires, bring ye him nigh;
For although all his sleights may be sly,
Yet ere he pass hence we shall test him.
O my heart hops for joy,
To see now this prophet appear;
We shall have good game with this boy;
Take heed, for in haste ye shall hear.
I lay we shall laugh and have liking,
To see how this lewd lad alleges our laws.

2 DUKE ¶Hark, cousin; thou comest to chat with a king;
Take tent and be cunning in chat; you have cause.

1 DUKE ¶Yea, and look that thou be not a sot of thy saying,
But sober, and soon set out all thy saws.

2 DUKE ¶He seemeth full sulky, this boy that they bring,
And yet of his babbling men boast broad and free.

240

HEROD	¶Why, therefore I sought him to see.
	Look, fair sirs; as we bid you, be ready.
1 DUKE	¶Kneel down here to the king on your knee.
2 DUKE	¶Nay, no need for that will he see.
HEROD	¶Lo, sirs, he shows meekness no more unto me
	Than it were to a man of his tithing
1 DUKE	¶Out on thee, mudclot; go learn thee to lout,
	Before it more blame on thee bring.
HEROD	¶Nay, nay, I dare say without doubt,
	He knows not the course of a king,
	And here bides to our bale. Now, boaster, begin.
	Say first at beginning withal, where wast thou born?
	Do, fellow, for thy faith let us fall in
	First of thy marvels, who fed thee before?
	What, deign'st thou not? Lo, sirs, he deafens us with din.
	Say, whence led ye this lewd lad? His language is lorn.
1 KNIGHT	¶My lord, his marvels to more and to less
	He musters among us both midday and morn.
2 KNIGHT	¶My lord, they are too many to tell, as I guess,
	His wonders; he works them so mightily.
1 KNIGHT	¶Ho, man! Mumbling may nothing avail.
	Go to the king; tell him from top unto tail.
HEROD	¶Come, bring us that boy unto bale,
	For truly we leave him not lightly.
1 DUKE	¶This fool feigns he may mark men to their meed;
	He means many masteries and marvels to make.
2 DUKE	¶Five thousand folk did he go feed
	With five loaves and two fishes to take.
HEROD	¶How many folks sayest thou he fed?
2 DUKE	¶Five thousand, lord, came at his call.
HEROD	¶Yea, boy, and how much was the bread?
2 DUKE	¶But five loaves; that I wager was all.
HEROD	¶Now, by the blood that Mahound bled,
	What! this was the wonder of all.
2 DUKE	¶Yea, lord, and two fishes blessed he then,
	And gave them, and none was forgotten.
1 DUKE	¶Yea, lord; and twelve lapfuls was left
	Of relief, when all men had eaten.
HEROD	¶Of no such a munching imagine man may.
2 DUKE	¶My lord, for his masteries thus musters he his might.
HEROD	¶But say, sirs, are these sayings sooth that ye say?

241

2 KNIGHT	¶Yea, lord, and more marvels were shewed to our sight.
	One Lazar, a lad that in our land lay,
	Lay locked under loan from life and from light;
	And his sister came raking in rueful array,
	And, lord, for her roaring he raised him full right,
	And up from his grave let him gang
	Out forth, without any evil.
HEROD	¶O such lyings last sadly too long.
I KNIGHT	¶Why, lord, think ye these words be wrong?
	This same lad dwells here us among.
HEROD	¶Why, I think they be deeds of the devil.
	But why should ye haste him to hang?
	Your hurt to no harm he pursues.
2 KNIGHT	¶My lord, since he calls him a king,
	And claims to be king of the Jews.
HEROD	¶But say, is he king in his kindred and town?
I KNIGHT	¶Nay, he calls him a king, sir, his cares for to quell.
HEROD	¶Little wonder it is, then, if woes weigh him down,
	To be wearied with wrongs when he works well.
	But he shall sit by myself, since ye say so.
	Come near, king, into Court. Say, can ye not kneel?
	We shall have gauds full good and games ere we go,
	How likest thou? Well, lord? Say, what?
	The devil! ne'er a deal?
	I fail in my reverence. Inutile, moy.
	I am of favour, lo, fairer by far.
	Halloo ha Hallali! Ut ho! Oy, Oy!
	By all wit that I wot it waxes worse, sure.
	Servicia primet such lozels and lurdans as thou, lo.
	Respicias timet. What the devil and dam shall I do now?
	Do chatter away, churl, for I can thee cure.
	Say, may thou not hear me? Hoy man; art thou mad?
	Now, tell me truly how formerly you fared.
	Forth, friend; by my faith, thou art a fond lad.
I DUKE	¶My lord, it astounds him; you steven it so stout.
	He would rather have stayed stock still where he stood.
HEROD	¶If the boy were abashed of Herod's big shout,
	'Twere a joke of the best, by Mahound's blood.
2 DUKE	¶My lord, I trow 'tis your falchion that frights
	And stops him.

HEROD	Why, true; I believe thee;
	And so I will waft it away,
	And softly with a sceptre assay.
	Now, sir, be pert, I thee pray,
	For none of my grooms shall now grieve thee.
	Si loqueris tibi laus, pariter quoque prospera dantur;
	Si loqueris tibi fraus, fel fex ac bella parantur.
	My men, go ye honour him amain,
	As best may a great one beseem.
I DUKE	¶Fair sir, and my lord sovereign.
2 DUKE	¶Monseigneur, je baise la main.
HEROD	¶Go, answer them nicely again.
	What the devil! We dote or we dream!
I KNIGHT	¶Nay; we get not a word, that dare I well lay,
	For he is wrested of wit or bewildered, I say.
HEROD	¶Ye say, he lacked of your laws as ye that lad led?
2 KNIGHT	¶Yea, lord; and made many tricks by the way.
HEROD	¶Now, since he comes as a knave and as a knave clad,
	Wherefore call ye him king?
I DUKE	Nay, my lord, he is none,
	But a harlot is he.
HEROD	¶What a devil! I am hard bested.
	A man might as well stir a stock or a stone.
I SON	¶My lord, this fraud is so foully afraid;
	He never looked so long on a lord all alone.
HEROD	¶No, son. The ribald sees us so richly arrayed,
	He thinks we be angels each one.
2 DUKE	¶My lord, I hold him aghast of your gay gear.
HEROD	¶Great lords ought so to be gay.
	Here shall no man make thee to fear,
	And therefore now name in mine ear;
	For by the great god, if thou make me swear,
	Thou hadst never dole till this day.
	Come, chat on quick, churl, of thy kin.
I DUKE	¶Nay, needs must he names to you none.
HEROD	¶Yet shall he abide ere he ceases.
2 DUKE	Ah, stay, lord.
HEROD	Let me alone.
I DUKE	¶Now, good lord, if you may move you no more,
	It is not fair to fight with a fond fool;
	But go to your council and comfort you there.

HEROD   ¶Thou sayest sooth; we shall see if so will be good.
For surely our sorrows are sad.

2 SON   ¶What a devil ails him?
My lord, I can make you be glad,
For in truth this master is mad;
He lurks low and looks like a lad.
He is mad, lord, or else his wit fails him.

3 SON   ¶My lord, you have moved you as much as you may,
For you might honour him no more, were he Mahound.
And since it seems to be so, let us now assay.

HEROD   ¶Look, beaux sires, ye be to our bidding bound.

1 DUKE   ¶My lord, how should he fear us? He dreads not your array.

HEROD   ¶Now, come on—might the devil him draw—, son,
And since he feigns falsehood and makes foul affray.
Roar on him rudely, and see ye not run.

1 SON   ¶My lord, I shall enforce myself, since ye say so.
Fellow, be not afeared, nor feign not therefore,
But tell us now some trifles between us two,
And none of our men shall meddle here more.
And therefore by reason array thee;
Some point for thy profit, come, tell now.
Hearest thou not what I say thee?
Thou mumbling midget, I may thee
Help, and turn thee from trouble, I trow.

2 SON   ¶Look up, lad, lightly, and lout to my lord here,
For from bale unto bliss he may thee now borrow.
Chat on, knave, carefully, and cast thee to accord here,
And tell us now somewhat, thou skipjack of sorrow.
Why stands thou as still as a stone here?
Spare not, but speak in this place here?
Thou gadling; it may gain thee some grace here.
My lord,
This fellow is so feared in your face here,
No answer in this need he names you with none here.

3 SON   ¶Do, beausire, for Belial's blood and his bones,
Say somewhat ere it will wax worse.

1 SON   ¶Nay; we get not one word in this dwelling.

2 SON   ¶Then cry we all on him at once . . . Oyez, Oyez, Oyez!

HEROD   ¶O ye make a foul noise with your yelling.

3 SON   ¶Needs must, my lord; we are never more near.

I SON	¶My lord, all your mouthing avails not a mite.
	To meddle with a madman is marvel to me.
	Command then your knights to clothe him in white,
	And carry him as he came to your country.
HEROD	¶Lo, sirs, we lead you no longer astray;
	My son has said soberly how it should be.
	But such an appointment for a page is too gay.
I DUKE	¶My lord, fools that are fond may find such a fee.
HEROD	¶What, in a white garment to go,
	Thus girt in a garment so gay?
2 DUKE	¶Nay, lord; as a fool force him fro.
HEROD	¶How say you, sirs? Should it be so?
ALL SONS	¶Yea, lord.
HEROD	Aye? Then there is no mo,
	But boldly go bear him away.
	Sir knights, see, we strive to make you be glad.
	Our council has warned us wisely and well.
	White clothes, we shall say, suits well a fond lad,
	And all his fool's folly, faith, truly we tell.
I DUKE	¶We will with good will for his weeds wend,
	For we know well enough what weeds he should wear.
2 DUKE	¶Lo, now is attire here as you intend,
	All fashioned and fit for this fellow to wear.
I SON	¶Lo, here is a jupon of joy,
	All such should be good for the boy.
I DUKE	¶In a king's dress shall he be displayed,
	And shall like a fool be arrayed.
2 DUKE	¶Now, thank them, a curse upon thee.
I SON	¶Nay, we get not a word, well I warrant.
2 SON	¶Man, make magic marvel for me.
I DUKE	¶What? Think ye he be wiser than we?
	Leave off, then, and let the king see
	How seemly the show we have made.
	See, my lord, if it pleases you so,
	For thus we have gotten him his gear.
HEROD	¶Why, what? Is the ribald arrayed?
	My blessing, fair sirs, may you bear.
	Go, cry in my Court, and let it be penned,
	All the deeds we have done in our dealing today.
	Whoso finds him aggrieved, let him speak soon, I say;
	If we find no default, his fate is to go free.

I DUKE ¶Oyez!
If any wight of this wretch worse doings may know,
Come, let him bear witness, whoso works wrong.
Busk boldly to the bar, his bales to bate so;
For my lord, by my loyalty, will not delay long.
My lord, there appears none to charge his estate.

HEROD ¶Why, then, for our turn he goes freely away.
Sir knights, then prepare you now presently to leave
And proceed to Sir Pilate, and unto him say,
We grant him our friendship, full free to receive,
And also our grievance forgive we this day

I KNIGHT ¶My lord, with your leave, this way we shall learn;
It likes us no longer here now to abide.

2 KNIGHT ¶My lord, if doubt comes to appear,
We come then again with good cheer.

HEROD ¶Nay, fair sirs, ye find us not here;
Our leave will we take at this tide,
And early betake us to rest,
For such needs have annoyed us ere now.

I DUKE ¶Yea, surely, lord; so hold I best,
For this gadling ungoldy has grieved you.

HEROD ¶Now look ye bear word as ye wot,
How well we have quit us this while.

I KNIGHT ¶Ho! Wise men will deem that we dote,
If we make not an end of our note.

HEROD ¶Wend forth, and the devil in thy throat!
We find no default him to slay.
Wherefore we should banish or flay him
We find not in rolls of record,
And since he is dumb, for to slay him.
Were this a good law for a lord?
Nay, lozels unloyal, ye learned all too late;
Teach those lords of your land such lessons to hear.
Repair with your presence and say to Pilate
We grant him our power all plain to appear,
And also our grievance we wholly abate,
And we grant him our grace with good cheer.
As touching this troubler that brawls in debate,
Bid him work as he will and work not in fear.
Go tell him this message from me.
And lead forth that midget—ill fortune have he!

1 KNIGHT	¶My lord, with your leave, let him be,
	For all too long led him have we.
2 DUKE	¶What now, sirs? My lord will ye see?
HEROD	¶What, fellows, take ye no heed what I tell you
	And bid you? That yeoman rule well.
2 KNIGHT	¶My lord, we shall wage him an ill way.
HEROD	¶Nay, fair sirs, be not so fell;
	Fare softly, for so will beseem.
1 KNIGHT	¶Now since we shall do as you deem,
	Adieu, sir.
HEROD	Dance on, in the devil's way.

32

THE CUKES AND
WATERLEDERS

*Pilatus, Anna, Cayphas, duo Judei, et Judas reportans eis
xxx argenteos.*

PILATE ❡Peace, beausires, I bid you, that bide here about me,
And look ye stir no strife but stand stone still;
Or by the lord that life lent me, I shall make you lout
me,
And all shall bide in my bale that work not my will.
Ye ribalds that reign in this rout,
Now stint of your stevening so stout,
Or with this brand that is fearful to flout,
All to death I shall drive you this day.
For Sir Pilate of Pontus as prince am I proved,
In strength most royal in richest array.
There's no baron in this borough has heaved me about,
But he seeks me as sovereign, in certain I say.
Then take heed to my lordly estate,
That none jangle nor jar at my gate.
Begin not to go on your gate,
Till I have said and set out all my saw.
For I am the loveliest lapped and laid,
With favour full fair in my face;
My forehead both brown is and broad,
And mine eyes they glitter like gleam in the glass;
And the hair that hides all my head
Is even like to the gold wire;
My cheeks are both ruddy and red,
And my colour as crystal is clear.
There is no prince proved under pall,
But I am most mighty of all,
Nor no king but shall come to my call,

248

Nor groom that dare grieve me for gold.
Sir Cayphas, in counsel thy clerkship I bid,
For thy counsel is known for cunning and clear;
And Sir Anna, thy answer ought not to be hid;
Thou art one who is able and ought to be near
In Parliament plain.
And I am prince peerless, your points to enquire.
How say you, ye Jews, of Jesus that swain?
Come now, sirs, say on your saws;
What title now have ye unto him?
And truly look ye on your laws;
Why sent ye so soon to undo him?

ANNAS ¶Good sir, that is prince and lord of our law,
That traitor untrue whereof you now tell us,
Now certain and soon the sooth shall I say,
It is Jesus that japer that Judas did sell us.
He mars our men in all that he may;
His marvels that many he musters compel us;
He does many grave deeds on our Sabbath day;
That uncunning caitiff, he casts him to quell us.
That lying deceiver so false
From man unto man will compel us,
And undo you and ourself else;
Your own self will he undo,
If he hold forth this space,
And all this Jewry too,
If ye grant to him grace.

PILATE ¶Sir Anna, this answer allow I no thing;
I hold it but hatred, this article whole.
And therefore, Sir Bishop, at my bidding,
Do tell me now truly the text of this tale.
Determine it truly and right,
And loyally lead it by law.
Felony or falsehood, even here I defy it;
Say now seriously the truth, for love or for awe.

CAYPHAS ¶Sir Pilate, the tales this traitor hath told,
It heaves us in heart full wholly to hear them.
The warlock with his wiles he weens them to mould;
This lad with his lies full lightly did steer them.
Full fast will he take them unto him,
If thus he go forth with his gauds,

Or speech overspread; yea, better to undo him,
This liar is so fell with his false frauds.

PILATE ¶Your answers are hideous and hateful to hear.
Had I not heard him and myself had him seen,
Yet ye might have made me believe you entire.
But fault in him I find not, but wise he is and clean.
For wise and for clean can I call him;
No fault can I find to refuse him.
I hope yet in haste ye may hear him
When he comes to the call; then may ye accuse him.

I KNIGHT ¶My lord, many of his marvels in faith have we found;
Yon harlot heaves our hearts full of hot ire.
He says himself that he is God's son,
And shall sit on the right hand beside his own sire.

2 KNIGHT ¶These tales are full true that we tell;
On the rainbow that ribald it reads.
He says he shall have us to heaven or hell,
One day, to deem us after our deeds.

PILATE ¶To deem us? In the devil's name!
Say, whither? Say whither, to the devil!
What, dastards, ye ween ye be wiser than we?

I KNIGHT ¶My lord, with your leave, we name it for no ill;
He has mustered his marvels to more than to me.
My sovereign lord, yon skipjack, he says
He shall cast down our Temple; no lying I mean;
And dress it up duly within three days,
As well as it was, full goodly again.

ANNAS ¶Yea, sir; and on our Sabbath day,
Then works he his works full well.

PILATE ¶Out, fie on him, false one, for aye!
For these are dark deeds of the devil.

CAYPHAS ¶Sir, a noisesomer note now newly is noised,
That grieves me more than any kind of thing;
He claims himself clearly a kingdom of Jews,
And calleth himself our comeliest king.

PILATE ¶King, in the devil's name! Why fie on him, dastard!
What! Weens that wild warlock to win us thus lightly?
A beggar of Bedlam, born as a bastard!
Now, by Lucifer, loathe I that lad. I will leave him not
lightly.

ANNAS ¶Sir, the harlot is at Herod's hall, even here at your hand.

PILATE   ¶I sent to that warlock, may the devil him weary.

CAYPHAS   ¶It belongs to your lordship, by the law of this land,
As sovereign yourself to sit in enquiry.

ANNAS   ¶Sir, the traitor has told us more trifles truly,
Which would grieve you full soon, if we you them told.

PILATE   ¶Now, by Belial's bones, that boy shall abide,
And bring on his back a burden to hold.

I SON   ¶My lord, that is leader of laws in this land,
You sent him yourself to Herod the king,
And said, "The doom of that dog lies wholly in your
    hand,
To doom him or loose him at your liking."
And thus you commanded your knights for to say,
"For Sir Herod will search him full sore,
So that he wend with no wiles away;"
And therefore, my good lord, move you no more.

CAYPHAS   ¶Now surely, this was well said.
But, sir, will ye cease now, and we shall soon see.

PILATE   ¶Sir Cayphas and Anna, right so now we think.
Sit, in Mahound's blessing, and ask we for wine.
Ye knights of my court, command for us drink.
> [*A note in the later hand says, "Here is missing a*
> *conversation of the First Son and others".*]

JUDAS   ¶Alas, for woe that I was wrought,
Ere ever I came by kind or kin.
I ban the bones that forth me brought;
Woe worth the womb that I bred in,
        So may I bid.
For I so falsely did to him
That unto me great kindness did.
The purse with his expense about I bore;
There was none trusted so well as I.
Than me he trusted no man more,
And I betrayed him traitorly
        With lies all vain.
Blameless I sold his blessed body
Unto the Jews for to be slain.
To slay my sovereign assented I,
And told them the time of his taking.
Shameless myself thus ruined I,
So soon to assent to his slaying.

Now wist I how he might pass that pain . . .
To look how best that boon might be . . .
Unto the Jews I will again,
To save him, that he might pass free.
     That were my will.
Lord, wealth and worship with you be.

PILATE ¶What tidings, Judas, tellest thou still?
["*Here is missing a great and diverse conversation.*"]

JUDAS ¶My tidings are painful, I tell you,
Sir Pilate, and therefore I pray,
My master that I did sell you,
Good lord, let him wend on his way.

CAYPHAS ¶Nay, needs must, Judas, that we deny.
What mind or matter has moved thee thus?

JUDAS ¶Sir, I have sinned full grievously,
Betrayed that righteous blood Jesus
     And master mine.

CAYPHAS ¶Fair sir, what is that to us?
The peril and the plight are thine.
Thine is the wrong, and thou hast wrought it;
Thou told us full truly to take him;
And ours is the bargain, for we bought it.
Lo, we all assent for to slay him.

JUDAS ¶Alas, that may I rue full ill,
If ye assent him for to slay.

PILATE ¶Why, what wouldst thou we did now still?

JUDAS ¶I pray you, good lord, let him go;
And have of me your payment plain.

CAYPHAS ¶Nay, nay; we will not so.
We bought him that he should be slain.
To slay him thyself thou didst assent;
This wottest thou wondrous well.
What right is now to repent?
Thou shapest thyself no weal.

ANNAS ¶Away, Judas? thou dost for nought;
Thy words, I warn thee, are in waste.
Thyself to sell him when thou sought,
Thou wast against him then the most
     Of us each one.

CAYPHAS ¶We shall be avenged on him in haste,
Whether that ever he will or none.

PILATE ¶These words that thou namest nought needs it.
Thou unhanged harlot, hark what I say.
Spare of thy speaking, for nought speeds it;
Or walk out at the door, in the devil's way.

JUDAS ¶Why, will ye then not let him pass,
And have of me again your pay?

PILATE ¶I tell thee, traitor, that I will not.

JUDAS ¶Then am I lorn this day, alas,
Both bone and blood.
Alas the while, so may I say,
That ever I assent to spill his blood.
To save his blood see, sirs, I pray you,
And take you there your payment whole.
Spare for to spill him, now I pray you,
Else brew ye me full mickle dole.

PILATE ¶Now hearest thou me, Judas, thou shalt take it again;
We will it not; what the devil art thou?
When thou sought us, thou wast full fain
Of this money; what ails thee now
For to repent?

JUDAS ¶Again, sirs, here I give it you,
And save him from ruin that is meant.

PILATE ¶To ruin him thyself has thee shamed;
Thou mayest loathe the life thou leads.
Fondly as a false fool thyself has famed;
Therefore the devil thee drown for thy dark deeds.

JUDAS ¶I know my trespass and my guilt,
So great it is in grisly guise.
I am full woe he should be spilt.
Might I save him in any wise,
Well for me then.
Save him, sirs, and to your service
I will bind me, to be your man . . .
Your bondman, Lord, to be,
Now ever will I bind me.
Sir Pilate, you may trust me;
Full faithful shall ye find me.

PILATE ¶Find thee faithful? Ah, foul might thee fall,
Ere thou comes in our company.
For, by Mahound's blood, thou would sell us all.
Thy service will we not thereby;

          Thou art well known.
False tyrant, for thy traitory
Thou art worthy to be hanged and drawn.
Hanged and drawn shouldest thou be, knave,
If thou hadst right, by all good reason.
Thy master's blood thou biddest us save,
And thou wast first that didst the treason.

JUDAS   ¶I cry you mercy, lord; on me have rue,
This wicked wight that wrong has wrought.
Have mercy on my master true
That I have to your disposal brought,
      I cry you sore.

PILATE   ¶Go, jape thee, Judas; now name it not,
Nor move us of this matter more.

ANNAS   ¶No more of this matter now move thee,
Thou mumbling mommet, I thee tell.
Our point express here reproves thee
Of felony falsely and fell.

CAYPHAS   ¶He grudges not to grant his guilt.
Why shuns thou not to show thy shame?
We bought him that he should be spilt;
All here were we consent to the same,
      And thyself else.
Thou feigned not then for to defame,
But said he was a traitor false.

PILATE   ¶Yea, and for a false faitour
Thyself full foully did sell him.
O that was the trick of a traitor,
So soon thou shouldest go to beguile him.

I KNIGHT   ¶What, wouldst thou that we let him go,
Thou wicked wight that wrought such wrong?
We will not lose our bargain so,
So lightly for to let him gang,
      And reason why?
Did we let that lout live at all long,
It will be fond, in faith, folly.

2 KNIGHT   ¶Yon fool for no fools shall he find us;
We wot all full well how it was.
His master when he did bring us,
He prayed you, my lord, let him not pass.

PILATE   ¶Nay, surely, he shall not pass free;

    For him we have our money paid.

JUDAS ¶Take it again that ye took of me,
    And save him from that direful dread;
      Then were I fain.

ANNAS ¶It serves for nought that thou hast said,
    And therefore take it up again.

PILATE ¶Quickly again, thou traitor, take it;
    We will not wield it within our hold.
    Yet shalt thou not, slight man, so soon forsake it;
    I shall search him myself, since thou hast him sold.

CAYPHAS ¶Forsake it! In faith, that never he shall,
    For we will hold him that we have.
    The payment chains thee close withal;
    Thou needst no other covenant crave,
      Nor mercy none.

JUDAS ¶Since you assent him for to slay,
    Vengeance I cry on you each one.
    On each I cry, the devil fordo you,
    And that might I both hear and see.
    Hard vengeance here I will unto you,
    For sorrow unsought you on me see.

CAYPHAS ¶Why, fie on thee, traitor attaint, at this tide;
    Of treason thou taxed him that trusted thee for true.
    Off with thee hence, brawler; no longer abide;
    For if thou do, all thy reasons sore shalt thou rue.
    Say, wottest thou not who am I?
    Now, by my conscience, might I nigh near thee,
    In certain, lad, soon should I learn thee,
    Of lords to speak more courteously.

PILATE ¶Go thy gates, gadling, and grieve us no more;
    Leave off thy talk, might the devil thee hang.

JUDAS ¶That which you took of me, take it you there;
    Therewith your mastery make you among,
    And claim it you clean.
    I loathe all my life, so live I too long;
    My treacherous turn torments me with pain.
    Since so my treason I have taken unto me,
    I need ask no mercy, for none shall I get.
    Therefore in haste myself shall I fordo me.
    Alas the hard while that I ever met yet.
    Thus shall I mark my miserable meed,

And work my vengance with heart and will;
To slay myself now will I speed,
For sadly have I served to ill.
     So welaway.
That ever I was in wit or will,
That trusty true one to betray.
Alas, who may I move unto?
No other counsel now I need;
Myself in haste I shall fordo,
And take me now unto my death.

CAYPHAS   ¶Come then now, Sir Pilate, let us see what you say
As touching this money that here we have,
That Judas in wrath has waved away
And cast to us crabbedly, that cursed knave.
How say ye thereby?

ANNAS   ¶Sir, since he it slung, we shall it save.

CAYPHAS   ¶Quick, carry it to our treasury.

PILATE   ¶Nay, sir, not so.

CAYPHAS   Why, sir, how then?

PILATE   ¶Sir, it shall not cumber us
Nor come in our Corbonan.

CAYPHAS   ¶No; to our treasury certain
Further shall come of it nought.
And see yourself reason good and true—
It is the price of blood that we with it bought.
Therefore some other point I purpose it to,
     And thus I devise.

PILATE   ¶A spot of earth for to buy, wait now I will
To bury the pilgrim that by the way dies,
Pilgrims and palmers to grave in ground,
(Sir Cayphas and Anna, assent you thereto?)
And also false felons that we have found.

ANNAS   ¶As you deem, lord, so will we do.

ESQUIRE   ¶Hail, Sir Pilate, peerless, and prince of this place;
Hail, gayest on ground; in gold there ye glide.
Hail, loveliest lord of limb and of face,
And all sovereigns seemly that sit by your side.

PILATE   ¶What would you?

ESQUIRE   A word ere I wend.

PILATE   ¶Now thou art welcome, I wis.
But deliver thee lightly, without any let;

	We have no time all day to attend unto thee.
ESQUIRE	¶A place here beside, lord, would I to pledge set.
PILATE	¶What title has thou thereto? Is it thine own free?
ESQUIRE	¶Lord, free by my freedom befals it.
	This tale is full true that I tell you,
	And Calvary Locus men calls it.
	I would it wedset, but not for to sell you.
PILATE	¶What wouldst thou borrow, fair sir, let me see?
ESQUIRE	¶If it were your liking, lord, for to lend it,
	Thirty pence I would that ye lent unto me.
CAYPHAS	¶Yea, fair sir, that you shall have.
PILATE	¶Shew us thy deeds, and have here thy money.
ESQUIRE	¶Have here, good lord, but look ye them save.
PILATE	¶Yea, sure, we shall save them full soundly,
	Or else do we not duly our devoir.
	Fast, fellow, for thy faith, afoot found be,
	For from this place, fair sir, I assoil thee for ever.
ESQUIRE	¶Now sorrow on such succour as I have sought,
	For all my treasure through treason I lose.
	I lose it untruly by treason;
	Therefore now my way will I wend,
	For ye do me no right nor no reason.
	I wish you all to the devil.
PILATE	¶Now sure, we are served at all;
	This place is purchased full properly.
	The Field of Blood look ye it call,
	I command you now each one hereby.
CAYPHAS	¶Sir, as you command us we shall call it so.
	But, my lord, with your leave, we may linger no longer.
	But fast let us foot it to fasten on our foe;
	Yon gadling ungodly has brewed us great anger.
ANNAS	¶Away then, sir Bishop, and be not abashed,
	For lost is all our liking, if he leap on light.
CAYPHAS	¶Nay, sir, he shall not truss so fast, and that ye may
	trust;
	For they win us no worship, the works of that wight,
	But great anger.
	Wherefore let us address us, his death for to dight,
	And let we this lewd lad live here no longer.
PILATE	¶Sir Cayphas, through counsel command we our
	knights,

To watch on that warlock, What way he may go.
Address you now duly; That dodderer now dight,
And stay not to seek him In land high and low,
    Nor leave him not lightly.

2 KNIGHT ¶In faith, we shall fetch him Full far from his friends.

PILATE ¶Walk on then, with a vengeance, And wend your way
    lightly.

33

THE TYLLEMAKERS

LATER, MYLNERS, ROPERS, SEVEOURS, TURNOURS, HAYRESTERS, and BOLLERS

Jesus, Pilatus, Cayphas, Anna, sex milites tenentes hastas cum vexillis, et alii quatuor ducentes Jesum ab Herode, petentes Baraban dimitti et Jesum crucifigi, et ibidem ligantes et flagellantes eum, ponentes coronam spineam super caput eius; tres milites mittentes sortem super vestem Jesu.

PILATE ¶Lordings, that are limited to the law of my alliance,
Ye shapely soldiers all shining to show,
I charge you as your chieftain that ye chat for no chance,
But look to your lord here and learn at my law.
As a duke I may condemn you and draw;
Many bold bairns are about me;
And what knight or knave I may know,
That lists not as a lord for to lout me,
  I shall learn him
In the devil's name, that dastard, to fear me.
Yea, who works any works without me,
I shall charge him in chains to cheer him.
Therefore, my lusty lads within this land lapped,
Stint now stepping softly and stoutly be bearing.
The traitor with tales who his tongue has trapped,
That fiend for his flattery full foul shall be falling.
What brat over broadly is brawling,
Or unsoftly will say in these halls,
That caitiff thus crying and calling,
As a boy shall be brought into bales.
  Therefore,
Talk not nor treat not of tales.
That fellow that grins here or yells,

I myself shall hurt him full sore.

ANNAS ¶Ye shall set him full sore, what fool will unease you;
If he like not your lordship, that lad, shall ye make him,
As a peerless prince full promptly to please you,
Or as dreadful duke with dints shall ye take him.

CAYPHAS ¶Yea, in faith, ye have force for to fear him;
Through your manhood and might he is marred;
No chivalrous chieftain may cheer him,
For that churl, his comfort is hard
And wasted;
In pining pain is he barred.

ANNAS ¶Yea, and with scathe of skelps ill scarred,
From the time that your wrath he has tasted.

PILATE ¶Now sure, as meseems, who so seriously sought you,
Your praising is profitable, ye prelates of peace.
Gramercy for your good word; ungain shall it not you
That ye will say the sooth, and for no subject cease.

CAYPHAS ¶Else were it pity we appeared in this press.
But see how your knights come at hand.

ANNAS ¶Yea, my lord, that lovest no lies,
I can tell you, there betide some tidings
Full sad.

PILATE ¶See, they bring yon brat in a band.
We shall hear now hastily at hand
What unhap before Herod he had.

I KNIGHT ¶Hail, loveliest lord that ever law led yet;
Hail, seemliest sire on every side;
Hail, stateliest in stead in strength that is stead yet ;
Hail, liberal; hail, lusty, to lords allied!

PILATE ¶Welcome. What tidings this tide?
Let no language lightly now let you.

2 KNIGHT ¶Sir Herod (it is not to hide)
As his good friend with grace did he greet you,
For ever.
In what manner soe'er he may meet you,
By himself full soon will he set you.
And says that ye shall not dissever.

PILATE ¶I thank him full throughly, and say him the same.
But what marvellous matters did this minion there tell?

I KNIGHT ¶For all the lord's language his lips, sir, were lame,
For any asking in that space no speech would he spill,

But dumb as a door did he dwell.
Thus no fault in him did he find,
For his deeds to deem him to quell,
Nor in bands him bitterly to bind,
And thus
He sent him to yourself, and assigned
That we, your knights, should be cleanly inclined
And quick with him to you to truss.

PILATE   ¶Sirs, hearken, Hear ye not what we have upon hand?
Lo, how these knights speak who to the king fared.
Sir Herod, they say, no fault in me found;
He fastens me in friendship, so friendly he fared.
Moreover, he spake and not spared
Full gently to Jesus that Jew;
And then to these knights here declared
How faults in him found he but few
      To die.
He tested him, I tell you for true,
For to fright him he deemed undue;
And, sirs, so soothly say I.

CAYPHAS   ¶Sir Pilate our prince, we prelates now pray you,
Since Herod tried no further this false one to slay,
Receive in your hall these sayings I say you;
Bring him to the bar; at his beard we shall bay.

ANNAS   ¶Yea; for if we wend thus by wiles away,
I wot well he works us some wonder.
Our company he mars all he may;
With his sayings he sets them asunder
      In sin.
With his bluster he breeds many a blunder.
While ye have him, now hold him well under;
We shall curse him all way if he win.

CAYPHAS   ¶Sir, no time now to tarry this traitor to test;
Against Caesar himself he speaks and he says
All the wights in this world work in waste
That take him any tribute; thus his teaching bewrays.
Yet further he feigns such affrays,
And says that himself is God's son.
And, sir, our law alleges and lays
The felon in whom falsehood is found
      Should be slain.

PILATE   ¶For no shame him to slight will we shun.
ANNAS   ¶Sir, witness of these words may be won,
          That will tell this is true, and not feign.
CAYPHAS   ¶I can reckon a rabble of fellows full right,
          Of pert men in presence from this place ere I pass,
          That will witness, I warrant, the words of this wight,
          How wickedly wrought this wretch ever has . . .
          Simon, Yarus and Judas,
          Dathan and Gamaliell,
          Nephtalim, Levi and Lucas,
          And Amys these matters can tell
                    Together;
          These tales for true they can tell
          Of this liar that false is and fell
          And in alleging our laws full lither.
PILATE   ¶Ah tush for your tales! They touch not the intent.
          These witnesses, I warrant, that to witness ye wage,
          Some hatred in their hearts against him have lent,
          And purpose by this process to put down this page.
CAYPHAS   ¶Sir, in faith it befits us not false to allege.
          They are trusty and true men, we tell you.
PILATE   ¶Your swearing, sirs, swiftly assuage;
          Mix no more in these matters, I will you
                    And charge.
ANNAS   ¶Sir, despise not this speech that we spell you.
PILATE   ¶If ye feign such false frauds, I shall fell you,
          For I like not this language so large.
CAYPHAS   ¶Our language is large, unless you will relieve us.
          But we both beseech you, bring him to the bar.
          What points we put forth, let your presence approve us;
          You shall hear how he moves out of order afar.
PILATE   ¶Yea, but be wise, witty and wary.
ANNAS   ¶Sir, dread ye not, for nothing we fear him.
          Fetch him; he is not right far.
          Go, bedell; bestir thee about him.
BEADLE   ¶I am here,
          My lord, for to lead him or lout him,
          Unclothe him or clap him and clout him;
          If ye bid, I obedient appear.
          Sir knights, ye are commanded with this caitiff to care,
          And bring him to bar, for so my lord bade.

1 KNIGHT	¶Is this thy message?
BEADLE	Yea, sir.
1 KNIGHT	Then move you no more,
	For we are light for to leap and bring forth this lad.
2 KNIGHT	¶Now step forth; in strife thou'rt bested;
	Full ill, I uphold, has thee happed.
1 KNIGHT	¶O man, thy mind is full mad,
	In our clutch to be clouted and clapped
	And closed.
2 KNIGHT	¶Ye be lashed, slashed and lapped.
1 KNIGHT	¶Yea, routed, rushed and rapped.
	Thus thy name with annoy shall be noised.
2 KNIGHT	¶Lo, this fellow, my sovereign, for which same ye sent.
PILATE	¶Well, stir not from that stead, but stand still there.
	Lest he shape some shrewdness in shame be he shent,
	And I will try in faith to taste of his fare.
CAYPHAS	¶Out, out! Stand I may not, so I stare.
ANNAS	¶Ha, haro! for this traitor with pain.
PILATE	¶Say, fellows, why roar you so there?
	Are ye mad, or witless, I ween?
	What ails you?
CAYPHAS	¶Out! That such a sight should be seen.
ANNAS	¶Yea, alas! We are conquered clean
PILATE	¶What, are ye fond, or your force fails you?
CAYPHAS	¶Ah sir, saw ye not this sight, how the shafts shook,
	And the banners to this beggar they bowed all abroad?
ANNAS	¶Yea; those cursed knights by craft let them crook,
	To worship this warlock whom they have in ward.
PILATE	¶Was it truly done this, indeed?
CAYPHAS	¶Yea, yea, sir; ourselves we it saw.
PILATE	¶Bah, spit on them! Ill might they speed.
	Say, dastards—the devil with you go—
	How dare ye
	These banners that broadly should blow
	Let bow to this lurdan so low?
	False fellows, with falsehood how fare ye?
3 KNIGHT	¶We beseech you and the seniors who sit by your side,
	With none of our governance be grieved so ill;
	For it lay not in our lot these lances to guide,
	And this work that we wrought, it was not our will.
PILATE	¶Thou liest—hearest thou, lurdan?—full ill;

Well ye know it, if ye would admit.

4 KNIGHT ¶Sir, our strength might not steady them still;
They yielded for aught we could hold
With our might.

5 KNIGHT ¶For all our force, faith, did they fold,
As to worship this warlock they would,
And it seemed to us that was not right.

CAYPHAS ¶Ah, liars unloyal, full false is your fable;
This fellow has fooled you to trust to his tale.

6 KNIGHT ¶You may say what you will, but these staves to hold
stable
What fellow tries force, full foul shall he fail.

ANNAS ¶Thou art doggedly dastard, by the devil's nail.
Ah, henheart, ill hap may you have.

PILATE ¶For a whip how he whined and did wail;
Yet no lash to this lurdan he gave.
Foul fall you!

3 KNIGHT ¶Sir, no trickery we cause in this case.

CAYPHAS ¶Yet you sit here in shameless disgrace.
Now curst clumsy caitiffs, I call you.

4 KNIGHT ¶Since you like not, my lord, our language to love,
Bring in now the biggest men that bide in his land
Properly in your presence their power to prove,
And see if they yield when they have them in hand.

PILATE ¶Now ye fear most foully that ever I found;
Fie now on your faint hearts for fear.
Stir thee; no longer there stand,
Thou beadle; this bidword go bear
All around.
The strongest of all men of war
And the stoutest these standards to bear,
Hither blithely bid them to be bound.

BEADLE ¶My sovereign, full soon shall I serve thee, and so
I shall bring to these banners right big men and strong.
A company of knaves in this country I know
That are sturdy and stout, and to such will I go.
Say, ye lads both lusty and strong,
Ye must pass to Sir Pilate a pace.

I SOLDIER ¶If we work not his will it were wrong;
We are ready to run in a race
Strong and stark.

BEADLE ❡Then stay not, but step on apace,
And follow me fast to his face.

2 SOLDIER ❡Lead on now; we like well this lark.

BEADLE ❡Lord, here be the biggest bairns that bide in this bound,
Most stately and strong, if with strength they be strained.
Believe me, I lie not; to look this land round,
They're the mightiest men who have manhood attained.

PILATE ❡Wot you well, or else hast thou weened?

BEADLE ❡Sir, I wot well, without words more.

PILATE ❡In thy tale be not tainted nor feigned.

BEADLE ❡Why, no, sir; why should I be so?

PILATE   Well, then;
We shall test ere they travel us fro.
To what game they begin them to go,
Sir Cayphas, declare them you can.

CAYPHAS ❡Ye lusty lads, list as I bid you. Prepare;
Shape you to those shafts that shine there so plain.
If you bairns bow the breadth of a hair,
Ye are put to perpetual pain.

1 SOLDIER ❡I shall hold it as straight as a line.

ANNAS ❡Whoso shakes, shame on him depends.

2 SOLDIER ❡Aye, certain. I say as for mine,
When it settles or sadly descends
          Where I stand,
When it wavers or wrongly it wends,
Or bursts, breaks, or bends,
Why then, let them hack off my hand.

PILATE ❡Sirs, watch on these wights, that no wiles may be
    wrought.
They are burly and broad; their boasts they have blown.

ANNAS ❡To name that now, sir, it needs right nought;
For who cursedly quits him, it soon shall be known.

CAYPHAS ❡Yea, that dastard to death shall be drawn;
Whoso fails, he foully shall fall.

PILATE ❡Now, knights, since 'tis past the cockcrow,
Have him hence with haste from this hall
          His ways.
So, smartly step up to this stall;
Make cry, and carefully call,
Even as Sir Anna he says.

ANNAS ❡Oyez!

Jesus thou descendant of Duke Jacob's kin,
Thou ne'erthrive of Nazareth, now named is they name.
All men who accuse thee, we bid them come in,
And answer thine accusers; defend now thy fame.

BEADLE ¶ *Judicatur Jesus.*

CAYPHAS ¶Ha, out! What disgrace, to our shame.
This is wrested all wrong, as I ween.

ANNAS ¶For all their boast, these boys were to blame.

PILATE ¶Such a sight was never yet seen.
Come sit.
My comfort was caught from me clean.
Up I start; I might not abstain
To worship in work and in wit.

CAYPHAS ¶Much marvelled we both what moved you in mind
In reverence of this ribald so rudely to rise.

PILATE ¶I was past all my power, though I pained me and
pined;
I wrought not as I would, in no manner of wise.
Sirs, heed well my speech, I advise.
Quickly his ways let him wend.
Thus my doom will I duly devise.
For I fear, in faith, him to offend
By lights.

ANNAS ¶Then our laws were drawn to an end,
To his tales if you truly attend;
For by witchcraft he worked on these wights.

CAYPHAS ¶By his sorcery, sir—yourself the truth saw—
He charmed our chevaliers and myself enchanted.
To reverence him royally we rose all in a row;
Doubtless we endure not of this dastard to be daunted.

PILATE ¶Why, what harms has this noble here haunted?
I know to convict him no cause.

ANNAS ¶To all men he God's son him granted,
And lists not to live by our laws.

PILATE   Say, man,
Conceive you not what cumbersome clause
That this clergy accusing you knows?
Speak; excuse thyself, if thou can.

JESUS ¶Every man has a mouth that is made upon mould,
In weal and in woe to wield at his will.
If he govern it goodly, like as God would,

For his spiritual speech he needs not to spill;
And what man shall govern it ill,
Full unhandy and ill shall he hap.
For each tale unto us that you tell
You account shall; you cannot escape.

PILATE   Sirs mine,
Ye found, in faith, all his design;
For in this lad no lies can I trap,
Nor no point to put him to pine.

CAYPHAS ¶Without cause, sir, we come not, this churl to accuse
him;
That will we ye wit, as well is worthy.

PILATE ¶Now I record well the right; ye will no sooner refuse
him
Till he be driven to his death and doomed to die.
But take him to you thereby,
And like as your law will decide,
Doom ye his body to abide.

ANNAS ¶O Sir Pilate without any peer,
            Now nay;
Ye wot well (no doubt can appear)
We may not, not all of us here,
Slay no man, to you truth to say.

PILATE ¶Shall I doom him to death, not deserving in deed?
But I have heard wholly why in heart ye him hate.
He is faultless, in faith, and so God might me speed,
I grant him my good will to gang on his gate.

CAYPHAS ¶Not so, sir; for well ye it wot,
To be king he claimeth with crown.
Who so stoutly will step to that state,
You should doom, sir, to be set down
            And dead.

PILATE ¶Sir, truly that touches to treason,
And ere I remove he shall rue that reason,
Ere I stalk or stir from this stead.
Sir knights that are comely, take this caitiff in keeping;
Skelp him with scourges and scathe him full sore;
Wrest him and wring him till for woe he is weeping,
And then bring him before us as he was before.

I KNIGHT ¶He may ban the time that he was born;
Soon shall he be served as ye bade us.

ANNAS	¶Come, whip off his weeds that are worn.
2 KNIGHT	¶All ready, sir, we have arrayed us;
	Have done.
	For this brawler soon ready we have made us,
	As Sir Pilate has properly prayed us.
3 KNIGHT	¶We shall set to him seriously anon.
4 KNIGHT	¶Let us get off his gear, God give him ill grace.
I KNIGHT	¶They are stripped off soon, lo, take there his trashes.
3 KNIGHT	¶Now knit him in this cord.
2 KNIGHT	I am keen in this case.
4 KNIGHT	¶He is bound fast; now beat on with bitter brashes.
	Go on; leap, hear ye, lordings, with lashes;
	And enforce we this fellow to flay him.
2 KNIGHT	¶Let us drive to him dreadfully with dashes;
	All red with our rods we array him
	And rend him.
3 KNIGHT	¶For my part, I am prompt for to pay him.
4 KNIGHT	¶Yea, send him sorrow; assay him.
I KNIGHT	¶Take him till I have time to attend him.
2 KNIGHT	¶Swing to this pillar; too swiftly he sweats.
3 KNIGHT	¶Sweat may this swain for weight of our swaps.
4 KNIGHT	¶Rush on this ribald and rapidly revive.
I KNIGHT	¶Revive him I rede you, with routs and with raps.
2 KNIGHT	¶For all our annoying, this niggard he naps.
3 KNIGHT	¶We shall wake him with wind of our whips.
4 KNIGHT	¶Now fling to this flatterer with flaps.
I KNIGHT	¶I shall heartily hit on his hips
	And haunch.
2 KNIGHT	¶From our skelps not scatheless he skips.
3 KNIGHT	¶Yet list he not lift up his lips,
	And pray us have pity on his paunch.
4 KNIGHT	¶To have pity on his paunch he proffers no prayer.
I KNIGHT	¶Lord, how likest thou this lark, and this lore that we learn you?
2 KNIGHT	¶Lo, I pull at his pelt; I am a proud payer.
3 KNIGHT	¶Thus your cloak shall we clout, to cleanse you and clear you.
4 KNIGHT	¶I am strong in this strife for to stir you.
I KNIGHT	¶Thus with chops this churl shall we chastise.
2 KNIGHT	¶I trow with this trace we shall tear you.
3 KNIGHT	¶All thine untrue teachings thus taste I,

Fool arrant.

4 KNIGHT ❡I think I be hardy and hasty.

1 KNIGHT ❡I wot well my weapon not waste.

2 KNIGHT ❡He swoons or he faints soon, I warrant.

3 KNIGHT ❡Let us loose him lightly; come, lay on your hands.

4 KNIGHT ❡Yea; for if he die for this deed, undone are we all.

1 KNIGHT ❡Now unbound is this boy, and unbraced are his hands.

2 KNIGHT ❡O fool, how fares thou now, foul might thou fall?

3 KNIGHT ❡Now because he our king did him call,
We will kindly him crown with a briar.

4 KNIGHT ❡Yea, but first this purple and pall
And this worthy weed shall he wear,
For scorn.

1 KNIGHT ❡I am proud at this point to appear.

2 KNIGHT ❡Let us clothe him in these clothes all clear,
As a lord that his lordship has lorn.

3 KNIGHT ❡'Twill be long ere thou meet with such men as thou
met with this morn.

4 KNIGHT ❡Do set him in this seat, as a seemly in hall.

1 KNIGHT ❡Now press to him tightly with this thick thorn.

2 KNIGHT ❡Lo, it holds so to his head that the brains out fall.

3 KNIGHT ❡Thus we teach him to temper his tales;
His brain begins for to bleed.

4 KNIGHT ❡Yea, his blunders brought him to these bales.
Now reach him a rush or a reed
So round;
For his sceptre it serves indeed.

1 KNIGHT ❡Yea, it is good enough in this need.
Let us goodly him greet on this ground.
Ave, right royal, and Rex Judeorum!
Hail, comely king, that no kingdom has kenned.
Hail, duke doughty; thy deeds are dumb.
Hail, man unmighty thy means to mend.

3 KNIGHT ❡Hail, lord without land to command.
Hail, king; hail, fool feeble of hand.

4 KNIGHT ❡Hail, fool with no force to defend.
Hail, strong man that may not well stand
To strive.

1 KNIGHT ❡Ho, harlot; here, heave up thy hand,
And us all that in worship are working,
Thank us. And ill might thou thrive.

2 KNIGHT	¶So; let us lead him now lively, and linger no longer.
	To Sir Pilate the prince our pride will we praise.
3 KNIGHT	¶Yea; he may sing ere he sleep for sorrow and anger,
	For many dread deeds has he done in his days.
4 KNIGHT	¶Now lightly let us wend on our ways;
	Let's truss us; no time is to tarry.
I KNIGHT	¶My lord, will ye list to our lays?
	Here this boy is you bade us go harry
	With blows.
	We are cumbered his corse for to carry.
	Many wights on him wonder and worry.
	Lo, his flesh, how its beatings it shows.
PILATE	¶Well, bring him before us. Ah, he blushes all blue.
	I suppose of his saying he'll cease evermore.
	Sirs, look here on high and see: ECCE HOMO
	Thus beaten and bound and brought you before.
	Methinks that it suits him full sore;
	For his guilt on this ground he is grieved.
	. . . [*A leaf is lost here.*[1]]
	*And the measure that now I shall move,
	It may move you to mercy the more
	And grace.
	For to doom him to death I deplore;
	I would fain set him free from this place.
	Your custom hath been to let go
	Some felon to freedom this day.
Cayphas	¶Barabbas in prison lies low;
	At this feast now release him, we pray.
Pilate	¶A rebel still raging to slay?
	Would ye rather that I should release
	This Jesus?
All	Barabbas, we say.
Pilate	Will ye cease?
	None is heard, for each howleth so loud.
All	¶Not this man; Barabbas.
Pilate	Ho, peace!
	Ye clamour and call in a crowd.
	If this is your will so to be,
	For Jesus now what is your mind?

[1] *-*. The matter of this lost leaf is so essential to the action that I have attempted to supply the sense of the missing lines.—J. S. P.

His evil deeds done show to me,
For in him no fault can I find;
Good he ever hath done to mankind.

Cayphas ¶Away with him now; let him die.

Pilate ¶Shall I scourge him again, and unbind?

All ¶Nay; crucify him. Crucify.
If thou loose him, thou art not Caesar's friend.

Pilate ¶On you be his blood, then, say I.

Cayphas ¶On us be his blood. Make an end

All Crucify!

Pilate ¶Then since your will I may not bend,
All my part in his bloodshed I henceforth deny.★
For properly by this process I will prove
I had no force from this fellowship this man to defend.

BEADLE ¶Here is all, sir, for which you did send.
Will you wash while the water is hot?

Pilate ★¶Bear witness, all ye that are here.
From the guilt of his blood I am clear,
For innocent he.

Cayphas ¶On us that same blood without fear,
And our children to come, let it be.

All ¶On us and our sons let it be.★

PILATE ¶From Barabbas his bonds now unbend;
With grace let him gang on his gate
Where you will.

BARABBAS ¶Ye worthy men goodly and great,
God increase all your comely estate,
For the grace ye have granted me still.

PILATE ¶Hear the judgement of Jesus, all Jews in this stead.
Crucify him on a cross, and on Calvary him kill.
I condemn him this day to die this same death;
Therefore hang him on high upon that high hill.
And on either side of him I will
That a harlot ye hang in this haste;
Methinks it both reason and skill
That amidst, since his malice is most,
Ye hang him.
Then torment him, some torture to taste.
More words I will not now waste;
But stay not, to death till ye bring him.

CAYPHAS ¶Sir, it seems in our sight that is soberly said.

271

Now, knights that are cunning, with this caitiff go fare;
The life of this looseling at your liking is laid.

1 KNIGHT ¶Let us alone, lord, and learn us no more.
Sirs, set to him sadly and sore.
Let the cords round his body be cast.

2 KNIGHT ¶Let us bind him in bands all bare.

3 KNIGHT ¶Here is one; full long will it last.

4 KNIGHT ¶Lay on hands here.

5 KNIGHT ¶I pull till my power is past.
Now fast is he, fellows, full fast.
Let us stir us; we may not long stand here.

ANNAS ¶Draw him fast; hence deliver you; have done.
Go, see him to death without longer delay;
For dead must he needs be by noon.
All mirth must we move tomorrow that we may;
It is soothly our great Sabbath day.
No dead bodies unburied shall be.

6 KNIGHT ¶We see well the truth that ye say.
We shall trail him fast to his tree,
Thus talking.

4 KNIGHT ¶Farewell; now quickly wend we.

PILATE ¶Now sure, ye are a brave company.
Forth with a wild vengeance be walking.

34

THE SHERMEN

Jesus sanguine cruentatus portans crucem versus Calvariam.
Simon Sereneus, Judei angariantes eum ut tolleret crucem,
Maria mater Jesu, Johannes apostolus intimans tunc proxime
dampnacionem et transitum filii sui ad Calvariam, Veronica
tergens sanguinem et sudorem de facie Jesu cum flammeolo
in quo imprimitur facies Jesu, et alie mulieres lamentantes
Jesum.

I KNIGHT ¶Peace, bairns and bachelors that bide here about.
Stir not once in this stead, but stand stone still,
Or by the lord that I believe on, I shall make you lout.
If ye spare not when I speak, your speech shall I spill
     Smartly and soon.
For I am sent from Sir Pilate with pride,
To lead this lad our laws to abide;
He gets no better boon.
Therefore I command you on every side,
Upon pain of imprisonment no man appear
To support this traitor by time nor by tide,
Not one of this press,
Nor not once so hardily for to enquire,
But help me wholly, all that are here,
This caitiff's care to increase.
Therefore make room and rule you now right,
That we may with this wicked wight
Smartly wend on our way.
He has napped not in all this night,
And this day shall his death be dight;
Let's see who dare say nay.
Because tomorrow we provide
For our dear Sabbath day,
We will nought amiss be moved,
But mirth in all that ever men may.

We have been busy all this morn
To clothe him and to crown with thorn,
As fits a foolish king.
And now methinks our fellows scorn;
They promised to be here this morn,
This felon forth to bring.
To nap now is not good.
Hey, where? High might he hang!

2 KNIGHT ¶Peace, man, for Mahound's blood.
Why make ye such crying?

1 KNIGHT ¶Why, wot you not as well as I,
This churl must unto Calvary,
And there on cross be done?

2 KNIGHT ¶Since doom is given that he shall die,
Let's call to us more company,
Or else we are over few.

1 KNIGHT ¶Our gear must be arrayed,
And mates assembled soon;
For Sir Pilate has said,
He must be dead by noon.
Where is Sir Wymond, wotst thou ought?

2 KNIGHT ¶He went to make a cross be wrought,
To bear this cursed knave.

1 KNIGHT ¶That would I soon were hither brought,
For then shall other gear be sought
That it behoves to have.

2 KNIGHT ¶We must have steps and ropes,
To rive him till he rave;
And nails and other japes,
If we ourselves will save.

1 KNIGHT ¶To tarry long we are full loath.
But, Wymond, come! Or by my faith,
We shall be blamed all three.
Hallo, Sir Wymond! Waiting's scathe.

2 KNIGHT ¶Hallo, Sir Wymond, ho!

3 KNIGHT ¶I am here; what say ye both?
Why cry ye so on me?
For I have been to make
This cross, as ye may see,
Out of that wood beside the lake;
Men call it the king's tree.

1 KNIGHT   ¶Now certainly I thought the same;
For that baulk . . . no man will us blame
To cut it for a king.

2 KNIGHT   ¶This churl has called himself a king,
And since the tree has such a name,
It is a fitting thing
That his own back on it may rest,
For scorn and for mocking.

3 KNIGHT   ¶Methought it seemed best
This bargain for to bring.

1 KNIGHT   ¶It is good ware, so might I speed;
If it be true in length and broad,
Then is this space well spent.

3 KNIGHT   ¶To look for that there is no need;
I took the measure ere I sped,
Both for the feet and hands.

2 KNIGHT   ¶Behold how it is bored
Full even at either end.
This work will well accord;
We shall not need to mend.

3 KNIGHT   ¶Nay, but I have ordained much more;
Yea, and these thieves are sent before,
That beside him shall hang.
And steps also are ordained there,
With stalwart steels as mystery were,
Both some short and some long.

1 KNIGHT   ¶For hammers and for nails
Let's see who soon shall gang.

2 KNIGHT   ¶Here are brags that will not fail,
Of iron and steel full strong.

3 KNIGHT   ¶Then is it as it ought to be.
But which of you shall bear this tree,
Since I have brought it hither?

1 KNIGHT   ¶By my faith, bear it shall he
That thereon hanged soon shall be,
And we shall teach him whither.

2 KNIGHT   ¶Upon his back shall it be laid,
For soon we shall come thither.

3 KNIGHT   ¶Look that our gear be all arrayed,
And go we all together.

JOHN   ¶Alas for my master that most is of might,

275

That yestereven late with lantern light
Before the bishop was brought.
Both Peter and I, we saw that sight,
And then we went our ways hard plight,
When the Jews wickedly wrought.
At morn they made false faith,
And subtleties up sought,
And doomed him to the death
That to them trespassed nought.
Alas for shame! What shall I say?
My worldly weal is gone for aye;
In woe ever may I wend.
My lord, that kept the law alway,
Is doomed to die the death this day,
Even by his enemies' hand.
Alas, that now my master mild
That all men's miss may mend,
Should falsely be defiled,
And no friends to defend.
Alas, for his mother and others mo;
My mother and her sisters also
Sit all with sighing sore.
They wot nothing of all this woe;
Therefore to warn them will I go,
Since I may mend no more.
Since he so soon shall die,
If they unwarned were,
Then how blameworthy I;
I will go fast therefore.
But in mine heart great dread have I
That his mother for dole shall die,
When she sees once that sight.
But sure I shall not fail thereby
To warn that careful company,
Ere he to death be dight.
. . . [*A whole leaf is lost here.*]

? JOHN   ¶Since he from us will part,
          I shall thee ne'er forsake.
? MARY   ¶Alas, the time and tide!
          I wot the day is come
          That once was specified

By Prophet Simeon.
The sword of sorrow, he said, should run
Through this heart subtily.

2 MARY   ¶Alas, this is a pitiful sight!
He that was ever lovely and light,
And lord of high and low,
How dolefully now is he dight.
In world is none so woeful wight,
Nor so troubled to know.
They that he mended most,
In deed and word also,
Now have they full great haste
To death him for to draw.

JESUS   ¶Daughters of Jerusalem City,
See, and mourn no more for me,
But think upon this thing.
For yourselves mourn shall ye
And for sons that born shall be
Of you, both old and young.
For such fare shall befal
That ye shall give blessing
To barren bodies all,
That no bairns forth may bring.
For sure ye shall see such a day
That with sore sighing ye shall say
Unto the hills on height,
"Fall on us, mountains; fall down here,
And cover us from that fell fear
That on us soon shall light."
Turn home to town again,
Since ye have seen this sight;
It is my Father's will,
All that is done and dight.

3 MARY   ¶Alas, this is a cursed case.
He that all heal in his hand has
Shall here be blameless slain.
Ah lord, give leave to clean thy face. . . .
Behold! how he has shewed his grace,
He that is most of main.
This sign shall bear witness
Unto all people plain,

How God's Son here guiltless
Is put to peerless pain.

1 KNIGHT ❡Say, whereto bide ye here about,
Ye crones, with screaming and with shout?
What do these stevenings here?

2 KNIGHT ❡Go home, thou baldhead, with thy clout,
Or, by that lord we love and lout,
Thou shalt abide full dear.

3 MARY ❡This sign shall vengeance call
On you all that are here.

3 KNIGHT ❡Go, hie thee hence withal,
Or ill hail come thou here.

JOHN ❡Lady, your weeping grieves me sore.

MARY ❡John, help me now or nevermore,
That I to him might come.

JOHN ❡My lady, wend we on before,
To Calvary; when we come there,
You shall say what you will.

1 KNIGHT ❡What a devil is this to say?
How long shall we stand still?
Go, hie you hence away,
In the devil's name, down the hill.

2 KNIGHT ❡These queans so cumber us with their clack,
He shall be served for their sake
With sorrow and with sore.

3 KNIGHT ❡If they come more such noise to make,
We shall go lay them in the lake,
If they were half a score.

1 KNIGHT ❡Let now such boasting be,
Since our tools are before.
This traitor and this tree,
Would I full fain were there.

2 KNIGHT ❡We shall no more so still be stead,
For now those queans are from us fled
That falsely would us fear.

3 KNIGHT ❡Methinks this boy is so forbled,
With this load may he not be led;
He swoons, that dare I swear.

1 KNIGHT ❡It needs not hard to haul;
Such hurt we may now spare.

2 KNIGHT ❡I see here comes a churl

	'Shall help him forth to bear.
3 KNIGHT	¶That shall we see one soon essay.
	Good man, whither is thou away?
	You walk as if in wrath.
SIMON	¶Sir, I have a great journey,
	That must be done on this same day,
	Or else it may do scathe.
1 KNIGHT	¶Thou mayest with little pain
	Ease thyself and us both.
SIMON	¶Good sirs, that would I fain,
	But to dwell were I loath.
2 KNIGHT	¶Nay, fair sir, you shall soon be sped.
	Lo, here a lad that must be led
	For his ill deeds to die.
3 KNIGHT	¶And he is bruised and all forbled,
	That makes us here thus still bested.
	We pray thee, sir, thereby,
	That thou wilt take this tree,
	And bear it to Calvary.
SIMON	¶Good sirs, that may not be,
	For full great haste have I.
	My ways are long and wide,
	And I may not abide,
	For dread I come too late.
	For surety have I plight,
	Must be fulfilled this night,
	Or 'twill impair my state.
	Therefore, sir, by your leave,
	Methinks I dwell full long.
	I were loath you for to grieve,
	But, good sirs, let me gang;
	No longer here may I stay on.
1 KNIGHT	¶Nay, sure, thou shalt not go so soon,
	For ought that you can say.
	This deed has most haste to be done,
	For this boy must be dead by noon,
	And now 'tis near midday.
	Go, help him in his need,
	And make no more delay.
SIMON	¶I pray you, do your deed,
	And let me go my way.

And, sirs, I shall come soon again,
To help this man with all my main,
And even at your own will.

2 KNIGHT ¶What? Wouldst thou trick us so, and feign?
Nay, for thy shifts thou shalt be fain
This order to fulfil.
Or, by mighty Mahoun,
Thou shalt rue it full ill.
Let's ding the dastard down,
If he speeds not thereto.

SIMON ¶Sure, sir, that was not wisely wrought,
To beat me, though I trespassed nought,
Either in word or deed.

1 KNIGHT ¶Upon his back it shall be brought
To bear it, whether he will or not.
What the devil! Whom should we dread?
Go, take it up. Be alive,
And bear it with good speed.

SIMON ¶It helps not here to strive;
Bear it then must I need.
And therefore, sirs, as ye have said. . . .
To bear this cross I hold me glad,
Right as ye would it were.

2 KNIGHT ¶Yea, now are we right well arrayed;
Look that our gear be ready made,
To work when we come there.

3 KNIGHT ¶I warrant all ready,
Our tools both less and more.
Let him go hardily
Forth with the cross before.

1 KNIGHT ¶Since he has his load, now let him gang;
For with this warlock work we wrong,
If we thus with him hied.

2 KNIGHT ¶Now is not good to tarry long.
What should we do more us among;
Say, son, So might thou speed.

3 KNIGHT ¶Name us none other need,
Till we have done this deed.

1 KNIGHT ¶Ay me!
Methinks our wits do doting speed;
He must be naked now indeed.

Although he call himself a king,
In all his clothes he shall not hang,
But naked as a stone be stead.

2 KNIGHT ¶That call I a full fitting thing.
But to his sides I trow they cling,
For blood that he has bled.

3 KNIGHT ¶Whether they cling or cleave,
Naked shall he be led;
And for the more mischief,
He shall be buffeted.

1 KNIGHT ¶Take off his clothes at once; let's see.
Aha!
This garment will fall well for me,
And so I think it shall.

2 KNIGHT ¶Nay, nay, sir; so may it not be.
They must be parted among us three;
Take even as shall fall.

3 KNIGHT ¶Yea; if Sir Pilate meddle him,
Your part will be but small.

1 KNIGHT ¶Sir, if ye list, go tell him;
Yet shall he not have all,
But even his own part and no more.

2 KNIGHT ¶Yea, let them lie still there in store,
Until this deed be done.

3 KNIGHT ¶Let's bind him as he was before,
And heave on hard, that he were there
And hanged ere it be noon.

1 KNIGHT ¶He shall be fast of fee,
And that right sore and soon.

2 KNIGHT ¶So it befals him for to be;
He gets no better boon.

3 KNIGHT ¶This work is well now, I warrant;
For he is bound as beast in band
That is doomed for to die.

1 KNIGHT ¶Then let us here no longer stand,
But each man fasten on a hand,
And heave him hence on high.

2 KNIGHT ¶Yea, now is time to truss,
To all our company.

3 KNIGHT ¶If any ask after us,
Call them to Calvary.

35

THE PYNNERS, LATONERS, PAYNTOURS

Crux, Jesus extensus in ea super terram; iiii Judei flagellantes et trahentes eum cum funibus, et postea exaltantes crucem et corpus Jesu cruci conclavatum super montem Calvarie.

1 KNIGHT   ¶Sir knights, take heed hither on high.
This deed untroubled we may not draw;
Ye wot yourselves as well as I
How lords and leaders of our law
Have given doom that this dolt shall die.

2 KNIGHT   ¶Sir, all their counsel well we know.
Since we are come to Calvary,
Let each man help as he did owe.

3 KNIGHT   ¶We are all ready, lo,
That order to fulfil.

4 KNIGHT   ¶Let's hear how we shall do,
And go to it with a will.

1 KNIGHT   ¶It may not help here to hang on,
If we will any worship win.

2 KNIGHT   ¶He must be dead—needs must—by noon.

3 KNIGHT   ¶Then is good time that we begin.

4 KNIGHT   ¶Let's ding him down; then is he done;
He shall not daunt us with his din.

1 KNIGHT   ¶He shall be set and taught full soon,
With grief to him and all his kin.

2 KNIGHT   ¶The foulest death of all
Shall he die for his deeds.

3 KNIGHT   ¶That means, cross him we shall.

4 KNIGHT   ¶Behold, how right he redes.

1 KNIGHT   ¶Then to this work we must take heed,
So that our working be not long.

2 KNIGHT   ¶None other task to name is need,
                  But let us haste him for to hang.

3 KNIGHT   ¶And I have gone for gear, good speed,
                  Both hammers and nails full large and long.

4 KNIGHT   ¶Then may we boldly do this deed;
                  Come on, let's kill this traitor strong.

1 KNIGHT   ¶Fair might befall your turn,
                  That has wrought on this wise.

2 KNIGHT   ¶We need not for to learn
                  Such caitiffs to chastise.

3 KNIGHT   ¶Since everything is right arrayed,
                  The wiselier now work may we.

4 KNIGHT   ¶The cross on ground is ready spread,
                  And bored even as it ought to be.

1 KNIGHT   ¶Look that this lad along be laid,
                  And made even unto this tree.

2 KNIGHT   ¶For all his force he shall be afraid;
                  That to essay soon shall ye see.

3 KNIGHT   ¶Come forth, thou cursed knave;
                  The comfort soon shall cool.

4 KNIGHT   ¶Thine hire soon shall thou have.

1 KNIGHT   ¶Walk on; now work we well.

JESUS   ¶Almighty God, my Father free,
                  Let these matters be made in mind.
                  Thou badest I should obedient be,
                  For Adam's plight for to be pined.
                  Here to the death I have bound me,
                  From that sin for to save mankind,
                  And sovereignly beseech I thee
                  That they for me may favour find.
                  From the fiend them defend,
                  So that their souls be safe
                  In wealth without an end;
                  I have nought else to crave.

1 KNIGHT   ¶Ha, hark, sir knights. For Mahound's blood!
                  Of Adam's kind is all his thought.

2 KNIGHT   ¶This warlock waxes worse than mad;
                  This doleful death he dreadeth nought.

3 KNIGHT   ¶Thou shouldest have mind, with main and mood,
                  Of wicked works that thou hast wrought.

4 KNIGHT   ¶I thought that he had been as good

As cease of sayings that he upsought.

1 KNIGHT   ¶These sayings shall rue him sore,
For all his sauntering, soon.

2 KNIGHT   ¶Ill speed them that him spare,
Till he to death be done.

3 KNIGHT   ¶Have done in haste, boy; make ready anon,
And bend thy back unto this tree.

4 KNIGHT   ¶Behold, himself has laid him down
In length and breadth as he should be.

1 KNIGHT   ¶This traitor here attainted of treason,
Go fast and fix him then, ye three.
And since he claimeth kingdom with crown,
Even as a king here have it shall he.

2 KNIGHT   ¶Now sure, I shall not feign,
Ere his right hand be fast.

3 KNIGHT   ¶The left hand, then, is mine;
Let's see who bears him best.

4 KNIGHT   ¶His limbs along then shall I lead,
And even unto the bore them bring.

1 KNIGHT   ¶Unto his head shall I take heed,
And with mine hand help him to hang.

2 KNIGHT   ¶Now since we four shall do this deed,
And meddle with this unthrifty thing,
Let no man spare for special speed,
Till we have made a full ending.

3 KNIGHT   ¶This order may not fail;
Now are we right arrayed.

4 KNIGHT   ¶This boy here in our bail
Shall bide full bitter trade.

1 KNIGHT   ¶Sir knights, say here . . . how work we now?

2 KNIGHT   ¶Why sure, I think I hold this hand.

3 KNIGHT   ¶And to the bore I have it brought
Full fittingly without a band.

4 KNIGHT   ¶Strike on, then, hard, for him thee bought.

1 KNIGHT   ¶Yes, here's a stub will stiffly stand;
Through bones and sinews it shall be sought.
This work is well, I will warrant.

2 KNIGHT   ¶Say, sir, how do we there?
This bargain will we win.

3 KNIGHT   ¶It fails a foot or more;
The sinews are so gone in.

4 KNIGHT	¶I think that mark amiss be bored.
2 KNIGHT	¶Then must he bide in bitter bale.
3 KNIGHT	¶In faith, it was over scantly scored,
	That makes it foully for to fail.
1 KNIGHT	¶Why chat ye so? Fasten on a cord,
	And tug him to, by top and tail.
3 KNIGHT	¶Thou commands lightly as a lord;
	Come help to haul, with an ill hail.
1 KNIGHT	¶Now certes that shall I do,
	Full surely as a snail.
3 KNIGHT	¶And I shall attach him too,
	Full nimbly with a nail.
	This work will hold; it is complete;
	Fastened now fast are both his hands.
4 KNIGHT	¶Go we all four then to his feet;
	So shall our space be speedily spent.
2 KNIGHT	¶Let's see what jest his bale might beat;
	Thereto my back now would I bend.
4 KNIGHT	¶Out, out! This work is all unmeet;
	This boring all must we amend.
1 KNIGHT	¶Ah, peace, man, for Mahound!
	Let no man know that wonder.
	A rope shall rive him down,
	Though all sinews go asunder.
2 KNIGHT	¶That cord full kindly can I knit,
	The comfort of this churl to cool.
1 KNIGHT	¶Fasten on then fast all that be fit;
	It has no force how fell he feel.
2 KNIGHT	¶Lug on ye both a little yet.
3 KNIGHT	¶I shall not cease, as I do well.
4 KNIGHT	¶And I shall try him for to hit.
2 KNIGHT	¶Out hail!
4 KNIGHT	How now? I hold it well.
1 KNIGHT	¶Have done. Drive in that nail,
	So that no fault be found.
4 KNIGHT	¶This working would not fail,
	If four bulls here were bound.
1 KNIGHT	¶These cords have evil increased his pains,
.	Ere he was to the borings brought.
2 KNIGHT	¶Yea. Asunder are both sinews and veins
	On every side; so have we sought.

3 KNIGHT	¶Now all his gauds nothing him gains.
	His sauntering shall with bale be bought.
4 KNIGHT	¶I will go say to our sovereigns
	Of all these works how we have wrought.
1 KNIGHT	¶Nay, sirs; another thing
	Falls first to you and me.
	I bade we should him hang
	On height that men might see.
2 KNIGHT	¶We wot well that so these words were;
	But, sir, that deed will hurt us dear.
1 KNIGHT	¶It may not mend to moot it more;
	This harlot must be hangèd here.
2 KNIGHT	¶The mortice is made fit therefor.
3 KNIGHT	¶Fasten on your fingers, then, all here.
4 KNIGHT	¶I ween it will never come there;
	We four can't raise it right, this gear.
1 KNIGHT	¶Say, man, why chatter so?
	Thy lifting was but light.
2 KNIGHT	¶He means there must be mo,
	To heave him up on height.
3 KNIGHT	¶Now, sure, I think it shall not need
	To call to us more company.
	Methinks we four should do this deed,
	And bear him to yon hill on high.
1 KNIGHT	¶It must be done, no doubt indeed.
	No more, but look ye be ready;
	And this part shall I lift and lead.
	At length shall he no longer lie.
	Therefore how all prepare;
	Let's bear him to yon hill.
4 KNIGHT	¶Then down here will I bear;
	Attend to his toes I will.
2 KNIGHT	¶We two shall see to either side,
	For else this work will wry all wrong.
	We are ready.
3 KNIGHT	¶In God, sirs, abide,
	And let me hoist his feet along.
2 KNIGHT	¶Why attend ye so to tales this tide?
1 KNIGHT	¶Lift up!
4 KNIGHT	Let's see.
2 KNIGHT	Oh! Lift along.

3 KNIGHT ⁋From all this harm he should him hide,
If he were God.

4 KNIGHT The devil him hang.

1 KNIGHT ⁋With great pain am I pent;
My shoulder is in sunder.

2 KNIGHT ⁋And sure, I am near spent,
So long have I borne under.

3 KNIGHT ⁋This cross and I in two must twin,
Else breaks my back in sunder soon.

4 KNIGHT ⁋Lay it down again, and leave your din;
This deed for us will never be done.

1 KNIGHT ⁋Essay, sirs; see if any gin
May help up, and delay be done.
Here active man might worship win,
And not with gauds all day be gone.

2 KNIGHT ⁋More active men than we
Full few I think ye'll find.

3 KNIGHT ⁋This bargain will not be,
For surely I want wind.

4 KNIGHT ⁋So at a loss never we were;
I think this churl some craft has cast.

2 KNIGHT ⁋My burden sets me wondrous sore;
Unto the hill I may not last.

1 KNIGHT ⁋Lift up, and soon he shall be there;
Then fasten on your fingers fast.

3 KNIGHT ⁋Now, lift!

1 KNIGHT Ha, lo!

4 KNIGHT A little more.

2 KNIGHT ⁋Hold, then.

1 KNIGHT How now?

2 KNIGHT The worst is past.

3 KNIGHT ⁋He weighs a wicked weight.

2 KNIGHT ⁋So may we all four say,
Ere he was heaved on height
And raised in this array.

4 KNIGHT ⁋He made us stand like any stones,
So hugely big was he to bear.

1 KNIGHT ⁋Now raise him nimbly for the nonce,
And set him by the mortice here,
And let him fall in all at once.
For sure that pain shall have no peer.

3 KNIGHT ¶Heave up!

4 KNIGHT   Let down, so all his bones
Asunder now on all sides tear.

1 KNIGHT ¶This falling was more fell
Than all the harms he had.
Now well may all men tell
The least bone of this lad.

3 KNIGHT ¶Methinks this cross will not abide,
Nor stand still in this mortise yet.

4 KNIGHT ¶At first was it made over wide;
That makes it wave, thou mayest well wit.

1 KNIGHT ¶It shall be set on every side,
So that it shall no further flit.
Good wedges shall we take this tide,
And fasten the foot; then is all fit.

2 KNIGHT ¶Here are wedges arrayed
For that, both great and small.

3 KNIGHT ¶Where are our hammers laid,
That we should work withal?

4 KNIGHT ¶We have them here, even at our hand.

2 KNIGHT ¶Give me this wedge; I shall it drive.

4 KNIGHT ¶Here is another yet ordained.

3 KNIGHT ¶Bring it me hither; be alive.

1 KNIGHT ¶Lay on, then, fast.

3 KNIGHT   Yes, I warrant.
I drive them all, so might I thrive.
Now will this cross full stably stand;
Although he rave, they will not rive.

1 KNIGHT ¶Say, sir, how like you now
This work that we have wrought?

4 KNIGHT ¶We pray you, tell us how
You feel, or faint you ought?

JESUS ¶All men that walk by way or street,
Take heed ye shall no travail miss.
Behold my head, my hands, my feet,
And fully feel, ere ending is,
If any mourning may be mete
Or mischief measured unto mine.
My Father, that all wrongs may right,
Forgive these men that do me pine;
For what they work that know they not.

Therefore, Father, I crave,
Let not their sins be sought,
But see their souls to save.

1 KNIGHT ¶Ha, hark! He jangles like a jay.

2 KNIGHT ¶Methinks he patters like a pie.

3 KNIGHT ¶He has been doing all this day,
And made great moving of mercy.

4 KNIGHT ¶Is this the same that we heard say
That he was God's son almighty?

1 KNIGHT ¶Therefore he feels full fell affray,
And he is doomed this day to die.

2 KNIGHT ¶Vah, qui destruis templum!

3 KNIGHT ¶His sayings were so, certain.

4 KNIGHT ¶And, sirs, he said to some
He might raise it again.

1 KNIGHT ¶To muster that he had no might,
For all the tricks that he could cast;
Although in words a witty wight,
For all his force now is he fast.

1 KNIGHT ¶As Pilate doomed is done and dight;
Therefore I reckon that we go rest.

2 KNIGHT ¶This race must be rehearsed right
Throughout the world both East and West.

3 KNIGHT ¶Yea. Let him hang there still,
And make mows at the moon.

4 KNIGHT ¶Then may we wend at will.

1 KNIGHT ¶Nay, good sirs, not so soon.
Agreement now must needs be got;
This kirtle would I of you crave.

2 KNIGHT ¶Nay, nay, sir; we will look by lot,
Which of us four falls it to have.

3 KNIGHT ¶I rede we draw cuts for this coat;
Lo, see how soon all sides to save.

4 KNIGHT ¶The short cut wins, that well ye wot,
Whether it falls to knight or knave.

1 KNIGHT ¶Fellows, ye need not take offence;
This mantle is my gain.

2 KNIGHT ¶Then quick let us go hence;
This travail is in vain.

36

THE BUTCHERS

Crux, duo latrones crucifixi, Jesus suspensus in cruce inter eos, Maria mater Jesu, Johannes, Maria, Jacobus et Salome, Longeus cum lancea, servus cum spongea, Pilatus, Anna, Cayphas, Centurio, Josep [ab Arimathia] et Nichodemus, deponentes eum in sepulcro.

PILATE ¶See, seignors, and see what I say;
Take tent to my talking entire.
Avoid all this din here this day,
And fall to my friendship all here.
Sir Pilate, a prince without peer
My name is full fitly to call,
And doomsman full worthy of fear
Of most gentle Jewry of all
      Am I.
Who makes oppression
Or does transgression,
By my discretion
Shall be doomed duly to die.
To die shall I doom them indeed,
Those rebels that rule them unright.
Whoso to yon hill will take heed
May see there the sooth in his sight,
How doleful to death they are dight
That list not our laws for to hear.
Lo, thus by my main and my might
The churls shall I chastise and cheer
      By law.
Each felon false gang
By neck shall hang;
Transgressors all
On the cross shall be knit for to know.

To know shall I knit them on cross;
To spoil them with shame shall I shape.
Their lives for to lose is no loss,
Such tyrants with trouble to trap.
Thus loyally the law I unlap,
And punish them piteously
Of Jesus I hold it ill hap
That he on yon hill hang so high,
   For guilt.
 His blood to spill
 Ye took him still;
 Thus was your will,
So spiteful your speed he were spilt.

CAYPHAS ¶To spill him we spake in a speed,
For falsehood he followed all way;
With frauds all our folk did he feed,
And laboured to learn them his law.

ANNAS ¶Sir Pilate, of peace we you pray;
Our law was full like to be lorn.
He saved not our dear Sabbath day.
For that to escape were a scorn,
   By law.

PILATE ¶Sir, before your sight
 With all my might
 I examined him right.
And no cause in him could I know.

CAYPHAS ¶Ye know well the cause in the case,
It touched unto treason untrue.
The tribute to take or to trace
Forbade he, our bale for to brew.

ANNAS ¶Of japes yet he jangled, yon Jew,
And cursedly called him a king.
To doom him to death it were due,
For treason it touches, that thing,
   Indeed.

CAYPHAS ¶Yet principal
 And worst of all
 He made them call
Him God's son—so, foul might he speed.

PILATE ¶He speeds for to spill in a space,
So wrought is your will and your way.

His blood shall your bodies embrace,
For that ye have taken to you.

ANNAS ¶That fortune full fain to fulfil
Indeed shall we dress us in haste.
That losel, he likes it full ill,
For turned all his tricks are to waste,
    I trow.

CAYPHAS ¶He called him king—
Ill joy him wring!
Yea, let him hang,
Full madly on the moon to mow.

ANNAS ¶To mow the moon has he meant.
Ha, fie on thee, false one and fey!
Who trusted thee, let him take tent.
Thou braggart, thyself thou didst say
The temple destroy you today.
By the third day were done every deal,
To raise it you should array. . . .
Lo, how was thy falsehood to feel,
    Foul befall thee!
For thy presumption
Thou hast thy last guerdon.
Do fast now come down,
And a comely king shall I call thee.

CAYPHAS ¶I call thee a coward to ken,
That marvels and miracles made.
You mustered among many men,
But, brawler, you boasted too broad.
You saved them from sorrows, they said;
To save now thyself let us see.
God's son if thou surely be made,
Deliver thee down from that tree
    Anon.
If thou be found
To be God's son
We shall be bound
To trust in thee truly each one.

ANNAS ¶Sir Pilate, your pleasure we pray;
Take tent to our talking this tide,
And wipe you yon writing away;
It is not best that it abide.

It becomes you to set it aside,
And set that he said in his saw,
As he that was print-full of pride,
"The Jews' King am I, comely to know,"
Full plain.

PILATE ¶*Quod scripsi, scripsi.*
Yon same wrote I;
I bide thereby,
Whoever may grudge there again.

JESUS ¶Thou man that amiss here has meant,
To me tent entirely now take
On the rood am I ragged and rent,
Thou sinful of soul, for thy sake.
For thy misdeed amends will I make;
I bide here, my back to bend low.
This woe for thy trespass I take
Who could thee more kindliness show
Than I?
Thus for thy good
I shed my blood.
Man, mend thy mood
For full bitter thy bliss must I buy.

MARY ¶Alas for my sweet son, I say,
That doleful to death here is dight.
Alas, for full lovely he lay
In my womb, this most wonderful wight.
Alas, that this blossom so bright
Untruly is tugged to this tree.
Alas!
My lord, my life,
With full great grief
Hangs as a thief.
Alas, he did never trespass.

JESUS ¶Thou woman, no more weep; be still;
For me may thou nothing amend.
To work out my Father's good will,
For all mankind my body I bend.

MARY ¶Alas, that thou mayest not stay.
How should I not weep for thy woe?
Grief takes all my comfort away.

Alas, must we part us in two
    For ever?

JESUS   ¶Woman, instead of me,
Lo, John thy son shall be.
John, see to thy mother free;
For my sake do thy devoir.

MARY   ¶Alas, son! I sorrow on height
Would that I were closed in clay,
A sword of such sorrow doth smite.
The death might I die this day.

JOHN   ¶Ah, mother, so shall you not say.
I pray you, even here be at peace.
For with all the might that I may
Your comfort I cast to increase
    Indeed.

Your son am I,
Lo, here ready
And now thereby
I pray you hence for to speed.

MARY   ¶My cry for to cease, or to stir,
How can I, such sight when I see?
My son, that is worthy and dear,
Thus doleful a death for to die.

JOHN   ¶Ah mother dear, cease this misery.
Your mourning, it may not amend.

MARY CLEOPAS   ¶Ah Mary, take trust unto me,
For succour to thee will he send
    This tide.

JOHN   ¶Fair mother, fast
Hence let us cast.

MARY   ¶Till he be passed
Will I be here near him to bide.

JESUS   ¶With bitterest bale have I bought
Thus, man, thy misdeeds to amend.
On me for to look stay thou not
How humbly my body I bend.
No wight in this wide world would ween
What sorrow I suffer for thy sake.
Man, my care for thy kind to be seen,
True tent unto me shalt thou take,
    And trust.

For foxes their dens have they,
Birds have their nests so gay,
But the Son of Man this day
Has not where his head he may rest.

THIEF ON LEFT ¶If thou be God's son so free,
Why hangest thou thus on this hill?
To save now thyself let us see,
And us, that speed so to spill.

THIEF ON RIGHT ¶Man, stint of thy sound and be still,
For doubtless thy God dreadest thou not.
Full well are we worthy of ill;
Unwisely much wrong have we wrought,
I wis.
No ill did he,
Thus for to die.
Lord, have mind of me,
When thou art come to thy bliss.

JESUS ¶Forsooth, son, to thee shall I say,
Since thou from thy folly wilt fall,
With me shalt thou dwell now this day
In paradise place principal.
Heloy! Heloy!
My God, my God full free,
Lama Sabatanye,
Wherefore forsook thou me
In care?
And I did never ill,
This death for to endure—
But be it at thy will.
Ah! I thirst sore.

BOY ¶A drink shall I dress thee indeed,
A draught that is daintily dight.
Full fast shall I spring for to speed,
I hope I shall hold what I plight.

CAYPHAS ¶Sir Pilate that most is of might,
Hark! "Hely", I now heard him cry.
He looks for that worthiest wight,
In haste for to help him on high
In his need.

PILATE ¶If he do so,
He shall have woe.

ANNAS ❡He were our foe
If he dress him to do us that deed.

BOY ❡That deed for to dress if he do,
For sure he shall rue it full sore.
Ne'ertheless, if he like it not, lo,
Full soon may he cover that care.
Now, sweet sir, your will if it were,
A draught here of drink have I dressed.
No need for expense that ye spare
But boldly bib it for the best.
For why?
Vinegar and gall
Are mixed withal.
Drink it ye shall.
Your lips, I hold them full dry.

JESUS ❡Thy drink, it shall do me no harm;
Know well, I will take of it none.
Now, Father who all things didst form,
To thy most might I make me my moan.
Thy will have I wrought all alone,
Thus ragged and rent on this rood.
Thus doleful to death am I done.
Forgive them, by grace that is good;
They knew not what it was.
My Father, hear my boon
For now all things are done.
My spirit to thee right soon
Commend I, *IN MANUS TUAS.*

MARY ❡Now, dear son Jesus so gentle,
Since my heart is as heavy as lead,
One word would I wit ere you went. . . .
Alas! Now my dear son is dead,
Full ruefully rent and forspent.
Alas, for my darling so dear!

JOHN ❡Ah, mother, now hold up thy head,
And sigh not with sorrows severe,
I pray.

MARY CLEOPAS ❡It grieves her heart
To see him part.
Hence let us start.
This mourning no help can convey.

CAYPHAS ¶Sir Pilate, perceive you, I pray;
Our customs to keep well ye can.
Tomorrow is our dear Sabbath day;
Of mirth must we move every man.
These warlocks are waxen full wan,
And needs now they buried be.
Deliver those dead, sir, and then
Shall we go to our solemnity
Indeed.

PILATE ¶That shall I do
In words full few.
Sir knights, go to;
To yon harlots now handily take heed.
Those caitiffs, kill them with the knife.
Deliver; have done; see them dead.

KNIGHT ¶My lord, I shall lengthen their life,
So that none of them more shall bite bread.

PILATE ¶Sir Longeus, step forth in this stead;
This spear, lo, hold here in thy hand.
To Jesus now set forth with speed,
And stay not till stiffly thou stand.
In Jesus' side
Shove it this tide.
No longer bide,
But go thou directly at hand.

LONGEUS ¶O maker unmade, full of might,
O Jesus so gentle and kind,
That sudden has sent me my sight—
Lord, loving to thee be assigned.
On rood thou art ragged and rent,
Mankind to amend when amiss.
Full spitefully spilt is and spent
Thy blood, Lord, to bring us to bliss
Full free.
Ah mercy, my succour;
Mercy, my treasure;
Mercy, my Saviour.
Thy mercy be marked in me.

CENTURION ¶O wonderful worker, I wis.
The weather is waxed full wan.
True token I trow that it is,

That mercy is meant unto man.
No cause in this case could they know,
That dolefully doomed him amain,
To lose thus his life by their law
      Unright.
Truly I say,
God's very son
Was he this day,
That doleful to death thus is dight.

JOSEPH OF ARIMATHEA ¶That true lord aye lasting in land,
Sir Pilate, now present in press,
May He save you by sea and by sand,
And all that are duly on dais.

PILATE ¶Joseph—this is truly no lies—
To me art thou welcome, I wis.
Now tell me the truth ere thou cease,
Thy worthy good will what it is,
      Anon.

JOSEPH ¶To thee I pray,
Give me today
Jesus' body
Under favour to bury it alone.

PILATE ¶Sir Joseph, I grant thee that gest.
I grudge not to get him in grave.
Deliver: have done he were dressed;
And seek, sir, our Sabbath to save.

JOSEPH ¶With hands and with heart that I have,
I thank thee in faith for my friend.
God keep thee, thy comfort to crave,
For swiftly my way will I wend
      On high.
To do that deed,
He be my speed
Whose arms were spread,
Mankind by his blood for to buy.

NICHODEMUS ¶Well met, sir. I moved in my thought
For Jesus that judged was amiss.
For licence you laboured and sought
To bury his body from rood.

JOSEPH ¶Full mildly that matter I would,
And that for to do will I dress.

NICHODEMUS ¶Together I would that we went,
And stay not for more nor for less.
For why?
Our friend was he,
Faithful and free.

JOSEPH ¶Therefore go we,
To bury that body on high.
Let each man now mark in his mind,
To see here this sorrowful sight
No falseness in him could they find,
That doleful to death thus is dight.

NICHODEMUS ¶He was aye a full worthy wight,
Now blemished and bloody and bruised.

JOSEPH ¶Yea, since that he showed not his might,
Full falsely our friend they abused,
I ween.
Both back and side,
His wounds are wide;
Therefore this tide
Take we now him down, us between.

NICHODEMUS ¶Between us now take we him down,
And lay him by length on this land.

JOSEPH ¶This reverend and rich of renown,
Let us hold him and lift him with hand.
A grave have I late here ordained,
That never was in need; 'tis new.

NICHODEMUS ¶To this corpse it is comely consigned,
To dress him with deeds full due,
This day.

JOSEPH ¶A sudary,
Lo, here have I;
Wind him thereby
And soon shall we grave him, I say.

NICHODEMUS ¶In ground let us grave him, and go;
Come, swift let us lay him alone.
Now, Saviour of me and of mo,
Keep us here in cleanness each gone.

JOSEPH ¶To thy mercy now make I my moan
As Saviour by sea and by sand;
So guide me that grief be all gone,
To live long and true in this land

At ease.

NICHODEMUS ¶Rich ointments have I
Brought for this fair body.
I anoint thee thereby
With myrrh and aloes.

JOSEPH ¶This deed, it is done every deal,
And well wrought this work is, I wis.
To thee, King, on knees here I kneel,
That closely thou keep me in bliss.

NICHODEMUS ¶He called me full clear to be his,
One night when I nighed him full near.
Have mind, Lord, and mend where I miss.
For done are our deeds here full dear,
This tide.

JOSEPH ¶This lord so good
That shed his blood,
Mend he your mood,
And bring in his bliss to abide.

37

THE SADDLERS

Jesus spolians infernum, xij spiritus, vi boni et vi mali.

JESUS ¶Man on mould, be meek to me,
And have thy maker in thy mind,
And think how I have borne for thee,
With peerless pains for to be pined.
The promise of my Father free
Have I fulfilled, as folk may find.
Therefore about now will I be
Those I have bought for to unbind.
The fiend with fraud did gain
Through fruit of earthly food;
I have them gotten again
Through buying with my blood.
And so I shall that state restore
From which the fiend fell for sin;
There shall mankind dwell evermore.
In bliss that never shall decline.
All that in work my workmen were,
Out of their woe I will them win,
And some sign shall I send before
Of grace to make their games begin.
A light I will they have,
To shew I shall come soon.
My body bides in grave
'Till all these deeds be done.
My Father ordained on this wise,
After his will that I should wend
For to fulfil the prophecies,
And I as spake my solace to spend.
My friends that on me in faith relies
Now from their foes I shall defend,

And on the third day right uprise,
And so to heaven I shall ascend.
Then shall I come again,
To judge both good and ill,
To endless joy or pain;
Thus is my Father's will.

ADAM ¶My brethren, hearken to me here.
Such hope of health we never had.
Four thousand and six hundred year
Have we been held here in this stead.
Now see I sign of solace clear,
A glorious gleam to make us glad;
Wherefore I hope our health is near,
And soon shall cease our sorrows sad.

EVA ¶Adam, my husband free,
This means solace certain;
Such light shall on us be
In Paradise full plain.

ISAIAH ¶Adam, we shall well understand.
I, Ysasias, whom God did send,
I preached in Nepthalim's fair land
And Zabulon even to my end.
I spake of folk in darkness set,
And said a light should on them land.
Thus learned I then while living yet,
Now see I God the same did send;
This light comes all of Christ,
That seed to save us now.
Thus is my point published;
But Symeon, what sayest thou?

SYMEON ¶Yes; my tale of wonders now I tell,
For in this Temple his friends me found;
I had delight with him to deal,
And held him homely in my hand.
I said, "Lord, let thy servant leal
Pass now in peace to lasting life,
For now myself has seen thy heal
I list no longer live in land."
This light thou hast purveyed
To folks that live on mould;
The same as I then said

(handwritten marginal notes:)

these prophesies.

on Biblical calculation
" to convey a thousand years are momene their word
— The myra.
7000 yrs = 2000 AD

Joy for having done penence for sine
→ preview to the event of
Purg. to announ K's 2nd coming.

fulfilling of prophesies.

Nunc Dimittis

gospel proof.
N.D. must seem may have ?
familiar ?

THE SADDLERS

I see fulfilled indeed.

JOHN BAPTIST ¶As voice crying I told all lands
The ways of Christ, as well I can.
I baptised him with both my hands,
Even in the flood of flowing Jordan.
The Holy Ghost did from heaven descend
As a white dove down on him then;
The Father's voice, my mirth to mend
Was made to me even as man—
"This is my son", He said,
"In whom I am pleased full well."
His light is on us laid;
He comes our cares to heal.

MOYSES ¶Of that same light learning have I.
To me Moyses he mustered his might,
And also to another, Hely,
When we were on a hill on height.
White as the snow was his body,
And his face like to the sun to sight.
No man on mould was so mighty
Fully to look against that light.
That same light see I now
Shining on us certain;
Wherefore truly I trow
We shall soon pass from pain.

1 DEVIL ¶Help, Belzabub, to bind these boys!
Such harrow was never heard in hell.

2 DEVIL ¶Why roarest thou so, Rybald?
What may betide? Canst thou ought say?

1 DEVIL ¶What! Hearest thou not this ugly noise?
These lurdans that in Limbo dwell,
They make meaning of many joys,
And muster them great mirth to tell.

2 DEVIL ¶Mirth?
Nay, nay; that point is past;
More help shall they not have.

1 DEVIL ¶They cry on Christ full fast,
And say he shall them save.

BELZABUB ¶Yea, if he save them not, we shall,
For they are sparred in special space;
While I am prince and principal

303

Shall they not pass out of this place.
Call up Astrot and Anabal,
To give their counsel in this case,
Baal, Berit and Belial,
To mar them that such masteries make.
Say to Satan our sire,
And bid them bring also,
Lucifer lovely to see.

I DEVIL ¶All ready, lord, I go.

JESUS ¶*ATTOLLITE, PORTAS, PRINCIPES.*
Open up, ye princes of pains severe,
ET ELEVAMINI ETERNALES,
Your endless gates that ye have here.

SATAN ¶What page is there that makes such press,
And calls him king of us all here?

DAVID ¶When living learned I, without lies,
He is a king of virtues clear.
With him ye may not fight,
For he is king and conqueror.
A lord mickle of might,
And strong to strive with power,
In battle fierce to fight,
And worthy to win honour.

SATAN ¶Honour? In the devil's way, for what deed?
All earthly men to me are thrall;
The lad that calls him lord indeed
Had never yet harbour, house nor hall.

I DEVIL ¶Hark, Belzabub! I have great dread,
For hideously I heard him call.

BELIAL ¶Ho! Spar our gates, ill might you all speed!
And set forth watches on the wall.
And if he call or cry,
To make us more debate,
Lay on him then hardily
And make him gang his gate.

SATAN ¶Tell me what boy dare be so bold
For dread to make such disarray.

I DEVIL ¶It is the Jew that Judas sold.
To die the death, the other day.

SATAN ¶Out, out! This tale in time is told;
This traitor crosses us alway.

304

He shall be here full hard to hold;
Look that he pass not, I thee pray.

2 DEVIL ¶Nay, nay; he shall not go
Away ere I be aware.
He shapes him to undo
All Hell ere he go far.

SATAN ¶Nay, fainthearts; thereof shall he fail;
For all his fare I him defy.
I know his tricks from top to tail;
He lives with gauds and guilery.
Thereby he brought out of our bail
Now lately, Lazar of Betannye.
Therefore I gave the Jews counsel
That they should all way make him die.
I entered in Judas
That purpose to fulfil;
Therefore his hire he has,
Always to dwell here still.

BELZABUB ¶Sir Satan, since we hear thee say
That thou and the Jews did all assent,
And knew he won Lazar away,
That to us was brought for to tent,
Trust thou then that thou mar him may
To muster might as he has meant?
If he deprive us of our prey,
We would ye wit well where they went.

SATAN ¶I bid you be no more abashed,
But boldly bring your armour soon,
With tools on which ye trust,
And ding that dastard down.

JESUS ¶*PRINCIPES, PORTA TOLLITE;*
Undo your gates, ye princes of pride,
ET INTROIBIT REX GLORIE,
The king of bliss comes in this tide.

SATAN ¶Out, haro! What harlot here is he,
That says his kingdom shall be cried?

DAVID ¶That may thou in my Psalter see,
For that point of prophecy.
I said that he should break
Your bars and bands by name,
And on your works take wreak;

305

Now shall ye see the same.

JESUS ¶This stead shall stand no more, by token;
Open up, and let my people pass.

I DEVIL ¶Out! Behold, all our bailey is broken,
And burst are all our bands of brass.
Tell Lucifer all is unlocken.

BELZABUB ¶What then? Is Limbo lorn, alas?
Make, Satan, help! We are forsaken.
This work is worse than ever it was.

SATAN ¶I bade he should be bound,
If he made masteries more;
Go, strike him to the ground,
And set him sad and sore.

BELZABUB ¶Yea, "set him sore"—that is soon said;
But come thyself and serve him so.
We may not bide his bitter blow;
He will us mar, even were we mo.

SATAN ¶What, fainthearts? Wherefore are ye feared?
Have ye no force to flit him fro?
See quick that all my gear's prepared;
Myself shall to that gadling go.
Now, bel ami; abide,
With all thy boastful cheer;
And tell to me this tide
What masteries make you here?

JESUS ¶I make no masteries but for mine;
Them will I save, I say again.
You had no power them to pine
But as my gaoler for their gain.
Here have they sojourned, not as thine
But in thy ward, thou wottest well how.

SATAN ¶Then what the devil didst thou since then,
Who ne'er came near them until now?

JESUS ¶Now is the time certain
My Father ordained before,
That they should pass from pain
And dwell in mirth ever more.

SATAN ¶Thy Father knew I well by sight;
He was a wight his meat to win;
And Mary I know, thy mother hight,
And the uttermost end of all thy kin.

306

       Who made thee be so mickle of might?
JESUS   ❡Thou wicked fiend, let be thy din.
       My Father dwells in heaven on height,
       With bliss that never wanes therein.
       His own Son I full well,
       His promise to fulfil;
       Together shall we dwell
       Or sunder, when we will.
SATAN   ❡God's Son? Then shouldst thou be full glad;
       After no chattels needst thou crave.
       But thou hast lived aye like a lad,
       And in sorrow as a simple knave.
JESUS   ❡That was for hearty love I had
       Unto man's soul, it for to save,
       And for to make thee mazed and mad.
       And by that reason duly to have,
       My Godhead did I hide
       In Mary, mother mine,
       That it should not be spied
       By thee nor none of thine.
SATAN   ❡Ah! This would I were told in town.
       So since thou sayest God is thy sire,
       I shall thee prove by right reason
       Thou movest thy men into the mire.
       To break his bidding they were bound.
       And since they did at thy desire,
       From Paradise he put them down
       Into hell here to have their hire.
       And thyself day and night
       Hast taught, all men among,
       To do reason and right
       And here workest thou all wrong.
JESUS   ❡I work not wrong, that shalt thou wit,
       If I my men from woe will win.
       My prophets plainly preached it,
       All these matters that now begin.
       They said that after my obit
       To hell then I should enter in,
       And save my servants from that pit
       Where damned souls shall sit for sin.
       And each true prophet's tale

Must be fulfilled in me;
I bought them by my bale,
And in bliss shall they be.

SATAN ¶Now since thou wilt allege the laws,
Thou shalt be attainted ere we go.
For them that thou to witness draws,
Full even against thee will they show.
Salamon has said in his saw
That whoso enters hell within
Shall never come out, as clerks know,
And therefore, fellow, leave thy din.
Job, thy servant also,
Thus in his time did tell,
That neither friend nor foe
Should find release in hell.

JESUS ¶He said full sooth, that shalt thou see,
That in hell may be no release,
But of that place then preached he
Where sinful care shall ever increase.
In that bale ever shalt thou be
Where sorrows sore shall never cease;
And that my folk therefrom were free,
Now shall they pass to the place of peace.
They were here with thy will
And so forth shall they wend,
And thyself shalt fulfil
Their woe without end.

SATAN ¶Oho!
Then see I how thou movest along,
Some measure with thy malice to tell,
Since thou sayest all shall not gang,
But some shall alway with us dwell.

JESUS ¶Yea, wit thou well, else were it wrong—
As cursed Cayne that slew Abell,
And all that haste themselves to hang,
As Judas and Archedefell,
Datan and Abiron
And all of their assent,
As tyrants every one
That me and mine torment.
All that list not to learn my lore

That I have left in land now new,
That is, my coming for to know
And to my sacrament pursue,
My death, my rising, read by row—
Who will not trust they are not true,
Unto my doom I shall them draw,
And judge them worse than any few.
And all that like to learn
My law and live thereby
Shall never have harms here
But weal, as is worthy.

SATAN ¶Now here's my hand. I hold me glad
This plan will plain our profit save.
If this be sooth that thou hast said,
We shall have more than now we have.
This law that thou now late hast laid
I shall teach men not to allow;
If they take it, they be betrayed,
For I shall turn them soon, I trow.
I shall walk East and West,
And make them work worse far.

JESUS ¶Nay, fiend, thou shalt be fast,
That thou shalt flit not far.

SATAN ¶Fast! That were a foul reason!
Nay, bel ami, thou must be smit.

JESUS ¶Michael, my angel, hither soon!
Fasten yon fiend, that he not flit.
And, devil, I command thee, go down
Into thy cell where thou shalt sit.

SATAN ¶Out, ah, haro! Now help, Mahound!
Now wax I woe out of my wit.

BELZABUB ¶Satan, this said we ere.
Now shalt thou feel thy fit.

SATAN ¶Alas, for dole and care!
I sink into hell pit.

ADAM ¶Ah, Jesu Lord, mickle is thy might
That meek art made in this manner,
Us for to help by promise plight
When I and she both forfeit were.
Here have we lived long without light
Four thousand and six hundred year;

Now see I by this solemn sight
How thy mercy has made us clear.

EVA ❡Ah lord, we were worthy
More torments for to taste;
But mend us with mercy,
As thou of might art most.

JOHN BAPTIST ❡Ah lord, I love thee inwardly,
That would make me thy messenger,
Thy coming on earth for to cry
And teach thy faith to all folk here;
And then before thee for to die
And bring thy bidding to them here,
That they should have thy help on high.
Now see I all thy points appear,
As David, prophet true,
Oft times told unto us;
Of this coming he knew,
And said it should be thus.

DAVID ❡As I have said, yet say I so;
NE DERELINQUAS, DOMINE
ANIMAM MEAM IN INFERNO:
Leave not my soul, Lord, after thee
In deep hell where the damned shall go,
Nor suffer souls from thee to be,
The sorrow of them that dwell in woe
Aye full of filth and may not flee.

ADAM ❡We thank his great goodness
Who fetched us from this place;
Make joy now more and less.

OMNES ❡We laud God of his grace.

JESUS ❡Adam and all my friends now here,
From all your foes come forth to me;
Ye shall be set in solace clear,
Where ye shall never sorrows see.
And Michael, my archangel dear,
Receive these souls all unto thee,
And lead them that they may appear
To Paradise in glad plenty.
Now to my grave I go,
Ready to rise upright;
And then fulfil I so

310

What I before have plight.

MICHAEL ¶Lord, wend we shall after thy law
To solace sure at thy command.
But that no devil's draught us draw
Lord, bless us with thy holy hand.

JESUS ¶My blessing have ye all in row;
I shall be with you where you wend.
All loyal ones that love my law
They shall be blessed without an end.

ADAM ¶To thee, Lord, be loving,
That us hast won from woe
For solace will we sing
LAVS TIBI DOMINO
          CUM GLORIA.

38

THE CARPENTERES

Jesus resurgens de sepulcro, quatuor milites armati, et tres Marie lamentantes. Pilatus, Cayphas et Anna. Juvenis sedens ad sepulcrum indutus albo, loquens mulieribus.

PILATE   ¶Lordings, listen now unto me.
I command you in each degree,
As deemster chief in this country,
    For counsel known,
At my bidding you ought to be
    And bend each one.
And Sir Cayphas, chief of clergy,
Of your counsel late here on high,
By our assent since he did die—
    Jesus—this day,
That we maintain and stand thereby,
    That work all way.

CAYPHAS   ¶Yes, sir; we shall maintain that deed;
By law it was done and agreed
You know yourself—of doubt's no need—
    As well as we.
His sayings now are on his head,
    And aye shall be.

ANNAS   ¶The people, sir, in this same stead
Before you spoke with a whole head,
That he was worthy to be dead,
    And thereto sware.
Since all was ruled by righteous rede,
    Name it no more.

PILATE   ¶To name I think it needful thing.
Since he was had to burying,
Heard we neither of old nor young
    Tidings between.

CAYPHAS ⁋Centurion, sir, will tidings bring
Of all, I ween.
We left him there for man most wise,
If any rebels should arise
Our righteous doom for to despise,
Or it offend,
To seize them to the next assize,
And then make end.

CENTURION ⁋Ah, blessed lord! Ah, Adonay!
What may these marvels signify;
That here were showed so openly
Unto our eyes,
This day on which that man did die
Righteous and wise?
This thing a mystery must mean;
So strange a sight was never seen.
Our princes and our priests, I ween,
Fear now they may.
I will go find, by knowledge clean,
What they can say.
God save you, sirs, on every side.
Worship and wealth in this world wide
And mickle mirth on you abide
Both day and night.

PILATE ⁋Centurion, welcome this tide,
Our comely knight.
You have been missed, us here among.

CENTURION ⁋God give you grace goodly to gang.

PILATE ⁋Centurion, our friend full long,
What is your will?

CENTURION ⁋I dread me that you have done wrong,
And wondrous ill.

CAYPHAS ⁋Wondrous ill, sir? I pray thee, why?
Declare it to this company.

CENTURION ⁋So shall I, sirs, tell you truly,
And will not feign.
That righteous man, him then mean I,
That you have slain.

PILATE ⁋Centurion, cease of such saw.
Thou art a man learned in the law,
If we should any witness draw,

    Us to excuse.
   To maintain us always you owe,
    And not refuse.
CENTURION ¶To maintain truth is well worthy.
   I told you, when I saw him die,
   That he was God's son almighty,
    That hangeth there.
   Yet say I so, and stand thereby,
    For evermore.
CAYPHAS ¶Yea, sir; such reasons may you rue.
   You should not name such note anew,
   Unless you could any tokenings true
    Unto us tell.
CENTURION ¶Such wondrous case ne'er yet ye knew
    As now befell.
ANNAS ¶We pray thee, tell us of that thing.
CENTURION ¶All elements, both old and young,
   In their manner made their mourning
    In each place plain,
   And knew by countenance that their king
    Was sadly slain.
   The sun for woe he waxed all wan,
   The moon and stars to wane began,
   The earth trembled, and as a man
    Began to speak;
   The stones that never stirred ere then
    Asunder brake.
   And dead men rose, both great and small.
PILATE ¶Centurion, beware withal.
   You know our clerks eclipses call
    Such sudden sight;
   Both sun and moon that season shall
    Lack of their light.
CAYPHAS ¶Yea, and if dead men rose bodily,
   That might be done through sorcery;
   Therefore we set nothing thereby,
    To be abased.
CENTURION ¶All that I tell for truth shall I
    Evermore trust.
   In this same work that ye did work,
   Not alone then the sun was murk,

But how the veil reft in your kirk,
  That say to me.
PILATE ¶Such tales full soon will make us irk,
  If told they be.
ANNAS ¶Centurion, such speech withdraw;
  Of all these words we have no awe.
CENTURION ¶Now since ye set nought by my saw,
  Sirs, have good day.
  God grant you grace that you may know
  The truth alway.
ANNAS ¶Withdraw then fast, since so you dread,
  For we shall well maintain our deed.
PILATE ¶Such reasons strange as he would rede
  Was ne'er before.
CAYPHAS ¶To name this work no more we need
  By even or morn.
  Therefore look no man make ill cheer;
  All this doing may make no fear.
  But to beware yet of more care
  That folk may feel,
  We pray you, sirs, of these saws here
  Advise you well.
  And to these tales take heed on high,
  For Jesus said even openly—
  A thing that grieves all this Jewry,
  And rightly may—
  That he should rise up bodily
  On the third day.
  If it be so, as might I speed,
  His latter death is more to dread
  Than is the first if we take heed
  Or tent thereto.
  To name this work methinks most need
  And best to do.
ANNAS ¶Yea, sir; for all that he said so,
  He has no might to rise and go.
  But if his men steal him us fro
  And bear away,
  That were to us and others mo
  A foul affray.
  For then would they say, every one,

That he rose by himself alone;
Therefore let him be kept anon
   By knights, I say,
Until three days be come and gone
   And passed away.

PILATE   ¶In certain, sirs, right well ye say.
For every point now to purvey
I shall ordain, if that I may,
   He shall not rise,
Nor none shall win him hence away
   In any wise.
Sir knights, that are in deeds doughty,
Chosen for chief of chivalry,
As we aye in your force rely
   By day and night,
Go ye and keep Jesus' body
   With all your might,
And for that thing—be what it may—
Keep ye him well to the third day,
And let no man take him away
   Out of that stead;
For if they do, in truth I say
   Ye shall be dead.

I KNIGHT   ¶Lordings, we tell you for certain,
We shall keep him with might and main;
No traitors there with wiles all vain
   Shall steal him so.
Sir knights, take gear that most may gain,
   And let us go.

II

At the Sepulchre

2 KNIGHT   ¶Yes, sure; we are all ready found.
We shall keep him, for our renown.
On every side let us sit down,
   Now all are here,
And surely we shall crack his crown,
   Whoso comes near.
     (*Then Jesus rises.*)

I MARY   ¶Alas! To death I would be dight.
So woe in work was never wight.

316

My sorrow is all for that sight
    That I did see,
How Christ, my master most of might,
    Is dead to me.
Alas! That I should see his woes.
Or yet that I his life should lose.
All mischief there its medicine knows,
    And meed of all,
Help and hold in grief for those
    To him would call.

2 MARY   ¶Alas! Who may my bales now beat,
When I may think on his wounds wet?
Jesus, that was of love so sweet,
    And ill did ne'er,
Is dead and graved under the grit;
    No cause was there.

3 MARY   ¶No cause was there. The Jews each one
That lovely lord have lately slain;
And trespass did he never none
    In any stead.
To whom now shall I make my moan,
    Since he is dead?

1 MARY   ¶Since he is dead, my sisters dear,
Wend on we will in mild manner
With our anointments fresh and clear
    That we have brought,
To anoint his wounds sore and severe
    That Jews have wrought.

2 MARY   ¶Go we alone, my sisters free;
Full fair we long his corse to see.
But I wot not how best may be;
    Help have we none,
And who shall now here of us three
    Remove the stone?

3 MARY   ¶If we were more, that might we do,
For it is huge and heavy also.

1 MARY   ¶Sisters! A young child, as we go
    Making mourning. . . .
I see it sit where we wend to,
    In white clothing.

2 MARY   ¶Sure, sisters, there is nought to hide;

The heavy stone is put aside.

3 MARY ¶Surely to see what may betide
                      Near will we wend,
To seek that lord and with him bide
                      That was our friend.

ANGEL ¶Ye women mourning in your thought,
Here in this place whom have ye sought?

1 MARY ¶Jesus, that unto death was brought,
                      Our Lord so free.

ANGEL ¶Women, certain here is he not;
                      Come near and see.
He is not here, the sooth to say;
The place is void wherein he lay;
The sudary here see ye may—
                      'Twas on him laid.
He is risen and gone his way,
                      As once he said.
Even as he said, so done has he.
He is risen through great mastery.
He shall be found in Galile
                      In flesh to show.
To his disciples now wend ye,
                      And tell them so.

1 MARY ¶My sisters dear, since it is so,
That he is risen from death to go,
As the angel told me and you too,
                      Our Lord so free,
Hence from this place I never go,
                      Ere I him see.

2 MARY ¶Mary, no time now need we spend;
To Galilee now let us wend.

1 MARY ¶Not till I see that faithful friend,
                      My lord and leech.
Therefore all this, sisters, I say,
                      Go forth and preach.

3 MARY ¶As we have heard, so shall we say;
Mary our sister, have good day.

1 MARY ¶Now very God, as well he may,
                      Man most of might,
Guide you, sisters, well in your way,
                      And rule you right.

Alas! What shall become of me?
My caitiff heart will break in three,
When I think on that body free,
                How it was spilt;
Both feet and hands nailed on a tree,
                Without his guilt.
Without his guilt true Man was slain,
For trespass did he never none;
The wounds he suffered, many a one,
                Were for my miss.
It was for my deed he was slain,
                And none of his.
Alas for me who loved him so,
That for me suffered wound and blow,
And then was graved in earth below,
                Of kindness king.
Until we meet, I nothing know
                That joy may bring.

1 KNIGHT ¶What! Out, alas! What shall I say?
Where is the corpse that herein lay?

2 KNIGHT ¶What ails the man? Is he away?
                Is our charge gone?

1 KNIGHT ¶Rise up and see.
                Haro! For aye
We are undone.

3 KNIGHT ¶What the devil is this? What ails you two,
Such noise and cry for to make so?
                Why is he gone?
Alas, where is he that here lay?

4 KNIGHT ¶Out, haro! The devil! Where is he away?

2 KNIGHT ¶What? If he thusgates from us went,
That false traitor that here was pent,
And we truly here for to tent
                Had underta'en:
Now certainly I count us spent
                Wholly each one.

3 KNIGHT ¶Alas! What shall we do this day,
Since thus that warlock went his way?
And safely, sirs, I dare well say
                He rose alone.

2 KNIGHT ¶If Pilate hear of this affray,

We are dead and done.

3 KNIGHT ❡Why, can none of us better rede?

4 KNIGHT ❡There is not else, but we be dead.

2 KNIGHT ❡When that he stirred out of this stead,
None could it ken.

1 KNIGHT ❡Alas! Hard hap was on my head,
Among all men.
When Sir Pilate knows of this deed,
That we were sleeping when he fled,
He will forfeit, we may well dread,
All that we have.

2 KNIGHT ❡We must make lies, for that is need,
Ourselves to save.

3 KNIGHT ❡That I advise, so might I go.

4 KNIGHT ❡And I assent thereto also.

2 KNIGHT ❡An hundred, shall I say, and mo,
Armed every one,
Did come and take his corse, although
We were near slain.

1 KNIGHT ❡Nay, sure; I hold there's nought so good
As say the truth even as it stood,
How that he rose with main and mood
And went his way.
To Sir Pilate, though he be mad,
This dare I say.

2 KNIGHT ❡Why, dare you to Sir Pilate go
With these tidings, and tell him so?

1 KNIGHT ❡So I advise; if he us slay
We die but once.

3 KNIGHT ❡Now he that wrought us all this woe,
Woe worth his bones.

4 KNIGHT ❡Go we then, gentle knights at hand,
Since we shall to Sir Pilate wend.
I trow that we shall part no friends,
Ere that we pass.

1 KNIGHT ❡I shall tell him each word to the end,
Even as it was.

III
Pilate's Hall Again

1 KNIGHT ❡Sir Pilate, the prince without peer,

Sir Cayphas and Anna his peer,
And all ye lordings that are here,
    To name you by name,
God save you all everywhere
    From sin and shame.

PILATE ¶You are welcome, our knights so keen.
Of mickle mirth now may we mean;
Some tales tell us therefore between,
    How ye have wrought.

1 KNIGHT ¶Our watching, lord, I tell thee plain,
    Is come to nought.

CAYPHAS ¶To nought? Alas, cease of such saw.

2 KNIGHT ¶The prophet Jesus that ye know
Is risen and gone, to all our awe,
    With main and might.

PILATE ¶Then the devil himself may thee draw,
    False recreant knight.
Cumbered and cowards I you call.
Have ye let him go from you all?

3 KNIGHT ¶Sir, there was none that did but small,
    When he was sped.

4 KNIGHT ¶We were so feared, down we did fall
    And faint for dread.

ANNAS ¶Had ye no strength him to gainstand?
Traitors, ye might have bound in band
Both him and them that there ye found,
    And seized them soon.

1 KNIGHT ¶That deed all living men in land
    Might not have done.

2 KNIGHT ¶We were so frightened, every one,
When that he put aside the stone,
We were so astonished we durst stir none
    And so abashed.

PILATE ¶What! Rose he by himself alone?

1 KNIGHT   Yea, sir. That may ye trust.

4 KNIGHT ¶We never heard since we were born,
Nor all our fathers us before,
Such melody midday nor morn
    As was made there.

CAYPHAS ¶Alas! Then all our law is lorn
    For evermore.

2 KNIGHT ¶What time he rose good tent I took;
The earth that time trembled and shook;
All kindly force then me forsook,
Till he was gone.

3 KNIGHT ¶I was afeared; I durst not look,
Nor might had none.
I might not stand, so was I stark.

PILATE ¶Sir Cayphas, ye are a cunning clerk;
If we amiss have taken our mark,
I trow we fail.
What then shall come now of this work?
Say now your counsel.

CAYPHAS ¶To say the best forsooth I shall,
That shall be profit to us all.
Yon knights their words again must call,
How he is missed.
We would, for ought that might befall,
That no man wist.

ANNAS ¶Now, Sir Pilate, since it is so
That he is risen from death below,
Tell them to say, where'er they go,
That he was ta'en
By twenty thousand men and mo,
And they near slain.
And thereto from our treasury
Give them reward for this their lie.

PILATE ¶Of this purpose well pleased am I,
And further thus,
Sir knights that are in deeds doughty,
Take tent to us,
And hearken what ye are to say
To every man, both night and day.
Ten thousand men in good array,
Who would you kill,
With force of arms bare him away
Against your will.
Thus shall ye say in every land.
And more on that same covenant,
A thousand pound have in your hand
To your reward;
And friendship, sirs, ye understand,

Shall not be spared.

CAYPHAS ❡Each one your state we shall amend;
And look you say as we intend.

I KNIGHT ❡To any country where ye send,
By night or day,
Whereso we come, whereso we wend,
So shall we say.

PILATE ❡Whereso ye tarry in each country,
Of our doing in no degree,
See that no man the wiser be,
Nor question share;
Nor of the sight that ye did see
Name it nowhere.
For we shall maintain you alway,
And to the people shall we say
It is greatly against our law
To trust such cries.
So shall they think both night and day
That all is lies.
Thus shall the truth be bought and sold,
And treason shall for truth be told.
Therefore aye in your hearts now hold
This counsel clean.
And fare ye well, both young and old
Who here are seen.

39

THE WYNEDRAWERS

Jesus, Maria Magdalena cum aromatibus.

MARY
MAGDALENE ¶Alas! In this world was no wight
Walking with so mickle woe.
Thou dreadful death, draw hither and dight
And mar me, as thou hast done mo.
In loam is it locked, all my light;
Wherefore on ground unglad I go;
For Jesus, he of Nazareth hight,
The false Jews from me have slain so.
My wit is wasted now indeed;
I reel as I walk; now woe is me.
For laid is the lovesome one in grave;
The Jews nailed him unto a tree.
My doleful heart is ever in dread;
To ground now gone is all my glee;
I stumble where one time I sped;
Now help me, God in Persons three.
Beloved Lord in every land,
As thou didst shape both day and night,
Sun and moon shining bright and clear,
Grant grace that I may have a sight
Of my Lord or his messenger here.

JESUS ¶Thou woman wandering in this way,
Why weepest thou and takest no heed,
As thou on field would fall down fey?
Whom seekest thou this livelong day?
Say me the sooth, as Christ thee speed.

MARY ¶My Lord Jesus, true God, I say,
Whose side for sins did sorely bleed.

JESUS ¶I shall thee tell, if thou wilt hear,

The sooth of him that thou hast sought.
Without a doubt, faithful compeer,
He is full near that mankind bought.

MARY   ¶Sir, I would look both far and near
To find my Lord; I see him not.

JESUS   ¶Woman, weep not, but mend thy cheer;
I wot well whither he was brought.

MARY   ¶Sweet sir, if thou bare him away,
Tell me the truth and there me lead
Where thou him hid, without delay;
I shall him seek again, good speed.
Therefore, good gardener, tell me,
I pray thee for the prophet's sake,
Of these tidings that I ask thee—
For it would do my sorrow to slake—
Where God's own body found might be,
That Joseph from the cross did take.
If in my keeping he might be,
Of all my woe I'd comfort make.

JESUS   ¶What would'st thou with that body bare
That buried was with baleful cheer?
Thou mayest not salve him of his sore
Or pains so sad and so severe.
But he shall free mankind of care;
What clouded was shall he make clear,
And make the folk well for to fare
Who were defiled in bitter fear.

MARY   ¶Ah! Might I ever with that man meet,
The which that is so mickle of might,
Dry would I wipe what now is wet.
I sorrow but for worldly sight.

JESUS   ¶Mary, of mourning amend thy mood,
And here behold my wounds so wide.
Thus for man's sins I shed my blood,
And all this bitter bale did bide.
Thus was I raised on the rood
With spear and nails so sharp and rude.
Believe it well; it turns to good,
When men in earth their flesh shall hide.

MARY   ¶Ah, Rabboni! I have thee sought,
My Master dear, full fast this day.

JESUS ❡Away, Mary, and touch me not;
But take good heed what I shall say.
I am he that all things has wrought,
That thou callest Lord and God very;
With bitter death mankind I bought,
And I am risen, as see thou may.
And therefore, Mary, speak now with me,
And stay thou here thy weeping yet.

MARY ❡My Lord Jesus, I now know thee.
Thy wounds, they are still wet.

JESUS ❡Come near me not, my love; let be,
Mary, my daughter sweet,
To my Father in Trinity
Because I rise not yet.

MARY ❡Ah, mercy, comely conqueror!
Through thy might death is o'ercome indeed.
Mercy, Jesus, man and saviour!
Thy love is sweeter than the mead.
Mercy, thou mighty comforter,
For ere I was all reft of rede.
Welcome, my lord, all my honour,
My joy, my love, in every stead.

JESUS ❡Mary, in thine heart now write
Mine armour rich and good.
My haketon covered all in white,
As body of man behued,
With stuff good and perfect
Of maiden's flesh and blood.
When they did pierce and smite,
My head for hauberk stood.
My plates were spread abroad—
That was my body upon a tree.
My helm covered all my manhood;
The strength thereof can no man see.
The crown of thorn that made me bleed
Points out my dignity;
My diadem says, doubt banished,
Dead shall I never be.

MARY ❡Blest body, all ill right to set,
How dearly hast thou bought mankind!
Thy wounds have made thy body wet

With blood that was within confined.
Nailed thou wast through hands and feet,
And all was for our sin.
Full grisly must we caitiffs greet.
Of woe how should I not begin,
To see this man so good
Thus ruefully bedight,
Rived and rent on a rood?
This is a rueful sight,
And all is for our good
And nothing for his plight,
Since spilt thus is his blood
For every sinful wight.

JESUS ¶To my God and Father dear,
To him full soon I shall ascend
For I shall now not long dwell here;
I have done all he did intend.
And therefore learn now, each man here,
How all on earth their life may mend.
To all that love me I draw near,
To bring him bliss that ne'er shall end.

MARY ¶Now all for joy I like to sing.
My heart is gladder than the glee.
And all for joy of thy rising
That suffered death upon a tree.
Of love now art thou crowned king;
Is none so true living so free.
Thy love passes all earthly thing.
Lord, blessed might thou ever be.

JESUS ¶To Galile now shalt thou wend,
Mary, my daughter dear.
My brethren this attend
Now all together there.
Tell them each word to the end
That thou spake with me here.
My blessing on thee land,
And all that we leave here.

40

THE SLEDMEN

Jesus, Lucas et Cleophas in forma peregrinorum.

1 PILGRIM   ¶That lord who has lent me this life for to lead,
            In my ways mayst thou guide me thus wandering alone,
            When all other men have most mirth to their meed,
            Then here as a mourning man make I my moan.
            For doubtless indeed may we dread us.
            Alas, they have reft us our rede.
            With dole have they dight him to death,
            That lord who was pleasant to lead us.

2 PILGRIM   ¶He led us full loyally, that lord; now, alas,
            My lord for his loyalty his life has he lorn.

1 PILGRIM   ¶Say, who comes here clattering?

2 PILGRIM   I, Cleophas.
            Abide, my dear brother. To bale am I borne.
            But tell me now, where are you bound?

1 PILGRIM   ¶To Emmaus, this castle beside us;
            There may we both harbour and bide us.
            Let us tarry therefore at no town.

2 PILGRIM   ¶At towns for to tarry take we no intent,
            But take leisure at this time to talk of some tales,
            And jangle of Jews and of Jesus so gent,
            How they beat that body, the help of all bales.
            With buffets they beat him full barely.
            In Sir Cayphas' hall did they him call,
            And then before Pilate in his hall
            On that morn thereafter, full early.

1 PILGRIM   ¶Full early the judge-men there doomed him to die,
            Both priests and prelates to Pilate applying,
            All curst caitiffs and keen, on Christ did they cry,
            And of that true lord made many a lying.
            They spit in his face to despise him;
            To spoil him no thing did they spare him,

But none the less naked they bared him,
With scourges smart going they smote him.

2 PILGRIM ¶They smote him full smartly that the blood out burst,
That all his hide with hurt was hastily hid;
A crown of thorns on his head then tightly they thrust;
It is great dole for to deem the deeds that they did.
With binding and buffets and beating,
Then on his back bare he by
A cross unto Calvary
Who sorely was swooning for sweating.

1 PILGRIM ¶For all the sweat that he sweat with swings they him
swang
And rived him full ruefully with ropes on a rood;
Then heaved him up highly on high for to hang;
Without sin by this man so served they his mood.
He ever was truest for trusting.
Methinketh my heart is bound for to break,
Of his pitiful pains when we here speak,
So friendly we found him in testing.

2 PILGRIM ¶In testing we found him full faithful and free;
In his mind meant he never amiss to no man;
It was sorrow forsooth in sight for to see
When that spiteful spear into his heart ran.
With grief was he sorely acquainted;
And into his heart then they thrust,
When his pitiful pains were past.
That sweeting full swiftly he fainted.

1 PILGRIM ¶He fainted full soon with swooning, that sweet.
Alas, for that lovely that laid is so low.
With groaning full grisly on ground may we greet,
For so comely a corse can I never know.
With dole unto death so they brought him,
For all their wise works that he wrought them;
These false folks when they had bethought them,
That with great unkindness they caught him.

2 PILGRIM ¶Unkindness they did him, those caitiffs so keen,
And as unwitty wights such woe did they wreak.

JESUS ¶What, sirs, are these marvels that now ye mean,
And this mickle mourning in mind that ye make,
Walking thus wild by the ways?

2 PILGRIM ¶Why, art thou a pilgrim, and hast been

At Jerusalem, and hast thou not seen
What dole has been done in these days?

JESUS ❡In these days, dear sir? What dole was there done?
Of that work would I wit, if your will were.
And therefore I pray you now tell me soon,
Was there any hurling in hand? Now let me hear.

I PILGRIM ❡Why, heard thou no telling or crying
At Jerusalem, where thou has been,
When Jesus the Nazarene
Was dolefully dight to the dying?

2 PILGRIM ❡To be dying they dight him that deft was and dear,
Through procuring of princes that there were in press.
Thus as wights that are wild so walk we now here,
So pant we as pilgrims that must hold their peace.
For mourning of our master thus mourn we,
As wights that wander thus walk we,
Of Jesus in telling thus talk we,
And from taking to towns thus turn we.

I PILGRIM ❡Thus turn we from towns, but take we intent
How they murdered that man of whom we now tell.
Full ruefully with ropes on rood they him rent,
And tacked him thereto in fury full fell.
Upright then full rudely they raised him,
Then mightily to annoy him withal
In a mortice fast let they him fall;
To pain so they put and pressed him.

2 PILGRIM ❡They pressed him to pain him, that peerless of peace,
On that wight that was wise thus wrought they great
wonder.
And yet with that sorrow still would they not cease,
They shook him and shot him his limbs all asunder.
His brains thus brake they and burst him.
A blind knight—such was his good hap—
In with a spear point at the pap
To the heart full throughly he thrust him.

I PILGRIM ❡He thrust him full throughly, there was no debating
With dole was that dear one thus unto death dight.
His back and his body were bruised with beating;
It was, I say sooth, a sorrowful sight.
But oft times we have heard say,
And we trust it as we heard tell,

330

That he was to ransom Israel—
But now is this the third day.

2 PILGRIM ¶These days now our wits are waxen unsure,
For some of our women for certain they said
That they saw in their sight a solace secure,
How all was gleaming light where he was laid;
They told us, as e'er might they thrive,
For certain they saw it in sight,
A vision of angels all bright,
Who told them their Lord was alive.

1 PILGRIM ¶Alive, as they told, that Lord lived here in land;
These women came quickly to warn us, I ween.
Some of our folk hied forth, and soon did they find
All sooth that they said of the sight they had seen.
For truly they looked where he lay;
They thought to have found that man there;
Then was his tomb empty as air.
Then wist they that wight was away.

2 PILGRIM ¶Away is that wight whose guidance we miss.
JESUS ¶Ah, fools, that are faulty and fail of your faith!
This bale must he abide to bring you to bliss.
Unless loyal to your law, your life hold I loath.
To prophets he proved it and preached,
And also to Moses did say,
That he must needs die on a day,
And Moses forth told it and teached;
And told it and taught it full many times then.

1 PILGRIM ¶Ah, more of this talking we pray you to tell us.
2 PILGRIM ¶Yea, sir; by your speaking full kindly we ken.
It is of your master, this tale that you tell us.

1 PILGRIM ¶Yea, good sir; now see what I say.
See ye this castle beside here?
All night we think for to bide here;
Bide with us, sir pilgrim, we pray;
We pray you, sir pilgrim, ye press not to pass.

JESUS ¶Yea, sir, I must need.
1 PILGRIM   Nay, the night is over near.
JESUS ¶And I have far for to go.
1 PILGRIM   I think well thou hast.
We pray thee, sir, heartily, all night hold thee here.
JESUS ¶I thank you of this kindness you pay me.

1 PILGRIM	¶Go in, sir, indeed, and right soon.
2 PILGRIM	¶Sir, danger doubt not; have done.
JESUS	¶Sir, I must needs do as ye pray me.
	Ye bid me so kindly; I bide for the best.
1 PILGRIM	¶Lo, here is a seat, good sir, I say you.
2 PILGRIM	¶With such good as we have we gladden our guest.
1 PILGRIM	¶Of this poor pittance partake now, we pray you.
JESUS	¶Now bless I this bread that brought is on the board
	Taste thereon faithfully, friends, you to feed.—
1 PILGRIM	¶To feel thereon entirely have we intent—
	Oh! I trow some disaster betides us!
	Say, where is this man?
2 PILGRIM	Away he went!
	Right now sat he beside us.
1 PILGRIM	¶Beside us we both saw him sit
	And by no point could I perceive him to pass.
2 PILGRIM	¶Nay, by the works that he wrought full well might we wit.
	It was Jesus himself; I wist who it was.
1 PILGRIM	¶It was Jesus thus wisely that wrought,
	That raised was and ruefully rent on the rood.
	From bale and bitterness has he us bought,
	Bound was and beaten and all burst in blood.
2 PILGRIM	¶All burst in blood, so sore was he beat
	By those wicked Jews that wrathful were ever,
	With scourges and sharp thorns on his head set.
	Such torture and torment heard I tell of never.
1 PILGRIM	¶I never heard tell of such pitiful pain
	As suffered our Sovereign hanging on height.
	Now is he risen with might and with main,
	I tell thee for sure; we saw him in sight.
2 PILGRIM	¶We saw him in sight, now take we intent,
	By the bread that he brake us, so near as between.
	Such wonderful ways as ever we went
	Of Jesus the gentle was never none seen.
1 PILGRIM	¶Was never none seen, such wonderful works
	By sea nor by sand, in this world so wide.
	With worship in mind these matters now mark,
	And preach we them presently on every side.
2 PILGRIM	¶On every side presently preach it shall we.
	Go we to Jerusalem, these tidings to tell.

Our fellows from trying now turn we;
More on this matter here may we not dwell.

I PILGRIM ¶Here may we not dwell on it more at this tide,
For process of plays that presses in plight.
May he bring you to bliss on every side
That sovereign lord that most is of might.

42

THE ESCREVENERS

Jesu, Petrus, Johannes, Jacobus, Philippus et alii apostoli cum parte piscis assi et favo mellis, et Thomas apostolus palpans vulnera Jesu.

PETER   ¶Alas! To woe how are we brought!
Had never men so mickle thought,
Since that our Lord to death was brought
         With Jews so fell.
Out of this stead go durst we not,
But here aye dwell.

JOHN   ¶Here have we dwelt with pining strong.
Our life we loathe; we live too long.
For since the Jews wrought us that wrong,
         Our Lord to slay,
We durst not ever come them among,
         Or go away.

JAMES   ¶The wicked Jews hate us full ill,
And bitter pains would bring us still,
Therefore I rede that we dwell still
         Here where we land,
Until that Christ our Lord us will
         Some succour send.

                              (*Jesus appears . . .*

JESUS   ¶Peace and rest be with you.   *. . . and vanishes.*)

PETER   ¶Ah, brethren dear, what may we trow,
What was this sight that we saw now
         Shining so bright,
And vanished thus, we know not how,
         Out of our sight?

JOHN   ¶Out of sight now is it sought.
It makes us mad, the light it brought.

JAMES   ¶Certes, I wot not securely

What may it be.
It was all vanity in our thought;
Nought else I trow it be.

JESUS ¶Peace unto you evermore might be.
Dread you not, for I am he.

PETER ¶In God's name, *benedicite!*
What may this mean?

JAMES ¶It is a spirit, forsooth thinketh me,
That we have seen.

JOHN ¶A spirit it is; that trow I right,
All thus appeared here to our sight;
It makes us mad of main and might,
And all dismayed.
Yon is the same that brought the light
That us affrayed.

JESUS ¶What think ye, madmen, in your thought?
What mourning in your hearts is brought?
I am the Christ, and dread ye nought.
Here may ye see
The same body that has you bought
Upon a tree.
That I have come you here to meet,
Behold and see my hands and feet,
And closely clasp my wounds still wet,
All that here is.
Thus was. I dight your bales to beat,
And bring to bliss.
For you thus-gates then have I gone.
Follow me freely, every one,
And see that I have flesh and bone;
Grope me here now.
For so has not a spirit none;
That shall you trow.
To make you ken and know me clear,
I shall show you examples here.
Then bring now forth unto me here
Some of your meat,
If among you as you appear
You have ought to eat.

JAMES ¶Thou loving lord that last shall aye,
Lo, here is meat that eat you may,

335

A honeycomb, the sooth to say,
    Roast fish as well.
To eat thereof here we thee pray,
    With full good will.

JESUS ¶Now since ye have brought me this meat,
To make your trust steadfast and great,
And for ye shall faint hope forget
    And trust in me,
With you all here then shall I eat;
    That ye shall see.

Now have I done, ye have seen how,
Bodily eating here with you.
Steadfastly look then that you trow
    Henceforth in me,
And take this remnant soon to you
    That left may be.

For you thus was I riven and dressed;
Therefore some of my pain ye taste;
And speak nowhere my word in waste;
    That learn ye clear,
And unto you the Holy Ghost
    Relieve you here.

Be ye now true and trust in me;
And here I grant you in your degree,
Whom that ye bind bounden shall be
    Right as you say,
And whom ye loose, loosed shall be
    In heaven for aye.

THOMAS ¶Alas for sight and sorrows sad!
Mourning makes me mazed and mad.
On ground now may I go unglad,
    Both even and morn.
That friend of whom my help I had
    His life has lorn.

Thus lorn have I that lovely light,
That was my master most of might;
So dolefully as he was dight
    Was never none,
Such woe was wrought of that worthy wight
    With wounds so wan.
When as his weals and wounds all wet . . .

With skelps sore was he swung; he sweat;
All naked nailed through hands and feet—
     Alas, for pine!
That blest, who best might woes abate
     Must life resign.
Alas! For sorrow myself I spend,
When heartily my thought I lend;
I found him aye a faithful friend,
     Truly to tell.
To my brethren now will I wend,
     Whereso they dwell
Ah, blissful sight was never none.
Our joy and comfort all is gone;
Of mourning may we make our moan
     In every land.
God bless you, brethren, blood and bone,
     There where ye stand.

PETER   ¶Now welcome, Thomas. Where has thou been?
Now wit thou well, and not in vain,
Jesus our Lord late have we seen
     On ground to go.

THOMAS   ¶What say ye, men? Alas! For pain
     You are mazed, I trow.

JOHN   ¶Thomas, truly we do not feign;
Jesus our Lord is risen again.

THOMAS   ¶Away! These tales are tricks and vain,
     Of fools unwise.
For he that was so foully slain,
     How should he rise?

JAMES   ¶Thomas, truly he is alive,
That bore the Jews his flesh to rive.
He let us feel his wounds five,
     Our Lord very.

THOMAS   ¶That trow I not, so might I thrive,
     Whatso ye say.

PETER   ¶Thomas, we saw his wounds wet,
How he was nailed through hands and feet;
Honey and fish with us he ate,
     That body free.

THOMAS   ¶I lay my life 'twas some spirit
     You thought were he.

337

JOHN   ¶Nay, Thomas, nay; thou hast misgone.
       For why? He bade us every one
       To clasp him closely, blood and bone
                 And flesh to feel.
       Such things, Thomas, has spirit none;
                 That wot you well.

THOMAS ¶What? Leave, fellows; let be your fare.
       Till that I see his body bare,
       And then my finger put in there
                 Within his hide,
       And feel the wound the spear did shear
                 Right in his side—
       Ere shall I trow no tales between.

JAMES ¶Thomas, that wound we all have seen.

THOMAS ¶Bah! Ye know never what ye mean;
                 Your wit you want.
       Ye must think, since ye thus me pain,
                 With tricks to taunt.

JESUS ¶Peace, brethren, now be unto you.
       And, Thomas, tent to me take thou.
       Put forth thy finger to me now;
                 My hands you see;
       For man's profit was I nailed so
                 Upon a tree.
       Behold, my wounds still bleeding stand;
       Here in my side put in thy hand
       And feel my wounds, and understand
                 That this is I.
       Thy misbelief be at an end,
                 But trust truly.

THOMAS ¶My Lord, my God! Full well is me!
       Ah, blood of price, blest might thou be!
       Mankind on earth, behold and see
                 His blessed blood.
       Mercy now, Lord, I ask of thee
                 With main and mood.

JESUS ¶Thomas, since thou hast seen this sight,
       That I am risen as I you hight,
       Therefore you trust it; but each wight
                 Blest be he ever,
       That trusts wholly in my rising right,

338

Yet saw it never.
Now all fare forth, my brethren dear,
On all sides in each country clear;
My rising tell both far and near;
Preach it shall ye.
And my blessing I give you here,
And this company.

43

THE TAILOURES

Maria, Johannes Evangelista, xi apostoli, ij angeli, Jesus ascendens coram eis, et iiij angeli portantes nubem.

PETER ❡O mightful God, how stands it now?
In world thus wild was I not ere.
If he comes—but I know not how
He parts from us when he will fare.
Yet that may for our profit show,
And all his working less and more.
Ah, king of comfort, good art thou,
And true and liking is thy lore.

JOHN ❡The missing of my master true,
That dwells not with us lastingly,
Makes me to mourn each day anew,
For wanting of his company.
His peer of goodness ne'er I knew,
Of might nor wisdom equally.

PETER ❡That we want him sore may we rue,
For he loved us full faithfully;
And yet in all my misliking
A word that Christ said comforts me.
Our heaviness and our mourning,
He said, to joy should turned be.
That joy, he said in his teaching,
To rob us none of power should be.
Wherefore above all other thing
That joy I long to know and see.

MARY ❡Thou Peter, when my son was slain
And laid in grave, you were in care
Whether he should rise, almost each one;
But now you see through knowing clear.
Some things foretold he that are gone

And some to come, but each one sure.
Whether it be to come or none,
We ought to know all will appear.
JESUS ¶Almighty God, my Father free,
In earth thy bidding have done,
And glorified the name of thee;
To thyself glorify thy Son.
As thou hast given me authority,
Of all flesh grant me now my boon,
That those thou gavest might living be
In endless life, and all be one.
That life is this that has no end,
To know the Father most of might,
And me the Son whom thou didst send
To die for man without ill plight.
Mankind was thine; thou didst me send,
And took me to thy ruling right;
I died for man, man's miss to mend,
And unto spiteful death was dight.
Thy will unto them taught have I
That would unto my lore incline;
My lore they took obediently;
None of them shall for grief decline.
Thou gavest them me, yet not thereby,
Yet are they thine as well as mine.
Drive them not from our company,
Since they are mine, and mine are thine.
Since they are ours, if they need ought,
Help thou them, if it be thy will;
And as thou knowest I them bought,
For want of help let them not spill.
From the world to take them pray I not,
But that thou keep them aye from ill.
All those so keep who set their thought
In earth my teaching to fulfil.
My tidings take my company
To teach the people where they fare;
In earth shall they live after me,
And suffer sorrows sad and sore;
Despised and hated shall they be,
As I have been, by less and more,

341

And suffer death in sore degree;
For soothfastness shall none them spare.
Then hallow them, Father, thereby,
In soothfastness so that they may
Be one as we are, you and I,
In will and work both night and day,
And know that I am verily
But soothfastness and life alway;
By which each man of willing way
May win the life that last shall aye.
But ye, my apostles here I mean,
That long have gone about with me,
In great faint-trusting have ye been,
And wondrous hard of hearts are ye.
Worthy to be reproved, I ween,
Are ye forsooth, if ye will see,
In as much as ye all have seen
My work proved and my authority.
When I was dead and laid in grave,
Of my rising ye were in doubt;
And some for my uprising strave
When I was lifelessly laid out
So deep in earth; but since I have
Been walking forty days about,
Eaten with you, your troth to save,
Coming among you in and out.
And therefore be no more in fear
Of mine uprising, day or night;
Your misbelief leave each one here.
For wit ye well, as man of might
Over whom no death shall have power,
I shall be endless life and light.
But for to show you figure clear,
Show I me thuswise to your sight——
How man by course of kind shall rise,
Though he be rotten unto nought,
Out of his grave in this same wise.
At the day of doom shall he be brought
Where I shall sit as true justice
And doom man even as he has wrought.
The wicked to wend with their enemies,

The good to bliss shall they be brought.
Another cause forsooth is this:
On a tree man was betrayed and slain;
I, man, therefore, to mend that miss,
On a tree bought mankind again,
To confusion of him and his
That falsely to forge that fraud was fain,
Mankind to bring again to bliss,
His foe the fiend to endless pain.
The third cause is, truly to tell,
Right as I wend, as well will seem,
So shall I come in flesh and fell
At the day of doom, when I shall deem
The good in endless bliss to dwell,
My foemen from me for to flee,
Without an end in woe to dwell.
Each living man, heed well the same.
But into all the world at hand
The Gospel truly preach shall ye
To every creature alive on land.
Who trusts, if he baptised be,
He shall, if ye shall understand,
Be saved and of all thralldom free;
Who trusts not, as unbelieving found,
For fault of truth condemned is he.
But all these tokens clear and clean
Shall follow them that trust it right——
In my name devils cruel and keen
Shall they cast out of any wight;
With new tongues speak; serpents unclean
Destroy; and if they day or night
Drink venom quick, it shall be seen
To harm them it shall have no might.
On sick folk they their hands shall lay,
And well shall they be soon to wield;
The poor men shall ye have alway,
My company, both in town and field.
And wit ye well, so shall all they
That work my will in youth or eld
Have there a place which I purvey
In bliss with me ever to dwell.

Now is my day's work brought to end,
My time that here to stay was lent.
Up to my Father now I wend
And your Father that down me sent,
My God, your God, and each man's friend
That to his teaching will consent,
To sinners that with sin contend,
That sins amend and will repent.
But since I speak these sayings now
To you, your hearts have heaviness.
Be all fulfilled, profit to show,
That I wend hence, as needful is.
Unless I wend, comes not to you
The comforter of the comfortless;
And if I wend, ye shall find how
I shall send him of my goodness.
My Father's will fulfilled have I,
Therefore farewell, all ye near by.
I go to make a stead ready,
Endless to dwell with me on high.
Send down a cloud, Father, whereby
I come to thee, my Father dear.
My Father's blessing most mighty
Give I to all that I leave here.
Ascendo ad patrem meum.

(*Then the angels sing.*)

MARY ¶Ah, mightful God, aye most of might,
A wondrous sight is this to see!
My son thus to be ravished right,
In a cloud going up from me.
Both heavy is my heart and light;
Heavy that such parting should be,
And light that he holds what he plight,
And goes thus with authority.
His promise holds he in each sort;
That comforts me in all my care.
But unto whom shall I resort?
Bewildered so was I never.
To dwell among these Jews so keen . .
Me to despise will they not spare.

JOHN ¶Though he be not in presence seen,

344

Yet he is salve of every sore.
But, lady, since that he betook
Me for to serve you as your son,
You need nothing, lady, but look
What thing in earth you will have done.
I were to blame if I forsook
To work your will, mid-day or noon,
Or any time whereof you spoke.

MARY ¶I thank thee, John, for this thy boon.
My motherhood, John, shalt thou have,
And for my son I will thee take.

JOHN ¶That grace, dear lady, would I crave.

MARY ¶My Son's words will I never forsake.
It were not seeming that we strave
Nor contraried nought that he spake.
But, John, till I be brought in grave
Thou shalt not see my sorrows slake.

JAMES ¶Our worthy Lord, since that he went
From us, lady, as is his will,
We thank him that to us has lent
To live alive here longer still.
I say for me with full consent,
Thy liking all will I fulfil.

ANDREW ¶So will we all with great talent;
Wherefore, lady, give thee not ill.

1 ANGEL ¶Ye men of the land of Galilee,
Why wonder ye, to heaven looking?
This Jesus, whom from you ye see
Uptaken, ye shall well understand,
Right so again come down shall he.
When he so comes with wounds bleeding,
Who well has wrought full glad may be,
Who ill has lived full sore dreading.

2 ANGEL ¶Ye that have been his servants true,
And with him staying night and day,
Such working as with him ye knew
Look that ye preach it forth alway.
Your meed in heaven is each day new;
Who serve him, please him well each day.
Who trusts you not, it shall them rue;
They must have pains increasing aye.

JAMES ¶Loved be thou, Lord, aye, most of might,
That thus in all our great disease
Comfortest us with thine angels bright.
Now might these Jews their malice cease,
Who saw themselves this wondrous sight
Thus near them wrought under their nose.
And we have matter day and night
Our God more for to praise and please.

ANDREW ¶Now may those Jews be all confused,
If they will think on inwardly
How falsely they have him accused,
Unblemished blamed through their envy.
Their falsehood that they long have used,
Now is it proved here openly.
If they upon this matter mused,
It should stir them to ask mercy.

PETER ¶That will they not, Andrew; let be;
For they are full of pomp and pride.
It may not avail to thee nor me
Nor none of us with them to chide.
Profit to dwell can I none see,
Wherefore let us no longer bide,
But wend we into each country,
To preach through all this world so wide.

JOHN ¶That is our charge, for that is best
That we delay no longer here;
For here get we no place of rest,
To dwell so near the Jewish power.
Us to destroy will they them cast.
Wherefore come forth, my lady dear,
And go we hence. I am full pressed
With you to wend with full good cheer.
My trust is now in every deal
For you to work after your counsel.

JAMES ¶My lady dear, that shall you feel
In ought that ever we may avail.
Our comfort is your care to heal;
While we may live you shall not fail.

MARY ¶My brethren dear, I trust it well;
My Son shall quit you your travail.

PETER ¶To Jerusalem go we again,

346

And look what after may befall.
Our Lord and master most of main,
He guide you and be with you all.

44

THE POTTERES

Maria, duo angeli, xi apostoli, et spiritus sanctus descendens super eos, et iiij Judei admirantes.

PETER ¶Brethren, take tent unto my steven;
Then shall ye stably understand.
Our Master dear is hence to heaven,
To rest there on his Father's right hand,
And we are left alive, eleven,
To learn his laws truly in land.
Ere we begin, we must be even,
Else were our works not to warrant.
For perfect number it is none,
Eleven only to be here;
Twelve may be asunder ta'en
And severed into many a share.
  Nobis precepit dominus predicare populo et
    testificare
  quia prope est judex vivorum et mortuorum.
Our Lord commanded more and less
To rule us rightly after his rede;
He bade us preach and bear witness
That he should doom both quick and dead.
To him all prophets prove express,
All those that trust in his godhead,
Of sins they shall have forgiveness;
And so shall we say plain indeed.
And since we on this wise
Shall his counsel descry,
It needs we us advise
That we say not severally.

JOHN ¶Often he said that we should wend
In all this world his will to work,

348

And by his counsel to be kenned
He said he should set Holy Church.
But first he said he should send down
His messenger, that we should not irk,
His Holy Ghost, on us to land,
And make us to mix with matters mirk.
We mind he told us thus,
When that he fared us fro:
Cum venerit Paraclitus
Docebit vos omnia.

JAMES   ¶Yea, certainly he told us so,
And much more too than we have known.
Nisi ego abiero,
He said forsooth: "Unless I go,
The Holy Ghost shall not be seen."
Et dum assumptus fuero,
"Then shall I send you comfort clean."
Thus told he wholly how
That our deeds should be dight;
So shall we truly trow
He will hold what he hight.

4 APOSTLE   ¶He promised us from harm to hide,
And hold in health both head and hand;
When we take that he told that tide,
From all our foes it shall defend.
But thus in bayle behoves us bide,
Until that message to us he send.
The Jews beset us on each side,
That we may neither walk nor wend.

5 APOSTLE   ¶We dare not walk for dread,
Or comfort come unto.
It is most for our speed
Here to be still stuck so.

MARY   ¶Brethren, what mean you here, now tell,
To make mourning in every deal?
My Son, that of all weal is well,
To work full well he will reveal.
For the tenth day is this to tell
Since he said we should favour feel.
Believe that long it shall not dwell;
And therefore dread you never a deal,

But pray with heart and hand
That we his help may have;
Then shall it soon be sent,
His message that shall save.

1 DOCTOR ¶Hark, master, for Mahound his pain,
How that these mobards madden now!
Their master, that our men have slain,
Has made them on his trifles trow.

2 DOCTOR ¶The lurdan says he lives again.
That matter may they never avow;
For as they heard his preaching plain,
He was away, they wist not how.

1 DOCTOR ¶They wist not where he went,
Therefore fully they fail,
And say there shall be sent
Great help through his counsel.

2 DOCTOR ¶He may send neither cloth nor clout;
He was never but a wretch alway.
Assemble our men and make a shout;
So shall we best yon fools affray.

1 DOCTOR ¶Nay, nay; then will they die for doubt.
I rede we make not mickle bray,
But warily wait when they come out,
And mar them then, if that we may.

2 DOCTOR ¶Now, sure, thereto assent I will;
Yet would I not they wist.
Yon carles then shall we kill,
If they live as we list.

The Holy Ghost descends. Then the angel sings
(Veni Creator Spiritus).

MARY ¶Honour and bliss be ever now,
With worship in this world alway,
To my sovereign Son Jesus,
Our Lord alone that shall last aye.
Now may we trust his tales are true,
By deeds that here are done this day.
As long as you his path pursue,
The fiend shall fail you to affray.
For his high Holy Ghost
He lets here on you land,
All mirth and truth to taste

350

And all sin to amend.

PETER   ¶All sin to mend now have we might;
This is the mirth our Master meant.
I might not look, so was it light.
Ah, loved be he that such has lent.
Now has he held his promise plight.
His Holy Ghost in its descent,
Like to the sun it seemed in sight;
And suddenly then was it sent.

2 APOSTLE   ¶It was sent for our weal;
It gives us hap and heal;
Methinks such force I feel,
I might fell folk full well.

3 APOSTLE   ¶We have force for to fight in field,
And favour of all folk to bear;
With wisdom in this world to wield,
By knowing of all clerkship clear.

4 APOSTLE   ¶We have splendour to be our shield,
And language need we none to learn.
That Lord may give us well to wield
That has us guarded to this year.

5 APOSTLE   ¶This is the year of grace '
That musters us among;
As angels in this place
Have said thus in their song.

1 APOSTLE   ¶Yea; in their saying said they thus,
And told their tales between them two;
Veni creator spiritus;
Mentes tuorum visita.
They prayed the Spirit come to us,
And mend our minds with mirth also;
That learned they of our Lord Jesus,
For He said that it should be so.

2 APOSTLE   ¶He said he should us send
His Holy Ghost from heaven,
Our minds with mirth to mend.
Now is all ordained even.

3 APOSTLE   ¶Even as he said should to us come,
So has been showed unto our sight.
Tristicia implevit cor vestrum:
First sorrow in heart promised he;

Sed convertetur in gaudium:
Then said he that light should we be.
Now what he said thus, all and some,
Is moved among us through his might.

4 APOSTLE ¶His might with main and mood
May comfort all mankind.

1 DOCTOR ¶Hark, man; by Mahound's blood,
These men mad out of mind!
They make chatter of each country,
And learn language of every land.

2 DOCTOR ¶They speak our speech as well as we,
And in each stead they understand.

1 DOCTOR ¶And are not all of Galilee,
That take this hardiness in hand?
But they are drunk, all this company,
With must or wine, I well warrant.

2 DOCTOR ¶Now sure that was well said;
That makes their mind to mar.
Yon traitors shall be afraid,
Ere that they flit aught far.

4 APOSTLE ¶Hark, brethren; watch ye well about;
In our affair we find no friend.
The Jews with strength are stern and stout,
And sharply shape us to offend.

1 APOSTLE ¶Our Master has put all perils out,
And felled the falsehood of the fiend.
Undo your doors, and have no doubt,
For to yon warlocks will we wend.

2 APOSTLE ¶To wend we have no dread,
Nor for to do our debt;
For to name what is need
Shall none alive us let.

PETER ¶Ye Jews that in Jerusalem dwell,
Your tales are false, that shall ye find.
That we are drunken, we hear you tell,
Because you think we have been pined.
A prophet proved—his name's Johell,
A gentle Jew of your own kind—
He speaks thus in his special spell,
And of this matter makes his mind;
By points of prophecy

He told full far before;
Ye may not this deny,
For thus his own words were:
Et erit in novissimis diebus, dicit dominus,
Effundam de spiritu meo super omnem carnem.

3 APOSTLE   ¶Lo, losels, lo! Thus learn ye clear,
How that your elders wrote alway;
The Holy Ghost have we ta'en here,
As your own prophets preached aye.

4 APOSTLE   ¶It is the might of our Master dear,
All deeds that here are done this day.
He gives us might and plain power
To conclude all that ye can say.

1 DOCTOR   ¶These men have mickle might,
Through hap they here have ta'en.

2 DOCTOR   ¶Wend we out of their sight,
And let them even alone.

1 APOSTLE   ¶Now, brethren mine, since we all part,
To teach the faith to foe and friend,
Our tarrying may turn to ill part;
Wherefore I counsel that we wend
Unto our lady, and take our leave.

2 APOSTLE   ¶Surely, with gentle words we will.
My lady, take it not to grieve
I may no longer with you dwell.

MARY   ¶Now, Peter, since it shall be so
That you have divers gates to gang,
There shall none harm you so to do,
While my Son musters you among.
But, John and James, my cousins two,
Look that ye dwell not from me long.

JOHN   ¶Lady, your will in weal and woe,
It shall be wrought, else work we wrong.

JAMES   ¶Lady, we both are bound
At your bidding to be.

MARY   ¶The blessing of my Son
Be both with you and me.

353

45

THE DRAPERS

Jesus, Maria, Gabriell cum duobus angelis, duo virgines et tres Judei de cognacione Marie, viii Apostoli, et ii diaboli.

GABRIEL ¶Hail, mightful Mary, God's mother so mild.
Hail, be thou root of all the rest; hail, be thou royal.
Hail, flower and fruit not faded nor defiled;
Hail, salve to all sinful. Now say thee I shall
Thy Son to thyself has me sent,
His messenger; soothly he says
No longer than these three days
Are left thee this life that is lent.
And therefore he bids thee look that thou blithe be,
For to bigly bliss that lord will thee bring,
There to sit with himself, all solace to see,
To be crowned for his queen and he himself King,
In mirth that shall ever be new.
He sends to thee worthily, I wis,
His palm out of Paradise,
In token that it shall be true.

MARY ¶I thank my Son seemly of his messenger.
Unto Him lastingly be aye loving,
That me thus worthily would honour on this wise,
And to his high bliss my bones for to bring.
But, good sir, name me thy name?

GABRIEL ¶Gabriel, obedient to bring
The bright word of his bearing,
Forsooth, lady, I am the same.

MARY ¶Now, Gabriel, that soothly is from my Son sent,
I thank thee for these tidings thou tellest to me,
And loved be that Lord for the loan that has me lent;
(Obedient I bide to work all his will.)
And, dear Son, I beseech thee,

354

Great God, thou grant me thy grace,
Thine Apostles to have in this place,
That they at my bearing may be.

GABRIEL ¶Now, fairest of face, most faithful and free,
Thine asking thy Son has granted of his grace,
And says all together in sight thou shalt see
All his Apostles appear in this place,
To work all thy will at thy wending.
And soon shall thy sharp pains be past,
And thou be in life that shall last
Evermore, without any ending.

JOHN ¶Mary, my mother that mild is and meek,
Chief chosen for chaste, now tell me, what cheer?

MARY ¶John, son, I tell thee forsooth I am sick.
My sweet Son sent me promise; right now it is here,
And doubtless he says I shall die.
Within three days, I wis,
I shall be sheltered in bliss,
And come to his own company.

JOHN ¶Ah, by thy leave, lady, name it me not,
Nor tell me no tidings to part us in two;
For be thou, blessed lady, unto bier brought,
Evermore while I dwell in this world I have woe.
Therefore let it stay, and be still.

MARY ¶Nay, John, son, myself now I see,
After God's will must it needs be;
Therefore be it wrought at his will.

JOHN ¶Ah worthy, when thou art gone shall I be full woe.
But God grant the Apostles know of thy wending.

MARY ¶Yes, John, son; for certain shall it be so;
All shall they surely be here at my ending.
The messenger of my Son told me this,
That soon shall my penance be past
And I be in life that ever shall last,
Then near him to bide in that bliss.

PETER ¶O God omnipotent, the giver of all grace!
Benedicite domino! A cloud now full clear
Belapped me in Juda preaching as I was,
And I have much marvel how that I come here.

JAMES ¶Ah, cease. Of this assembling can I not say
How and in what wise that we are here met.

355

For suddenly in sight here soon was I set
Either mirth or mourning mean well it may.

ANDREW ¶Ah, brethren. By my thinking, as I wis, so were we.
In divers lands truly our time have we spent,
And how we are assembled thus can I not see,
But as God of his message has us all here sent.

JOHN ¶Ah, fellows, let be your lore,
For as God wills it must needs be;
For peerless of power is he;
His might is to do mickle more.
For Mary, that worthy, shall wend now, I ween,
Unto that great bliss that high bairn has us bought.
That we in her sight all assembled might be seen,
Ere she from us dissever, her Son she besought.
And thus has she wrought at her will,
When she shall be brought on a bier,
That we may be nighing her near
That time, to attend to her still.

MARY ¶Jesu, my darling that worthy is and dear,
I thank thee, my dear Son, of all thy great grace,
That all this fair fellowship at hand I have here,
That to me some comfort may give in this case.
This sickness, it sits me full sore.
My maidens, take care now of me,
And cast some cool water upon me—
I faint . . . so feeble I fare.

1 MAID ¶Alas for my lady that gleamed so light.
That ever I lived in this life thus long in the land,
That I on this seemly one should see such a sight!

2 MAID ¶Alas, help! She dies in our hand.
Ah, Mary, of me have thou mind,
Some comfort us two for to give;
(Full woe without thee must we live.)
Thou knowest we are come of thy kind.

MARY ¶What ails you women, with woe thus wanly to weep?
Ye do me harm with your din, for I must needs die.
Ye should, when ye saw me so drowsy to sleep,
Have left your lamenting and let me lie.
John, cousin, make them stay and be still.

JOHN ¶Ah, Mary, that mild is of mood,
When thy Son was raised on the rood,

356

To tend thee he gave thee to me,
And therefore at thy bidding obedient I will be.
If there be ought, mother, that I amend may,
I pray thee, mildest of mood, that thou move it to me,
And I shall, dearworthy dame, do it every day.

MARY ¶Ah, John, son, that this pain were overpast.
With good heart, all ye that are here,
Pray for me faithfully and clear,
For I must wend from you full fast.

1 JEW ¶Ah, maid fairest of face, most faithful to find,
Thou maiden and mother that mild is and meek,
As thou art courteous and come of our kind,
All our sins for to cease thy Son now beseech,
With mercy to mend our amiss.

2 JEW ¶Since, lady, you come of our kin,
Now help us, thou very virgin,
That we may be brought unto bliss.

MARY ¶Jesu my son, for my sake beseech I thee this . . .
As thou art gracious and good thou grant me thy grace . . .
They that come of my kin that amend their amiss
Now specially speed them and spare them a space,
And be their shield, if thy will be.
And, dearest Son, when I shall die,
I pray thee, of thy mercy
The fiend that thou let me not see.
And also, my blessed bairn, if thy will be,
I seriously beseech thee, my son, for my sake,
Men that are stiffly bested in storms or in sea
And are in will wisely my worship to wake,
And then name my name in that need,
Thou let them not perish nor spill.
Of this boon, my Son, at thy will,
Grant me especially to speed.
Also, my blest bairn, thou grant me my boon:
All that are in hurt or in need and name me by name,
I pray thee, Son, for my sake thou succour them soon,
In all assaults that are sharp thou shield them from
  shame.
And women also in their childing
Now specially thou them speed;
And if so be they die in that dread,

357

To thy bliss then directly them bring.

JESUS ¶Mary my mother, through the might now of me,
For to make thee in mind and in mirth to be mending,
Thine asking all wholly here promise I thee.
But, mother, the fiend must be needs at thine ending
In figure full foul to affright thee.
Mine angels shall then be about thee;
And therefore, dear dame, thou needs not doubt thee,
For doubtless thy death shall not fright thee.
And therefore, my mother, come mildly to me,
For after the sun my message will I send,
And to sit with myself all solace to see,
An everlasting life in liking to spend.
In this bliss shall be all thy dwelling;
Of mirth shalt thou never have missing,
But evermore bide in my blessing.
All this shalt thou have at thy wielding.

MARY ¶I thank thee, my sweet Son, for sure I am sick.
I may not now move me, for mercy . . . almost . . .
To thee, Son, that made me thy maiden so meek.
Here, through thy grace, my Son, I give thee my ghost.
My simple soul I thee send
To heaven that is highest in height,
To thee, Son, that most is of might;
Receive it here into thy hand.

JESUS ¶Mine angels lovely to see, lighter than the leven,
Into the earth swiftly I will that ye wend,
And bring me my mother to the highest of heaven,
With mirth and with melody, her mood for to mend.
For here shall her bliss be abiding;
My mother shall mildly by me
Sit next the high Trinity,
And never in two be dividing.

1 ANGEL ¶Lord, at thy bidding obedient I will be;
That flower never fading full fain will we bring.

2 ANGEL ¶And at thy will, good Lord, work so will we,
With solace on each side that seemly enclosing.

3 ANGEL ¶Let us fly to her fast with force to defend,
That bride for to bring to this bliss bright;
Body and soul we shall make her ascend,
To reign in this regally, by reason full right.

4 ANGEL ❡To bliss that bride for to bring,
Now, Gabriel, let us swiftly be wending.
This maiden's mirth to be mending,
A seemly song now let us sing.
Cum uno diabolo.
And they sing an antiphon, namely, Ave regina celorum.

46

THE WEVERS OF WOLLEN

Maria ascendens cum turba angelorum, viii Apostoli, et
Thomas Apostolus predicans in deserto.

THOMAS ¶In wailing and weeping, in woe am I wrapped,
In shame and in sorrow, in sighing full sad.
My lord and my love, lo, full low is he lapped;
That makes me to mourn now full dull and full bad.
What dragging and what hurling that headman he had;
What breaking of branches were bursten about him;
What bruising of beating of wretches full bad!
It learns me full loyal to love and to lout him,
That comely to ken.
God's son Jesus,
He died for us;
That makes me thus
To mourn among many men.
Among men may I mourn for the malice they meant
To Jesu, the gentlest of Jews' generation.
Of wisdom and wit were the ways that he went,
That drew all these doomsmen's deep indignation.
For doubtless full dear was his due domination.
Unkindly they showed him their king for token,
With comfort of care and cold recreation.
For he mustered his miracles among many men,
And to the people he preached;
But the Pharisees fierce
All his reasons reverse,
And to their headmen rehearse
That untrue were the tales that he teached.
He teached full true, but the tyrants were pained;
For he reproved their pride, they purposed do fast;
To mischief him with malice in their mind have they
meaned,
And to accuse him of cursedness the caitiffs have cast.

Their rancour was raised, no man might it rest.
They took him with treason, that turtle of truth;
They fed him with flaps, with fierceness held fast;
To tug him and rive him there reigned no ruth.
Unduly they doomed him.
They dushed him, they dashed him;
They lushed him, they lashed him;
They pushed him, they pashed him;
All sorrow they said it beseemed him.
It beseemed him all sorrow, they said in their saying.
They skipped and they scourged him; he 'scaped not with
　　scorns.
That he was leader and lord in their law lay no alleging,
But forced on and thrusted a crown of thick thorns.
Each tag of that turtle so tattered and torn is,
That that blessed body is blue and swollen for beating;
Yet the headmen to hang him with huge hideous horns
As brutish or bribers were baaling and bleating.
"Crucify him" they cried.
Soon Pilate in parliament
Of Jesus gave judgement;
To hang him the harlots were bent;
There was no deed of that doomsman denied.
Denied not that doomsman to doom him to death,
That friendly fair form that never offended.
They hied them in haste then to hang up their head—
What woe that they wrought, no wight would have
　　weened it.
His true title, they took them no time to attend it,
But as a traitor attainted they pulled him and tugged him;
They shunned for no shouts his shape for to rend it.
They raised him on rood, as full wrathfully they rugged
　　him.
They pierced him with a spear,
That the blood royal
To the earth 'gan fall,
In redemption of all
That his loyal laws like to learn here.
To learn he that likes of that law that is leal,
May find him our friend here full faithful and fast,
That would hang thus on high to enhance us in weal
And buy us from bondage by his blood that is best

Then the comfort of our company in cares were cast,
But that lord so alone would not leave us full long;
On the third day he rose right in his realm to rest.
Both flesh and fell freshly that figure put on,
And to me brethren did appear.
They told me of this,
But I believed amiss;
To rise fleshly, I wis,
I thought it past any man's power.
But the power of that prince was preciously proved,
When that sovereign shewed himself to my sight.
To mark of his manhood my mind was all moved,
But that reverend reduced me by reason and right.
The wounds full wide of that worthy wight,
He told me to feel them, my faith to make fast;
And so I did doubtless, and down I me dight,
Bent my back for to bow and obeyed him for best.
So soon he ascended;
And my fellows there
Far sundered were.
If they were here,
My mirth were mickle amended.
Amended were my mirth with that company to meet;
My fellows together for to find am I bound.
I shall not stay in no stead, but in stall and in street
Get ready by guides to get them on ground.
O sovereign! How soon am I set here so sound.
This is the Vale of Josaphat; in Jewry 'tis known.
I will stem of my saying, and stay here a tide,
For I am weary of walking the ways that I went
Full wildsome and wild.
Therefore I cast
Here for to rest;
I hold it best
To prepare on this bank for to bide.

  [*A page of music follows; the words are:* Surge proxina
  mea columba mea tabernaculum glorie vasculum vite
  templum celeste.]

1 ANGEL ¶Rise, Mary, thou maiden and mother so mild.
2 ANGEL ¶Rise, lily full lusty; thy love is full liking.
3 ANGEL ¶Rise, chieftain of chastity, in cheering thy child.
4 ANGEL ¶Rise, rose ripe redolent, in rest to be reigning.

5	ANGEL	¶Rise, dove of that doomsman who all deeds is deeming.
6	ANGEL	¶Rise, turtle, tabernacle, temple full true.
7	ANGEL	¶Rise, seemly in sight, of thy Son to be seeming.
8	ANGEL	¶Rise, gathered full goodly, in grace for to grow.
9	ANGEL	¶Rise up now anon.
10	ANGEL	¶Come, chosen child.
11	ANGEL	¶Come, Mary, mild.
12	ANGEL	¶Come, flower undefiled.
8	ANGEL	¶Come up to the King to be crowned.

Veni de Libano sponsa mea coronaberis.

THOMAS ¶O glorious God, what gleams are gliding?
I move in my mind what this may bemean.
I see a bride born in bliss to be biding,
With angels' company comely and clean.
Many strange sights in sooth have I seen,
But this mirth and this melody mingles my mood.

MARY ¶Thomas, away with thy doubts at my tiding,
For I am going forth to my fair son so good,
I tell thee this tide.

THOMAS ¶Who, my sovereign lady?

MARY ¶Yea, surely, I tell thee.

THOMAS ¶Wither wending, I pray thee?

MARY ¶In bliss with my bairn for to bide.

THOMAS ¶To bide with thy bairn, in bliss to be biding?
Hail, gentlest of Jesse in Jews' generation.
Hail, wealth of this world all weal that is wielding;
Hail, gentlest enhanced to high habitation.
Hail, precious and dear is thy due domination.
Hail, flower well flourished and fruit full of savour.
Hail, seat of our Saviour and see of salvation.
Hail, happy to hold to; thy help is full of favour.
Hail, peerless in pleasance.
Hail, precious and pure.
Hail, salve that is sure.
Hail, letter of languour.
Hail, help of our hurt in obeisance.

MARY ¶Go to thy brethren in sorrow abiding,
And say in what wise to weal I am wending.
Without any tarrying tell them this tiding,
Their mirth so best much increase giving.
They, Thomas, to me were attending,
When I drew to my death, all but thou.

363

THOMAS   ¶But I, lady? While in land I am living,
To obey thee obedient my bones will I bow.
But I, alas?
Where was I then,
When that trouble began?
An unhappy man
Both now and ever I was.
Unhappy, uncourteous, am I held at home.
What dreary deserting drew me from death's deed?

MARY   ¶Thomas, cease of thy sorrows. I am soothly the same.

THOMAS   ¶That wot I well, thou worthiest that wrapped is in weed.

MARY   ¶Then spare not a space my speech for to speed.
Go tell them soothly, you saw me ascending.

THOMAS   ¶Now doubtless, most worthy, I dare not for dread.
For to tales that I tell they are not attending,
For no spell that is spoken.

MARY   ¶I shall thee show
A token true
Full fresh of hue. . . .
My girdle, lo, take them this token.

THOMAS   ¶I thank thee as reverend root of our rest;
I thank thee as steadfast stock for to stand;
I thank thee as trusty tree for to trust;
I thank thee as bending bough to the band;
I thank thee as leaf the lustiest in the land.
I thank thee as beauteous branch for to bear.
I thank thee as flower that never fades here.
I thank thee as fruit that has fed us for fare.
I thank thee for ever.
If they reprove me,
Now shall they leave me.
Thy blessing give me,
And doubtless I shall do my devoir.

MARY   ¶Thomas, to do thy devoir is fitting.
He bid thee his blessing that dwelleth above,
And in sight of my own Son there sitting
Shall I kneel to that comely with crown.
For who in despair by dale or by down
With piteous plaint in perils will pray me,
If he sink or sweat, in fainting or swoon,
I shall sue to my sovereign son for to say me,
He shall grant them his grace.

Be it man in his mourning,
Or woman in childing,
All these to be helping
That Prince shall I pray in that place.

THOMAS ¶Gramercy, thou goodliest grounded in grace;
Gramercy, thou loveliest lady of allure;
Gramercy, the fairest in figure and face;
Gramercy, the dearest to do our desire.

MARY ¶Farewell. Now I pass to the peerless empire.
Farewell, Thomas; I tarry no longer tide here.

THOMAS ¶Farewell, shining shape that shinest so sheer;
Farewell, the best of all beauties to bide here.
Farewell, thou fair face;
Farewell, key of counsel;
Farewell, all this world's weal;
Farewell, our hap and our heal;
Farewell now, all goodness and grace.

> *Veni electa mea et ponam in tronum meum Quia concupivit*
> *rex speciem tuam.*

THOMAS ¶That I met with this here my mirths may amend;
I will hie me in haste and perform what I plight.
To bear my brethren this message my back shall I bend,
And tell them in certain the truth of this sight.
By dale and by down I shall dress me to dight;
I shall run and rest not to ransack full right.
Lo, the men I meant, I meet them even on my way.
God save you all here.
Say, brethren, what cheer?

PETER ¶What doest thou here?
Thou may on thy gate now be going away.

THOMAS ¶Why, dear brethren, what grief is begun?

PETER ¶Thomas, I tell thee, in trouble we run.

THOMAS ¶I thought that my friends full faithful were found.

JAMES ¶Yea, but in care little kindness you have done.

ANDREW ¶With brag and with boast is he busy to bid us;
If there come any cares he cares not to ken.
We may run till we rave, ere any truth rid us,
For all friendship he fetched us, by frith or by fen.

THOMAS ¶Sirs, I marvel, I tell you,
What moves in your mind.

JOHN ¶We can well find
Thou art unkind.

THOMAS ¶Now peace, then, and prove it, I pray you.
PETER ¶Then come not to court here; unkindness thou did us.
Our trust has turned us to trouble alway.
This year hast thou roved; thy ruth would not rid us.
For wit well, that worthy has gone on her way.
In a deep den is she delven this day,
Mary, that maiden and mother so mild.
THOMAS ¶That know I full well.
JAMES ¶Thomas, away.
ANDREW ¶It helps not to hear him; he will not be beguiled.
THOMAS ¶Sirs, with her have I spoken
Later than ye.
JOHN ¶That may not be.
THOMAS ¶Yes, kneeling on knee.
PETER ¶Then quick! Can you tell us some token?
THOMAS ¶Lo, this token full trusty she told me to take you.
JAMES ¶Ah Thomas, where got you that girdle we see?
THOMAS ¶Sir, my messages are moving some mirth for to make
you;
For fleeing fleshly I found her with her fair son to be;
And when I met with that maiden it mingled my mood.
Her message she sent you, so seemly to see.
ANDREW ¶Yea, Thomas, unsteadfast full staring you stood;
That makes thy mind now full mad for to be.
But hearken and hear now;
Let us look where we laid her,
If any folk have affrayed her.
JOHN ¶Go we, grope where we laid her,
If we find out that fair one together now.
PETER ¶Behold now! Hither all hie in haste.
This glorious and goodly is gone from this grave.
THOMAS ¶To my talking you took no intent for to trust.
JAMES ¶Ah Thomas, untruly now trespassed we have;
Mercy full kindly we cry and we crave.
ANDREW ¶Mercy, for foul is our fault, by my fay.
JOHN ¶Mercy, we pray thee; we will not deprave.
PETER ¶Mercy, for deeds we did thee this day.
THOMAS ¶Our Saviour so sweet
Forgive you all,
And so I shall.
This token tall
Have I brought you, your bales to abate.

PETER   ¶It is welcome, I wis, from that worthy wight,
For it was wont to wrap that worthy virgin.

JAMES   ¶It is welcome, I wis, from that lady so light,
For her form would she wrap it in, delighting therein.

ANDREW   ¶It is welcome, I wis, from that salver of sin,
For she bent it about her with blossoms so bright.

JOHN   ¶It is welcome, I wis, from the queen of our kin,
For about that reverend it reached full right.

PETER   ¶Now kneel we each one
Upon our knee.

JAMES   ¶To that lady free.

ANDREW   ¶Blest might she be,
Yea, for she is lady lovesome alone.

THOMAS   ¶Now, brethren, be busy; brisk prepare for the way;
To Ind will I turn me and travel to teach.

PETER   ¶And to Romans so royal, in secret to say,
Will I pass from this place, my people to preach.

JAMES   ¶And I shall Samaritans seriously seek,
To warn them by wisdom they work not in waste.

ANDREW   ¶And I to Achaia truly, in that land to be leech
Will hie me to help them and heal them in haste.

JOHN   ¶This covenant accords.
Sirs, since ye will so,
I must needs part you fro.
To Asia will I go.
May he lead you, the Lord of all lords.

THOMAS   ¶The Lord of all lords, in land shall he lead you,
While ye travel in trouble, the truth for to teach.
With fruit of your faith freely shall he feed you,
For that labour is lovesome, each land for to leech.
Now I pass from your presence, the people to preach,
To lead them and learn them the law of our Lord.
As I said, we must sunder and earnestly seek
Each country to keep clean and knit in one cord
Of our faith so great.
That lord so good
That died on rood,
With main and mood
He guide you by guides full straight.

47

THE OSTELERES

Maria, Jesus coronans eam, cum turba angelorum cantans.

JESUS ¶Mine angels that are bright of sheen,
On my message take ye the way
Unto Mary, my mother clean,
That lady brighter than the day.
Greet her all well, even as I mean.
And to that seemly shall ye say,
Of heaven I have her chosen queen,
In joy and bliss that last shall aye.
I will you tell what I have thought,
And why that you shall to her wend.
I will her body to me be brought,
To be in bliss without an end.
My flesh of her on earth was ta'en;
Unkindly thing it were, I wis,
That she should bide by her alone,
And I dwell here so high in bliss.
Therefore to her forth shall ye fare,
Full friendly for to fetch her hither.
There is no thing that I love more;
In bliss then shall we be together.

1 ANGEL ¶O blissful lord, now most of might,
We are ready with speed of flight
Thy bidding to fulfil,
To thy mother, that maiden free,
Chosen chief of chastity,
As it is thy will.

2 ANGEL ¶Of thy message we are full fain;
We are ready with might and main,
Both by day and by night.
Heaven and earth now glad may be

368

              That noble lady now to see
              In whom that thou didst light.

3 ANGEL   ¶Lord Jesu Christ our governour,
              We all are ready at thy bidding;
              With joy and bliss and great honour
              We shall thy mother to thee bring.

4 ANGEL   ¶Hail, daughter of the blessed Anne,
              The which conceived through Holy Ghost,
              And thou brought forth both God and man,
              The which felled down the fiendish host.

5 ANGEL   ¶Hail, root of right that forth has brought
              That blessed flower our Saviour,
              The same that made mankind of nought,
              And brought him up into his tower.

6 ANGEL   ¶Of thee alone he would be born
              Into this world of wretchedness,
              To save mankind that was forlorn
              And bring him out of great distress.

1 ANGEL   ¶Thou mayest be glad both day and night
              To see thy Son our Saviour;
              He will crown thee now,.lady bright,
              Thou blessed mother and fair flower.

2 ANGEL   ¶Mary mother and maiden clean,
              Chosen chief unto thy child,
              Of heaven and earth now art thou queen;
              Come up now, lady meek and mild.

3 ANGEL   ¶Thy Son has sent us after thee,
              To bring thee now unto his bliss;
              There shalt thou dwell and blithe shalt be;
              Of joy and mirth thou shalt not miss.

4 ANGEL   ¶For in his bliss without an end
              Shalt thou all kind of solace see,
              Thy life in liking for to spend
              With thy dear Son in Trinity.

   MARY   ¶Ah, blest be God for his command;
              Himself best knoweth what is to do.
              I thank him with my heart and hand,
              That thus his bliss would take me to.
              And you also, his angels bright,
              That from my Son to me are sent;
              I am ready with all my might

For to fulfil his commandment.

5 ANGEL ¶Go we now, thou worthy wight,
Unto thy Son that is so gent.
We shall bring thee into his sight,
To crown thee queen; thus has he meant.

6 ANGEL ¶All heaven and earth shall worship thee
Obediently at thy bidding.
Thy joy shall ever increased be;
Of solace sure then shall you sing.

Cantando.

1 ANGEL ¶Jesu, my lord and heaven's king,
Here is thy mother for whom you sent.
We have brought her at thy bidding;
Take her to thee as thou hast meant.

MARY ¶Jesu, my Son, loved might you be.
I thank thee heartily in my thought,
That in this wise ordained for me,
And to thy bliss thou hast me brought.

JESUS ¶Hail be thou, Mary, maiden bright;
Thou art my mother and I thy son.
With grace and goodness art thou dight,
With me in bliss aye to be one.
Now shalt thou have what I have plight;
Thy time is past of all thy care;
Worship thee shall the angels bright;
Annoy shalt thou wit never more.

MARY ¶Jesu, my Son, loved might thou be.
I thank thee heartily in my thought,
That on this wise ordains for me,
And to this bliss thou hast me brought.

JESUS ¶Come forth with me, my mother bright;
Into my bliss we shall ascend,
To dwell in weal, thou worthy wight,
That never more shall have an end.
Thy hurts, mother, to name them now,
Are turned to joy, and sooth it is,
All angels bright to thee shall bow
And worship worthily, I wis.
For mickle joy, mother, had you
When Gabriel greeted you by this,
And told thee trustfully to trow

370

You should conceive the king of bliss.

1 ANGEL ❡Now, maiden meek and mother mine,
It was full mickle mirth to thee,
That I should lie in womb of thine,
Through greeting of an angel free.

2 ANGEL ❡The second joy, mother, was thine,
Without pain when thou barest me.

3 ANGEL ❡The third, after my bitter pain
From death to life you saw me be.

4 ANGEL ❡The fourth was when I climbed up right
To heaven unto my father dear.
My mother, when you saw that sight,
To thee it was a solace clear.

5 ANGEL ❡This is the fifth, thou worthy wight;
Of all thy joys this has no peer.
Now shalt thou dwell in bliss so bright
For ever and aye, I tell thee here.

6 ANGEL ❡For thou art chief of chastity;
Of all women thou bearest the flower.
Now shalt thou, lady, dwell with me
In bliss that shall ever endure.

1 ANGEL ❡Full high on height in majesty,
With all worship and all honours,
Where we shall ever with thee be,
There dwelling in our blissful bowers.

2 ANGEL ❡All kind of sweetness is therein
That man may think upon or wife;
With joy and bliss that now begin,
There shalt thou, lady, lead thy life.

3 ANGEL ❡Thou shalt be worshipped with honours,
In heaven's bliss that is so bright,
With martyrs and with confessors,
With all virgins, thou worthy wight.

JESUS ❡Before all other created thing
I shall give thee both grace and might,
In heaven and earth succour to bring
To all that serve thee, day and night.
I grant them grace with all my might,
Through asking of thy prayer,
That to thee call by day or night,
In what disease soe'er they are.

371

THE OSTELERES

Thou art my life and my liking,
My mother and my maiden sheen.
Receive this crown, my dear darling;
Where I am king thou shalt be queen.
Mine angels bright, a song now sing;
In honour of my mother dear.
And here I give you my blessing
Wholly to have to all you here.

48

Return to stereotypes not the
landscape

Doctrinal & dogmatic –
in approach

Didactic style.

48

THE MERCERES

Jesus, Maria, xij apostoli, iiij angeli cum tubis et iiij cum corona, lancea et ij flagellis; iiij spiritus boni et iiij spiritus maligni, et vi diaboli.

GOD   ¶First when I this world had wrought,
Wood and wind and waters wan
And everything that now is aught,
Full well methought that I did then;
When they were made good I them thought.
Then to my likeness made I man,
And man to grieve me gave he nought.
Thus rue I that I the world began.
When I had made man at my will,
I gave him wits himself to wis;
In Paradise I put him still,
And bade him hold it all as his.
But of the tree of good and ill,
I said "What time thou eatest of this,
Man, thou speedest thyself to spill;
Thou shalt be brought out of all bliss."
But straightway man brake my bidding;
He thought to have been a god thereby;
He thought to have wit of every thing,
In world to have been as wise as I.
He ate the apple I bid should hang;
So he was beguiled through gluttony.
Then both him and his offspring,
To pine I put them all thereby.
Till long and late methought it good
To catch these caitiffs out of care.
I sent my Son with full blithe mood
To earth, to salve them of their sore.

For ruth of them he hung on rood,
And bought them with his body bare;
For them he shed his heart and blood.
What kindness might I do them more?
Then afterward he harried Hell,
And took out those wretches that were therein;
There fought he with those fiends fell
For them that sunken were for sin.
And since in earth he went to dwell,
Example he gave them, heaven to win;
In Temple himself did teach and tell
To buy them endless bliss therein.
So have they found me full of mercy,
Full of grace and forgiveness,
And they as wretches knowingly
Have led their life in wickedness.
Oft have they grieved me grievously;
Thus they requite me my kindness;
Therefore no longer, certainly,
Will I endure their wickedness.
Men see the world but vanity,
Yet will no man beware thereby;
Each day a mirror may they see,
Yet think they not that they shall die.
All that ever I said should be
Is now fulfilled through prophecy;
Therefore now is it time to me
To make ending of man's folly.
I have endured man many a year
In lust and liking for to spend,
And scarcely find I far or near
A man that will his miss amend.
In earth I see but sinners here;
Therefore mine angels will I send
To blow their trumpets, that all may hear
The time is come when I make end.
Angels, blow your trumpets high,
Every creature for to call;
Learned and lewd, both man and wife,
Receive their doom this day they shall.
Every one that e'er had life,

374

Be none forgotten, great or small;
There shall they see those wounds five
That my Son suffered for them all.
And sunder them before my sight;
All one in bliss they shall not be.
My blessed children, here on height
On my right hand I shall them see;
And then shall every wicked wight
On my left side for fearing flee.
This day their doom thus have I dight,
To every man as he has served me.

I ANGEL   ¶Loved be thou, Lord of might the most,
That angels made for messenger.
Thy will shall be fulfilled in haste,
That heaven and earth and hell shall hear.
Good and ill, each single ghost,
Rise, fetch your flesh that ye did bear;
For all this world is brought to waste;
Draw to your doom; nigh comes it near.

2 ANGEL   ¶Every creature both old and young,
Betimes I bid that you arise;
Body and soul now with you bring,
And come before the high justice.
For I am sent from heaven's King,
To call you to his great assise.
Therefore rise up and give reckoning,
How ye served him in every wise.

1 GOOD SOUL   ¶Loved be that Lord who bright does shine,
That in this manner made us rise,
Body and soul together clean,
To come before the high justice.
Let our ill deeds, Lord, be not seen,
That we have wrought in many wise;
But grant us grace and mercy clean,
That we may pass to Paradise.

2 GOOD SOUL   ¶Ah, loved be thou, Lord of all,
That heaven and earth and all hast wrought,
That with thine angels would us call
Out of our graves here to be brought.
Oft have we grieved thee, great and small;
Thereafter, Lord, now doom us not.

Suffer us not to be fiends' thrall,
That oft in earth with sin us sought.

1 BAD SOUL ¶Alas, alas! That we were born.
So may we sinful caitiffs say.
I hear well by this hideous horn
It draws full near unto Doomsday.
Alas, we wretches are forlorn
That ne'er to please God did essay;
But oft we have his flesh forsworn.
Alas, alas, and welaway!
What shall we wretches do for dread,
Or where for fearing may we flee,
When we may bring forth no good deed
Before him that our Judge shall be?
To ask mercy we have no need,
For well I wot condemned are we.
Alas, that we such life should lead
That drew us to this destiny.
Our wicked works will us destroy,
That we weened never should be witten;
That we did oft full privily,
Openly may we see it written.
Ah, wretches, dear must we abide;
Full smart with hell fire be we smitten;
Now may ne'er soul nor body die,
But with sharp pains evermore be beaten.
Alas, for dread sore may we quake;
Our deeds be our damnation;
For our mismoving must we make;
There is no help in excusation.
We must be set for our sins' sake
For ever far from our salvation,
In hell to dwell with fiends black,
Where never shall there be redemption.

2 BAD SOUL ¶As careful caitiffs may we rise;
Sore may we wring our hands and weep;
For cursedness and covetise
Damned we be to hell full deep.
Reckoned we never of God's service,
His commandments would we not keep;
But oft times made we sacrifice

376

To Satan, while others did sleep.
Alas, now wakens all our care;
Our wicked works we may not hide,
But on our backs we must them bear;
They will destroy us on each side.
I see foul fiends to fill our fear,
And all for pomp of wicked pride;
Weep now we may with many a tear.
Alas, that we this day should bide!
Before us plainly shall be brought
The deeds that shall us damn today,
That ears have heard or heart has thought
Since any time that we may say,
That foot has gone or hand has wrought,
That mouth has spoken or eye has seen;
This day full dear shall they be bought.
Alas, unborn that we had been!

3 ANGEL ¶Stand not together; part you in two;
All one shall ye not be in bliss.
The Father in heaven wills it be so,
For many of you have wrought amiss.
Ye good, on his right hand now go;
The way to heaven shall be this.
Ye wicked wights, now flee him fro
On his left hand, as none of his.

GOD [*the Son*] ¶This woeful world is brought to an end;
My Father in heaven wills it to be.
Therefore to earth now will I wend,
Myself to sit in majesty.
To deem my dooms I will descend;
This body will I bear with me;
How it was dight, man's sin to mend,
Now all mankind there shall it see.
My apostles and my darlings dear,
The dreadful doom this day is dight.
Both heaven and earth and hell shall hear
How I shall hold my promise plight,
That ye shall sit upon seats here
Beside myself to see that sight,
And for to deem folks far and near
After their working, wrong or right.

377

I said also, when I you sent
To suffer sorrow for my sake,
All they that would them right repent
Should with you wend and joyful wake;
Those to your tales who took no tent
Should fare to fire with fiends black.
Of mercy now may nought be meant,
But as their work was, weal or wrack.
My promise wholly I fulfil,
Therefore come forth and sit me by,
To hear the doom of good and ill.

> [*A XVI Century note suggests that some lines have been lost or altered here and six lines later. "De novo facto," and not copied into this text.*]

1 APOSTLE ¶I love thee, Lord God almighty,
Late and early, loud and still;
To do thy bidding fain am I;
I oblige me to do thy will
With all my might, as is worthy.

2 APOSTLE ¶Ah, mightful God, here is it seen
Thou wilt fulfil thy foreword right,
And all thy sayings will maintain;
I love thee, Lord, with all my might.
Therefore us that have earthly been
Such dignities have dressed and dight.

GOD [*the Son*] ¶Come forth; I shall sit you between,
And all fulfil that I have plight.

> *Here he goes to the Judgment seat with the song of angels.*

1 DEVIL ¶Fellows, array us for to fight;
Our fee to take fast let us go.
The dreadful doom this day is dight;
I dread me that we are full slow.

2 DEVIL ¶We shall be seen ever in their sight,
And warily wait, else work we wrong;
For if the doomsman do us right,
Full great party shall with us gang.

3 DEVIL ¶He shall do right to foe and friend,
For now shall all the sooth be sought;
All wicked wights with us shall wend;
To endless pain shall they be brought.

378

*. . . [A passage (?4 lines) "de novo facto" for 1 and 2
Bad Souls lost here.]*

GOD [*the Son*] ¶Every creature, take intent
What bidding now to you I bring.
This woeful world to nothing went,
And I am come as crowned king.
My Father in heaven has me sent
To deem your deeds and make ending.
Come is the day of judgment;
Of sorrow may every sinner sing;
The day is come of caitiffness,
All them to grieve that are unclean;
The day of bale and bitterness;
Full long abided has it been;
The day of dread to more and less,
Of care, of trembling, sorrow keen,
That every wight that wicked is
May say "Alas this day is seen!"
Here may ye see my five wounds wide
Which I endured for your misdeed,
Through heart and head, foot, hand and hide,
Not for my guilt, but for your need.
Behold my body, back and side,
How dear I bought your brotherhood.
These bitter pains would I abide,
To buy you bliss, thus would I bleed.
My body was scourged with cruel skill;
As thief full sorely was I threat;
On cross they hanged me on a hill
Bloody and blue as I was beat;
With crown of thorn thrust on full ill,
The spear into my side was set;
My heart blood spared they not to spill;
Man, for thy love I bore it yet.
The Jews spit on me spiteously;
They spared me no more than a thief;
When they struck me I stood full still;
Against them did I nothing grieve.
Behold, mankind, for it is I
That for thee suffered such mischief.
Thus was I dight for thy folly;

379

See how dear to me was thy life.
Thus was I dight thy sorrow to slake;
Man, thus was I made pledge for thee.
For this did I no vengeance take;
My will it was, for love of thee.
Man, sorely ought you for to quake,
This dreadful day such sight to see.
All this I suffered for thy sake:
Say, man, what suffered thou for me?
My blessed bairns on my right hand,
Your doom this day ye need not dread;
For all your comfort's at command;
Your life in liking shall ye lead.
Come to the kingdom's lasting land
For you prepared for your good deed.
Full blithe may ye be where ye stand,
For mickle in heaven shall be your meed.
When I was hungry, ye me fed,
To slake my thirst your heart was free;
When I was clotheless ye me clad,
Ye would no sorrow on me see.
In hard prison when I was stead,
On my pains then ye had pity;
Full sick when I was brought in bed,
Kindly ye came to comfort me.
When I was weak and weariest,
Ye harboured me full heartily;
Full glad then were ye of your guest,
Supplied my poverty piteously;
At once ye brought me of the best,
And made my bed full easily.
Therefore in heaven shall be your rest,
In joy and bliss to be by me.

1 GOOD SOUL ¶When had we, Lord that all hast wrought,
Meat or drink wherewith thee to feed,
Since we in earth had never nought
But through the grace of thy godhead?

2 GOOD SOUL ¶When was't that we clothes to thee brought,
Or visit thee in any need,
Or in thy sickness we thee sought?
Lord, when did we to thee this deed?

GOD [*the Son*]   ¶My blessed children, hear me say
What time this deed was to me done.
When any that need had, night or day,
Asked for your help and had it soon.
Your free hearts said them never nay,
Early nor late, midday nor noon;
But as ofttimes as they would pray,
They need but bide and have their boon.
Ye cursed caitiffs, kin of Cain,
That ne'er gave comfort in my care,
I and you for ever will be twain,
In dole to dwell for ever more.
Your bitter bales endless begin,
That ye shall have when ye come there;
Ye have deserved so for your sin,
Your grievous deeds that ye did ere.
When I had need of meat and drink,
Caitiffs, ye caught me from your gate;
When ye were set as sirs on bench,
I stood without, weary and wet.
Not one of you would on me think,
Pity to have of my poor state.
Therefore to hell I bid you sink,
And worthy well to go that gate.
When I was sick and sorriest,
Ye visited not, for I was poor;
In prison pent when I was fast,
None of you looked how I might fare.
When I knew never where to rest,
With dints ye drove me from your door;
But ever to pride ye promptly pressed;
My flesh, my blood, oft ye forswore.
Clothesless when I was oft and cold,
For need of you I went all naked;
House nor harbour, help nor hold,
Had I none of you, though I quaked.
My mischief saw ye manifold;
Not one of you my sorrow slaked,
But ever forsook me, young and old.
Therefore shall I now you forsake.

I BAD SOUL   ¶When hadst thou, Lord that all things has,

THE MERCERES

Hunger or thirst, since God thou is?
When was it thou in prison was?
When wast thou naked or harbourless?

2 BAD SOUL ¶When was it we saw thee sick, alas?
When did we this unkindliness,
Weary or wet to let thee pass?
When did we thee this wickedness?

GOD ¶Caitiffs, as oft as did betide
The needful asked ought in my name,
Ye heard them not, your ears ye hid,
Your help to them was not at home—
To me ye that unkindness did;
Therefore ye bear this bitter blame.
To least or most when ye it did,
To me ye did the self and same.
My chosen children, come to me;
With me to dwell now shall ye wend.
There joy and bliss shall ever be;
Your life in liking shall ye spend.
Ye cursed caitiffs, from me flee,
In hell to dwell without an end.
There shall ye nought but sorrow see,
And dwell by Satanas the fiend.
Now is fulfilled all my forethought,
For ended is each earthly thing.
All wights in earth that I have wrought
After their works have now winning;
They that would sin and ceased not,
Of sorrows sore now shall they sing;
And they that mended while they might
Shall dwell and bide in my blessing.

And so he makes an end with a melody of angels
passing from place to place.

382

Later than very
a text see Wolf
and the DMPr
& continued
decadence

49

THE INNHOLDERS

A fragment, ? of a Coronation.

GOD [*the Son*] ¶Hail, fulgent Phebus and Father eternal,
Perfect plasmator and God omnipotent,
By whose will and power perpetual
All things have influence and being verament.
To thee I give loving and laud right excellent,
And to the Spirit also, lord of all grace,
As by thy word and work omnipotent
Am I thy son and equal in that case.

In voices
Trinity

O *sapor suavitatis*, O succour and solace,
O life eternal and lover of chastity,
Whom angels above and the earth in his great
    space
And all things created love in majesty.
Remember, Father, in thy solemnity,
The wounds of thy Son, whom by thy providence
You made descend from thine equality
Into the womb of Mary, by meek obedience.
Of a virgin inviolate, for man's iniquity
Who for his sin stood mickle from thy grace,
By whole assent of thy solemnity
Thou made me incarnate and truly man I was.
Wherefore to speed me here in this same space
Hear thou me, Father, heartily I thee pray;
As for my mother truly in this case
Thou hear thy Son, and hark what I shall say.
For to myself it seems right great offence
My mother's womb in earth should putrify,
Since her flesh and mine were both one in
    essence . . .
I had no other but of her truly;
She is my mother to whom *legem adimplevi,*

She should
be uncorrupt
& undefiled
as he
is

Which thou hast ordinate as by thy providence.
Grant me thy grace, I beseech thee heartily,
As for the time of her meek innocence
In word nor deed nor thought never to offend,
She might be assumed, I pray thine excellence,
Unto thy throne, and so to be commend
In body and soul ever without an end
With thee to reign in thine eternity,
From sorrow and sadness sinners to defend.
O flagrant Father, grant it might so be.

GOD THE FATHER   ¶O lamp of light, O lumen eternal,
O coequal Son, O very sapience,
O mediator and mean, and life perpetual,
In whom dark clouds may have no aceidence,
Thou knowest right well by thine own providence
I have commit my powers general . . .
Tibi data est potestas and plenal influence.
Thou art my Son—— . . .